LIMITED CHOICES

LIMITED CHOICES

Mable Jones,
a Black Children's Nurse in
a Northern White Household

EMILY K. ABEL AND
MARGARET K. NELSON

UNIVERSITY OF VIRGINIA PRESS
Charlottesville and London

University of Virginia Press

Printed in the United States of America on acid-free paper

First published 2021

9 8 7 6 5 4 3 2 1

Library of Congress Cataloging-in-Publication Data

Names: Abel, Emily K., author. | Nelson, Margaret K., author.
Title: Limited choices : Mable Jones, a Black children's nurse in a northern white household / Emily K. Abel and Margaret K. Nelson.
Description: Charlottesville : University of Virginia Press, 2021. | Includes bibliographical references and index.
Identifiers: LCCN 2021023498 (print) | LCCN 2021023499 (ebook) | ISBN 9780813946658 (hardcover) | ISBN 9780813946665 (ebook)
Subjects: LCSH: Jones, Mable (Mable Walls), 1909–1995. | Abel, Emily K. | Nelson, Margaret K. | African American women household employees—Biography. | African American women civil rights workers—Biography. | African American women—Social conditions—20th century. | African Americans—Migrations—History—20th century. | Migration, Internal—United States—History—20th century. | United States—Race relations—History—20th century.
Classification: LCC E185.97.J7743 A64 2021 (print) | LCC E185.97.J7743 (ebook) | DDC 323.092 [B]—dc23
LC record available at https://lccn.loc.gov/2021023498
LC ebook record available at https://lccn.loc.gov/2021023499

Cover photos: Mable Jones and four Klein children (*top;* courtesy of the Klein family); Mable Jones holding one of her grandchildren (*bottom left;* courtesy of the Klein family); six of Mable Jones's grandchildren (*bottom right;* courtesy of Theresa Williams)

CONTENTS

FOREWORD

In the early days of conducting research for the Jefferson School African American Heritage Center's permanent exhibition, scholarship about African American postemancipation life in Charlottesville was sparse. A library search for Virginia landed you in Norfolk and Richmond but rarely in Charlottesville proper. Although former University of Virginia professors Scot French and Ed Schwartz had used the Black neighborhood of Vinegar Hill as a fodder for their classes, information about African American life of this era remained within the realm of the academy, unavailable to a larger public. French, Schwartz, and others like them are indebted to two groups of African American genealogist and researchers: first, the Burke Brown Steppe Afro-American Historical and Genealogical Society (1995), and then later, the Our Legacy group (2002). These organizations, along with the newly formed Preservers of the Daughters of Zion Cemetery continue to investigate family histories and have expanded the historical knowledge of Charlottesville's African American community. Currently, we are experiencing a resurgence in interest in local African American history as the city's glaring inequities were laid bare by activists before and after the 2017 Unite the Right rally. Where many Whites in the community assumed that Charlottesville, lacked a race problem and was invaded by White supremacists, local activists, especially Black activists, enumerated the area's long history of homegrown racism. Moreover, our youth activists are demanding that African American history be taught in local schools. Today, the emphasis is on authentic voices, a call that, in practice, reintegrates Black agency into the American narrative.

An authentic Black narrative has been elusive in the public realm in part because of the sporadic presence of a local Black press. The city's first African American newspaper, the *Charlottesville Messenger,* operated from 1901 through 1932. It was followed by the *Reflector* from 1934–1936, and then later by the *Tribune* (1951–50), an outgrowth of the *Roanoke Tribune.* The *Charlottesville-Albemarle Tribune* published from 1954 through 1992, has been the longest record of Black activity. There are few extant copies of the *Messenger* and the other subsequent periodicals centered on the activities of an aspiring middle class. Quotidian details were filled in by newspapers outside of Charlottesville, such as Robert Mitchell's *Richmond Times-Dispatch,* which published weekly commentary on Charlottesville's goings on as early as the 1890s. The dominant, White-led local newspaper, the *Charlottesville Chronicle* (1866–1904), which gave way to the *Daily Progress* (1892–present), provided cursory reporting on Black life and painted African Americans as social subordinates.

To fully grasp the nuances of Charlottesville's Black experience, researchers have relied heavily on oral histories. Many of these projects originated in the 1990s and were conducted with residents who lived during the height of Jim Crow and who have since passed away. We are now attempting to consolidate these histories into one repository and to record new oral histories. Mable Jones's oral history is part of the Ridge Street project conducted in the mid-1990s by Preservation Piedmont, a grassroots organization dedicated to the preservation of the city's built environment. Like others in the series, it is particularly informative because it addresses African American labor, a topic that has gained currency in the broader discourse about equity.

As authors Emily Abel and Margaret Nelson acknowledge, Jones's oral history and the additional conversations conducted with those who knew her were necessary to broaden their understanding of the person who they believe significantly impacted their lives. However, they have done more than script a biography. By contextualizing Jones's life within the broader subject of domestic labor, they have allowed us to consider the full implications of African American migration. The city directories after 1900 show that a vast majority of African Americans were laborers, involved in occupations much like those they were engaged in while enslaved. In the 1908 directory, the majority of occupations listed for Blacks was either laborer or domestic. These occupations would permit many in the community to purchase property, leading to greater overall stability. In fact, beginning in the 1890s, and by the final removal of Vinegar Hill, at least 50 percent of the African American community were homeowners. Such prosperity was hard fought, and by the time Mable Jones was born, it may have seemed impossible for most Black citizens. Virginia's 1902 constitution deliberately redressed whatever gains Black Virginians had achieved. Its ultimate goal to effect the complete disenfranchisement of Black men was successful—throughout the state, the 147,000 eligible African American voters were reduced to 21,000. In Charlottesville only eighty Black men were left with the ability to impact policy. Nonetheless, the Black community continued to make gains. They petitioned for a high school that would offer a modicum of communal security since it relieved the need to leave town in order to be educated past the seventh grade. Arguably, the building and the school's subsequent accreditation in 1929 reflected one of the last major gains for the Black community during the period. By the time Mable's family arrived in Charlottesville in 1925, additional curtailment of African American prosperity came in the form of de jure restrictions on property purchase. These race-based constraints established the boundaries of Black neighborhoods, where growth and wealth accumulation was further diminished through the denial of public services. For instance, the Ridge Street neighborhood where Jones eventually returned was one of the last Black neighborhoods to receive public utilities.

From her oral history, we learn that Mable went to the Jefferson School until she was sixteen and then quit. This was not an unusual occurrence even though by the 1920s school attendance was compulsory in Virginia. Mable had been working since she was thirteen—her decision to leave school three years later was probably a financial one, as she was responsible for helping her mother. By the time she ended her formal education, the Depression had reached Charlottesville and its negative impact on African Americans was significant. Jones's move to the North was certainly a result of scarce opportunities in the service industry, where Black labor had been relegated. Understanding Mable's working conditions in the

North further elucidates the realities of Black migration. We understand more clearly the circumstances under which Black domestics maintained familial ties to the South and are made to realize that migration does not break bonds but can strengthen them. Consequently, *Limited Choices: Mable Jones, a Black Children's Nurse in a Northern White Household* can be read as a cogent synthesis of modern African American history.

DR. ANDREA DOUGLAS
Executive Director
Jefferson School African American Heritage Center

ACKNOWLEDGMENTS

Many people helped us as we tried to document the life of Mable Jones. Above all we thank her many family members with whom we spoke either by phone or in person: Derrick Jones, Charles Jones, Walter Jones, Gregory Jones, Theresa Williams, Wayne Williams, and Thomas Edler.

We also owe a huge debt to a number of other people. Claudia Jessup shared her memories of Mable in the years after we knew her. We met several times with Gloria Gilmore and Robin Patton of One Shared Story. Robin spent one afternoon driving us around Louisa County and another helping us find land records. After our visits, both sent additional documents and photographs, and they continued to answer our myriad questions. In Charlottesville we also met Violet Price, Jean Hiatt, Eugene Williams, and Reverend Alvin Edwards, all of whom had known Mable and could tell us more about her.

Other people in Virginia provided invaluable assistance: Elizabeth Klacynski and Olivia Gabbay at the Jefferson School African American Heritage Center; Miranda Burnett, Margaret O'Bryant, Sandy DeKay, and Shelley Viola Murphy at the Albemarle-Charlottesville Historical Society; the staff at the Mount Zion First African Baptist Church; Penny White at the Albert and Shirley Small Special Collections Library at the University of Virginia; Karlene Kovalcik, who helped us locate critical documents at the Louisa County Historical Society; and Chris Farina, who gave us free access to his film *West Main Street*.

In Westchester County we received essential assistance from Mayra Cabrera at the Mamaroneck Public Library, Barbara Davis at the New

Rochelle Public Library, William Hegarty at the Larchmont Public Library, Patrick Raftery at the Westchester County Historical Society, and Mike Tripico at the Mamaroneck Historical Society. At the Middlebury College Library, Wendy Shook and Clement Ryan provided important support. Ilana Offen helped develop the chart illustrating the relationships among and geographical locations of Mable's ancestors. Emily French created the maps.

Colleagues, friends and family who read all or sections of the manuscript and provided insightful comments include Margaret Anderson, Carla Bittel, Charlotte Borst, Karen Brodkin, Janet Brodie, Susan Burch, Sharla Fett, Naomi Gerstel, Robert Gottlieb, Dorien Grunbaum, Karen V. Hanson, Elizabeth Hersh, Carollee Howes, Sarah Koch, Rachel Joo, Alaf Nash, Bill Nelson, Sonja Olson, Vivian Rothstein, Robert Schine, Jennifer Wang, Alice Wexler, and Maxine Baca Zinn. In addition, we benefited from advice from Rick Abel, Carla Cappetti, William Hart, Nazli Kibria, James Klein, Thomas Klein, Amy Morsman, James Ralph, Burke Rochford, and Ann Shalleck.

Margaret (Peggy) received funding from the Middlebury College Emeriti Research Fund and Emily from the UCLA Academic Senate.

At the University of Virginia Press, we thank Clayton Butler, Charles Bailey, and Helen Chandler, and Ellen Satrom. We owe a special debt of gratitude to Nadine Zimmerli, who supported this project from the beginning, offered wonderful advice, and in general did far more than most editors usually do.

Editorial Note: The two authors jointly wrote this book. The order of names is alphabetical.

CHRONOLOGY OF LIFE OF MABLE WALLS JONES

1909	Born in Green Springs, Louisa County, VA
1911	Birth of her brother Lawrence Marshall Walls
1913	Birth of her brother Thomas Walls
1917	Birth of her sister Beatrice Walls
1918	Birth of her brother Henry Philip Walls
1920	Death of her father, Oscar Walls
1925	Moved to Charlottesville with her mother (Dora Walls) and siblings
1929	Married to James Henry Jones
1930	Birth of her son James Henry Jones
1931	Birth of her son Thomas Marshall Jones
1935–?	Lived with employer, Paxson, in Ivy, Virginia
1944	Deserted by her husband James Henry Jones
1944–1946	Lived in Washington, DC, working for our parents, Miriam Borgenicht Klein and Milton Klein
1946–1953	Lived in Larchmont, NY, while working for Klein family, and in Charlottesville, VA
1947	Moved to 609 Parrott Street, Charlottesville, VA
1953–1995	Lived in Charlottesville, VA
195?–1994	Worked for Mamie Virginia Jessup and Claude Jessup
1956	Moved to 409 Ridge Street, Charlottesville, VA
1957	Divorced from husband
1978	Death of her mother, Dora Walls, and her son James Jones

1987	Death of her brother Henry Philip Walls
1984	Death of her brother Thomas Walls
1984	Death of her brother Lawrence Marshall Walls
1992	Death of her sister Beatrice Walls Frye
1992	Death of our mother, Miriam Borgenicht Klein
1994	Death of her employer, Mamie Virginia Jessup
1994	Tree fell on Ridge Street House
1995	Died; buried at Oakwood Cemetery, Charlottesville, VA

LIMITED CHOICES

INTRODUCTION

MABLE JONES, AN AFRICAN AMERICAN woman, was sixteen in 1925, when she first arrived in Charlottesville, Virginia, from a rural area with her widowed mother and four siblings. Three years earlier, she had begun her long career in domestic work, the occupation of most Black women in the early twentieth century. "I used to wash dishes for somebody in a home and go to school," she told an interviewer gathering information about life on a prominent Charlottesville residential street.[1] Mable left school after eighth grade because, she said, "I wanted to get a better job and help my mother. She raised five children." Mable was the "oldest and only ten or twelve when my father died. So my mother had a lot of responsibility."[2] In Charlottesville, Mable's mother hoped to find better schools for her younger children and higher paying jobs for Mable and herself. The tightening grip of Jim Crow, however, prevented her from fully attaining either goal. Mable remained a household worker until she was eighty-five, long after many Black women had found other occupations. The new opportunities that gradually opened for African American women after World War II were primarily for those who were younger and who had received more schooling.

Mable was born in Louisa County, Virginia, in 1909 and lived there until she was a teenager. At the time of her birth, her parents shared their home with both her father's brother and his ninety-nine-year-old grandmother, who had probably been enslaved. From the latter part of the nineteenth century until the middle of the twentieth century, the members of her large extended family earned money through farm labor, railroad work, and paid domestic work; they also relied on unpaid labor and each other for survival. After moving to Charlottesville, Mable returned to Louisa County many times, and her mother and sons lived there from some point during the Depression until the end of World War II. Louisa County remained an important place in her mind. Almost seventy years after she had left, when asked whether any of her relatives had remained in the area, she responded, "Yes, we had my home down there."[3]

Mable's Charlottesville life extended from the Jim Crow era, through the civil rights struggle, and almost to the end of the twentieth century. The city surrounds the University of Virginia, an institution that was built with the labor of enslaved African Americans and played a critical role in disseminating white supremacist ideas. During the civil rights era, Charlottesville gained notoriety as one of the Virginia communities that fought for years against school desegregation. Before that campaign ended, city officials decided to demolish its most prominent African American neighborhood, Vinegar Hill.[4] Yet the local Black press reveals that African Americans created a vibrant social life in the city in these decades. Even after the Great Depression struck, they "motored" to visit friends and relatives in other cities, held music festivals, played cards as members of bridge clubs, participated in quilting contests and 4-H clubs, and enjoyed canning and drying demonstrations. In Charlottesville, Mable married, raised two children, cared for a wide circle of family members, attended church, and spent time with friends, even while working in White people's homes. Over time Mable's mother owned two separate houses in the city. The second, on Ridge Street, was Mable's much-loved home for nearly forty years.

We originally decided to try to tell Mable's story because we had come to realize that although she played a major role in shaping our lives, we knew little about hers. Like so many African Americans, Mable regularly moved between the Black world and the White one. She began to work for our family in 1944, when our mother had a government job in Washington, DC, our father was in the navy overseas, our older sister was four, Emily was two, and Margaret (Peggy) was an infant. When the war ended, we moved to a New York suburb. At some point in the next couple of years, Mable followed. Until 1953 she lived with us for long periods of time, doing the cleaning, some of the cooking, and a lot of the childcare, especially after our two brothers were born in 1949 and 1951. We never doubted her importance to us. Whenever Mable left, we wrote to her. After 60 years, we still remembered her two addresses in Charlottesville.

Aside from those addresses and the names of her sons, however, we had no information about her when she wasn't with us. In his 1982 memoir, the theologian Frederick Buechner described his beloved nurse as "the mother of much that I was and in countless unrecognizable ways probably still am." "Yet," he continued, "I don't know where she came from or anything about her life apart from the few years of it that she spent with us. Nor do I know what became of her after she left, and there is a sadness in not knowing, in thinking of all the mothers and fathers we have all of us had who, for the little we remember them, might as well never have existed at all except for the deep and hidden ways in which they exist in us still."[5]

But it is not just sadness and a desire to honor Mable that motivated us to pursue this research. As a historian (Emily) and sociologist (Peggy), we realized that attempting to document her life would help us understand the constraints that forced so many Black women of her era to leave their families to care for Whites. Moreover, we have come to understand how our personal story is intertwined with hers in ways that extend beyond our few precious memories of the care she gave us. Anthropologist Leith Mullings states, "It was the working class and enslaved men and women whose labor created the wealth that allowed the middle class and upper middle class domestic life styles to exist."[6] We were brought together with Mable Jones by our privilege and her disadvantage in intersecting hierarchies of race and class.[7] Our family was White and upper-middle class; Mable was an African American working-class woman. To understand her story we had to tell some of ours; to understand our story we had to learn hers.

In writing these stories we have made critical decisions about language.

In our inegalitarian society, forms of address are inevitably fraught with overtones of race, class, and patriarchy. When we were children, everyone in our household called Mable Jones by her first name. That informality was definitely not reciprocal: Mable did not use first names for our parents although she did for us and our siblings. We have chosen to call her Mable in this book both because that is how we had always thought of her and because the alternatives grated: one was too formal ("Mrs. Jones"), another sounded rude ("Jones"), and a third was both awkward and repetitive ("Mable Jones"). We like to think that were we to meet Mable now, as adults, our use of first names with each other would be an acknowledgment of mutual respect.

We capitalize *Black* in this manuscript when referring to people and cultures of African origin. We do so out of respect for the history and identity shared by people of African ancestry in this country. We also capitalize *White*. We understand that in doing so we adopt a practice favored by hate groups and White supremacists. Nevertheless, we believe that pointed attention to racial identities as social creations outweighs that concern. As the philosopher Kwame Anthony Appiah wrote in the *Atlantic* in June 2020, "The point of the capital letter . . . isn't to elevate; it's to situate."[8] The White people we discuss in this book preserved their shared position and enjoyed its accompanying privileges. These people include upholders of Jim Crow laws, opponents to civil rights, suburbanites in the North living on property protected by racially restrictive covenants, women and men who hired Black domestic workers, and the children who benefited from the care the workers provided.

When we refer to the South, we include Washington, DC, as well as Virginia, where Mable Jones spent most of her life. In that South, Jim Crow laws limited the choices of African Americans. The civil rights movement that abolished those laws could not undo the harm wrought by centuries of racism. We grew up in the North where Mable spent portions of a half dozen years. There too, racism was rooted in both laws and social practices, albeit in very different ways. Our capitalization of *North* and *South* is designed to reflect those differences—and the impact they had on Mable's life—rather than to glorify either region.

As we began our research into Mable's life, we were lucky to find the oral history interview conducted with her in 1995, a few months before she died. (We include the transcript of the interview in the Appendix.) Through it, we learned Mable's middle name, her birthplace, the names of both her parents, and the name of another White family for whom she worked for more than four decades. Armed with that information, we began genealogical research on Ancestry.com to construct a family tree and a timeline of the major events in her life.[9] The interview also provided some access to Mable's voice. Whenever possible, we draw on her words to guide our interpretation of her life and we use them directly as the titles of chapters 1, 5, 6, and 7.

Our research gave us an opportunity to study the impact of the relational dynamics of race, class, and gender not only in the South but also in an affluent northern suburb. We grew up in the 1940s and 1950s in Larchmont in Westchester County, twenty miles from New York City. Almost everyone there was rich and White. And almost all the families had two parents—a working father and a housewife mother. Our family conformed precisely to this model. Our father commuted to his job as a lawyer in New York City. His earnings allowed our parents to buy a relatively small house and then, as the family expanded, a considerably larger and grander one a block away. Our mother wrote but, except for a few years during World War II, she did not work outside the home until her children were well into their teens. All of our relatives were White, as were all of our parents' friends and almost all of ours. Aside from Mable, the only African Americans any of us would have typically seen daily were other domestic workers, many of whom also lived in their employers' homes. Although Mable lived in our home on and off for nearly a decade, she remained an outsider in the community. She might have found this pattern familiar: she had worked for White people from a young age and had lived in the home of at least one White family before ours. But the North was different. In the South she had been close to her own family and church. Living in Larchmont she was far from home and had to travel on her days off to the adjacent city of New Rochelle to find a community and attend church. The difficulties of being so far from Charlottesville eventually drove her back there.

Several months into our research we visited Louisa County and Charlottesville for the first time to examine records and speak with people who had known Mable and especially with her relatives. On a second trip later that year we read through issues of the Black newspapers the *Charlottesville Tribune* and the *Charlottesville-Albemarle Tribune* in Special Collections at UVA and searched for documents at the Albemarle-Charlottesville Historical Society. Robin Patton, a founder of One Shared Story (a nonprofit organization in central Virginia that assists people researching their African American ancestry), spent hours lifting massive volumes in the Clerk's Office of the Louisa County Courthouse to help us locate the deeds of land purchased by and willed to Mable's ancestors.

We approached our first trip with great trepidation. How would people respond? How would her grandchildren make sense of two White women coming South to find out about the life of a woman whose work for their family had kept her from being with and caring for her own? Would her family view us as transgressing on a story that belonged to them? We were thus relieved when many people gave us what we experienced as a very warm reception—Mable's pastor, Reverend Alvin Edwards; one of her close friends, Violet Price; Robin Patton and Gloria Gilmore (the other founder of One Shared Story); and Eugene Williams, who had known Mable when he was a child and had subsequently played a central role in Charlottesville's civil rights struggle. We are grateful for the information they shared.

Meeting Mable's grandchildren was the highlight of that first trip. For several months we had been speaking on the telephone with Mable's grandson Charles Jones, who gathered two of his siblings, Theresa Williams (and her husband Wayne) and Walter Jones, to spend a couple of hours with us on our third day in Charlottesville. Charles is the head of a Masonic Lodge in Charlottesville. The grandchildren chose this, a relatively impersonal location, for our get-together. Before the meeting, Charles had asked Theresa to bring a framed picture of six of Mable's grandchildren, four crowded on a couch, two kneeling on the floor below. We, in turn, brought pictures that had been in our family album. One was a newspaper photograph of Mable's younger son in the hospital after he was wounded in the Korean War; another showed a forty-year-old Mable

Six of Mable Jones's grandchildren in her home on Parrott Street, between 1947 and 1956. (Courtesy of Theresa Williams)

sitting with us and our siblings. (We describe both of those in chapter 5.) The last photograph she had sent us years after she left. Her grandchildren tried to figure out which baby she had been holding on the piano bench they recognized from the Ridge Street house. Finally, Peggy displayed the family tree she had constructed. The grandchildren recognized only some of the names but suggested others she could add. One grandson living in the area, Gregory Jones, was about to leave for a week's vacation. Because he had no time to meet, we only talked to him on the phone. Like

Mable Jones holding one of her grandchildren in her home on Ridge Street. (Courtesy of the Klein family)

his cousins, he was interested in what we were doing and forthcoming with information about his parents and grandparents.

Understandably, we also encountered significant boundaries we could not cross, and much clearly remained unsaid. Paul Laurence Dunbar's poem "We Wear the Mask" speaks to the hesitation African Americans might have talking with Whites. It begins with this stanza:

> We wear the mask that grins and lies,
> It hides our cheeks and shades our eyes,—
> This debt we pay to human guile;
> With torn and bleeding hearts we smile,
> And mouth with myriad subtleties.[10]

Whatever constraints remained, the information family members, friends, and acquaintances shared with us enormously enhanced our understanding of Mable's history and enabled us to understand aspects of her life we had not known as children.

In order to place that life in context, we drew on the extensive literature about structural racism and discrimination in both the South and the North as well as about the civil rights movement. We also found a substantial body of scholarship dealing with the employment of Black workers in White southern households. We found little information, however, about the same kind of employment in postwar affluent Northern communities, work that was the only option for many African Americans who had left the South during the Great Migration.[11] As a result, along with our own memories, we relied on censuses, memoirs by and interviews with White men and women who recalled domestic workers in the New York area in the 1940s and 1950s, a sociological study of African American domestic workers in the Northeast, and newspaper accounts by African Americans in those years to contextualize Mable's life in the North. Those sources deepened our understanding of the sharp divide between White and Black perspectives on domestic work. As we show more fully in chapter 5, Whites (children and adults alike) often assumed that African Americans worked in their homes from a sense of devotion. For example, the White journalist John Darnton recalled that his mother had assumed that the dedication of her live-in housekeeper, Inell Jones, transcended their economic arrangement. Thus, when the family had difficulty "pulling together enough money to pay her on time every week," his mother "appeared to feel that, after being with us all those years, Inell had been less than loyal in not sticking around."[12] African Americans, by contrast, spoke of their involvement in domestic work as the result not of devotion to a White family but rather of their limited choices in a racist society.

Because we were part of Mable's experience in our household, we also had to delve into our own memories and interrogate our own feelings. Despite her domestic arrangement, our mother was a leftist, railing against McCarthyism, subscribing to *I. F. Stone's Weekly*, and supporting both the National Committee for a Sane Nuclear Policy (SANE) and the National Association for the Advancement of Colored People (NAACP). She taught us from a young age to view her relationship with Mable as a form of class and race exploitation. Later we added gender to that list, especially because we had always been told that Mable left her own children with her mother in Charlottesville to care for us. One story illustrates the gulf between our mother's politics and the reality of her life, as well as her desperate, sometimes bizarre attempts to close that gulf. When our mother died, we wrote to Mable. She responded with a long letter in which she reminded us of a time during elementary school when Peggy brought home a friend—a daughter in the only African American family living in Larchmont at the time—who asked our mother whether Mable was our maid. Our mother answered, "No, she's my cousin." After many decades, Mable remembered our mother's awkward attempt to relieve what we now would call liberal guilt.

And we had heard another story over and over. When our mother first met Mable, she asked whether Mable had children. Mable replied that she had two boys, James and Thomas. Our mother then responded, "What beautiful names. If I ever have boys, I will name them James and Thomas." Five and seven years later she did. We wondered how the people we met in Charlottesville would view our brothers having the same names as Mable's sons. Would our mother's use of James and Thomas seem like an act of appropriation? We were aware that given African American naming traditions, those names likely had distinct meanings in Mable's family that our mother knew nothing about. We were thus relieved when the people we met in Charlottesville and Louisa County expressed (at least to us) their belief that our mother's action revealed her love and respect for Mable. Charles Jones said, "Your mother must have cared a lot about Mable to name her sons after hers." And when we pointed to the generations of people named Thomas among Mable's ancestors (discussed in chapter 2), as a way of identifying her family, Gloria Gilmore added, "and now there is one in your family as well."

Yet we are not sure the interpretation of our mother's decision about names is quite so simple. We know our mother followed the Jewish proscription against naming children after living relatives. Even had she wanted to honor a parent, sibling, or cousin, she would not have used the name while that person was still alive. She would have been horrified had we done so when our children were born. And yet she felt comfortable using the names of two young men who, though still very much alive, she had never known. We can only guess she was attempting in some strange way to assuage her guilt from having benefited from what the scholar Sau-ling C. Wong calls "diverted mothering": when Mable came north to care for our growing family, she could not care for her own.[13] Over time, our mother transmitted her sense of guilt to us.

For both of us, guilt resulted in silence. Mable's experience in our family placed us on the wrong side of a critical divide, and for many years we expunged that relationship from the story we told of our lives.[14] Guilt also is a poor motivator for social action.[15] And it tends to reduce others to the status of victims. But Mable had sources of strength that were largely hidden from us as children. As a domestic worker, Mable represents a significant piece of Black women's history. As a woman deeply entrenched in an extended family structure and a strong religious community, she tells us even more about how African Americans survived oppression in the twentieth century.

Although we were aware that Mable was estranged from her husband and that her mother, Dora Walls, took care of Mable's sons when she lived in our house, it was not until we began this research that we learned how interdependent the two women were throughout their lives. As we delved further into her history, we also came to understand the extent to which their relationship was embedded in a large kinship network. Except when Mable was a live-in domestic worker, when she was first married, and for a few years when she lived in Washington, DC, she and her mother shared a home. Mable cared for Dora at the end of her life and was her main source of financial support for many years. In both Louisa County and Charlottesville, Mable and Dora lived close to other family members and could share resources with them. It is likely that we had no idea of the structure of Mable's family because it was so different from what we knew, living with two parents in an upper-middle-class, virtually all-White community far from our grandparents. Yet the two were connected: Mable's presence in our home enabled our family to assume that nuclear form; Mable's absence from her own family was underwritten by her kinship structure. As the sociologist Maxine Baca Zinn reminds us, "Racial differences in family life do not simply co-exist, but in any given period, they are sustained through interaction across racial and class boundaries."[16]

Mable said nothing (that we remember) about religion, but we have since learned that religion was at the center of Mable's life. From a young age, she regularly walked with her family to church in Louisa County. In Charlottesville, she filled multiple roles in the Mount Zion First African Baptist Church, which she joined soon after her arrival. She taught Sunday School, sang in the choir, attended worship services, and belonged to several benevolent societies. By not revealing this side of herself, perhaps she was deferring to our defiantly secular household. But perhaps she also engaged in what has been called "cultural dissemblance." The historian Darlene Clark Hine argues that widespread negative stereotypes of Black women encouraged them to conceal their "private, empowering definitions of self." Hine continues, "A secret, undisclosed persona allowed the individual Black woman to function, to work effectively as a domestic in white households, to bear and rear children, to endure the frustration-born violence of frequently under- or unemployed mates, to support churches, to found institutions, and to engage in social service activities, all while living within a clearly hostile white, patriarchal, middle-class America."[17]

The notion of cultural dissemblance raises another troubling issue. By recounting the story of a domestic worker, we contribute to the project of expanding a historical record that too long has focused primarily on powerful members of society. But are we simultaneously trespassing on aspects of Mable's life she wished to conceal from us? As White women writing about an African American domestic worker, we also are aware we are working within a controversial genre.[18] Criticisms of one of the most popular works in this genre, *The Help*, have helped us recognize (and we hope avoid) the major pitfalls. One problem is placing Whites at the center of the story while reducing Black women to stereotypes of devoted caregivers. Although we mention some of the priceless gifts Mable gave us, we try neither to give ourselves central billing nor to indulge in nostalgia about our early years with her. Another problem is allowing Whites to speak for African Americans. As much as possible, we depend on Mable's words to describe not only her experiences as a household worker but also her life apart from that role. Because she left so few records, we draw heavily on oral histories of people who shared some of her experiences (African Americans who were children in rural areas at the turn of the twentieth century, who traveled north, or who lived in Mable's neighborhood in Charlottesville) and on the self-published autobiography of one of Mable's relatives. In addition, we rely on our conversations with her grandchildren, friends, and acquaintances. When those sources are not available, we try not to insert our interpretations of what she might have thought or felt.

We spent parts of two afternoons in Charlottesville, talking with civil rights leader Eugene Williams on his front porch. In a letter making plans for our first visit, Mr. Williams urged us to highlight the constraints within which Mable fashioned her life: "I hope you will want to think about the segregation in Charlottesville that Mrs. Jones endured." He continued, "At my age, 92, I still don't understand how we endured it." In what follows, we try to fulfill the mission he gave us by telling Mable Jones's story within the context of the intersecting systems of power relations she encountered in the North as well as in the South.

1

"WE HAD MY HOME DOWN THERE"

DURING OUR GET-TOGETHER WITH Mable's grandchildren Charles, Theresa, and Walter, we sat on folding chairs in the women's area of the Masonic Lodge headquarters that Charles and other members had carefully renovated. We told them the names of the five children in our family; they listed the thirteen in theirs. When they got to their sister Jennifer, we recognized the middle name, Serena, as having been Mable's as well. They had not known that: they called her "Grandma Mable."

We were fortunate to learn Mable's middle name from her oral history because it helped guide us through the thicket of possible relatives on Ancestry.com. Although Serena is a relatively uncommon name, two Serenas show up on Mable's family tree, one on each side. Either or both might have been enslaved in Louisa County, Virginia. After our visit, Robin Patton of One Shared Story sent us records showing that a woman named Serena was in the will of James Watson Jr. who owned the Ionia Plantation in 1820. At Watson's death in 1825, that Serena, whose mother's name was Mima, was given to Watson's wife Elizabeth Shelton. In both 1820 and 1825 the number *twenty-five* is attached to Serena's name, perhaps indicating her monetary value. The name Serena (once misspelled as "Lerena") also

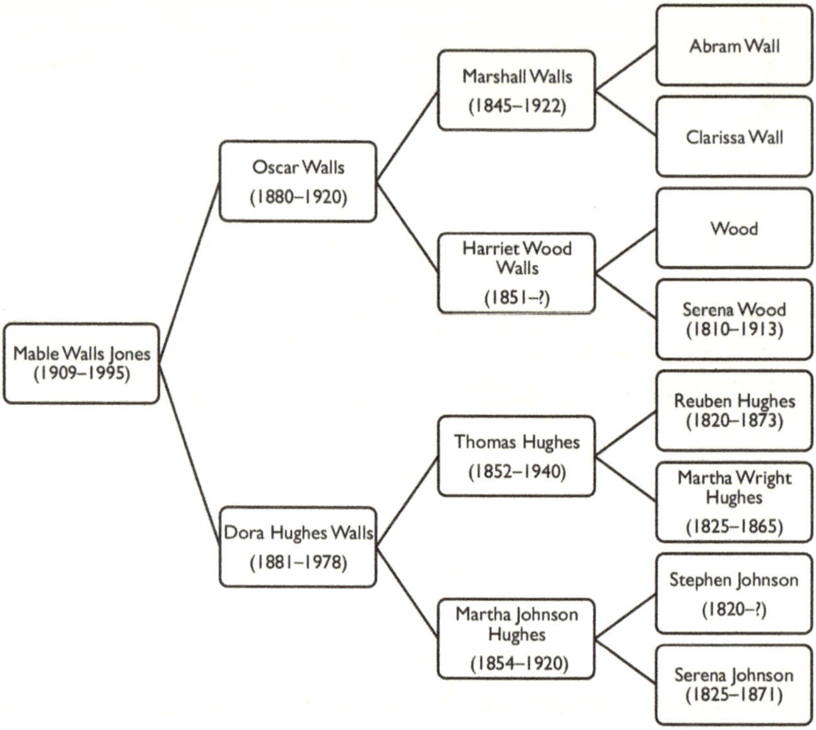

Abbreviated family tree. (*Source:* Ancestry.com)

appeared in a list of the enslaved people at the Green Springs Plantation dispersed by a Colonel Richards to a Dr. James Maury Morris, who took her to the Grassdale Planation. In 1844, when James Maury Morris died, she was included in the list of enslaved people dispersed to Morris's son, James Maury Morris Jr., and returned to Green Springs where the younger Morris lived. (In 1822, Serena's mother's name was listed as Louisa and her father's as Ben; she was valued at $125.) In addition, in both 1861 and 1862, the list of enslaved people at the Hawkwood Plantation included a Serena.[1]

It is possible that all these Serenas are the same person, moved after their enslavers died. In that case, she would have lived at four different plantations. Given the different names of the mothers, however, it is more likely that there were at least two Serenas: one enslaved originally by James Watson, the other enslaved by a Colonel Richards and then by the Morris family, first at Green Springs, then at Grassdale, and then at

Green Springs again. We do not know which of these—if either—is the enslaved woman included in the Hawkwood accounts. Even if neither is the Serena we hoped to find, Mable Jones's forbears might well have been considered chattel who could be sold or willed to another and moved from plantation to plantation against their wishes. And regardless of her identity, each Serena must have rejoiced in April 1865, when news of Lee's surrender and the presence of Union forces in Louisa County guaranteed the emancipation of enslaved people there.[2]

AFTER EMANCIPATION

In 1865 liberated African Americans represented 62 percent of the county's population of 16,701.[3] Like freedpeople throughout the South, they immediately began building their own schools, churches, and benevolent societies and gathering together family members who had been forcibly separated. The Freedmen's Bureau, a federal agency, provided direct relief, legalized marriages, and brought teachers from the North to staff their new schools. Federal laws and constitutional amendments promoted racial equality. By the time Mable Walls was born in 1909, however, Whites had violently overthrown legitimate biracial governments and reestablished control. A state constitutional convention in 1902 mandated racial segregation in schools and disenfranchised a high proportion of African Americans by instituting poll taxes and literacy tests. As a result, African Americans lost whatever political strength they had gained after emancipation. In 1906 the General Assembly passed legislation requiring streetcars to segregate White and Black passengers.[4]

Mable's parents were part of the first generation born after slavery, but she did have contact with at least one family member who might have been enslaved. We assume her middle name came from Serena Wood, the grandmother of Mable's father Oscar Walls, because she was living in the house he shared with his wife, Dora, when Mable was born. When Serena Wood died four years later, Oscar provided the following information for the death certificate: for occupation he wrote, "a domestic"; for parents, "unknown"; for color or race ,"African"; for marital status, "widowed"; and for her age, "supposed to be about 110."[5]

Mable Jones's father, Oscar Walls. (Courtesy of Piedmont Preservation)

Dora gave birth to four children after Mable: Lawrence Marshall in 1911, Thomas in 1913, Beatrice Montague in 1917, and Henry Philip in 1918. When Oscar died in 1920, his youngest child was not yet two and his eldest, Mable, not yet eleven. From then on, Dora's family was woman centered.[6] Dora's parents, aunts, uncles, and siblings, along with their offspring, were the primary actors in her and her children's daily lives. Mable used the name of her brother, Thomas, which he shared with other relatives on his mother's side of the family, for her own son. She chose not to use most of the names on her father's side, including his. Because Dora's family played a critical role in Mable's early life, we focus on them.

We can trace the contours of the lives of Mable's ancestors more easily after emancipation than before. Although we could not locate any letters, diaries, or oral history interviews, we found vital statistics at ten-year

Mable Jones's mother, Dora Walls. (Courtesy of Piedmont Preservation)

intervals in the enumeration censuses and information about landownership from deeds at the Louisa County Courthouse.[7] In addition, we relied on secondary sources and the accounts of people who lived in similar situations. We drew especially heavily on a collection of oral history interviews the Virginia Center for Digital History at the University of Virginia conducted in 2001 and 2002 with residents of Esmont, Virginia, to gain insight into the history and culture of African Americans in the segregated South.[8] Located in the southern part of Albemarle County, Esmont derived its name from a former plantation. Like Louisa County, the area had rich soil for farming.[9] Because the living conditions and means of survival there resembled those in Louisa County, we used these interviews to deepen our understanding of daily life among a rural Black population around 1900.

Historian Eric Foner notes that although strong family ties had existed under slavery, they "had always been vulnerable to disruption. Emancipation allowed blacks to reaffirm and solidify their family connections, and most freedmen seized the opportunity with alacrity."[10] Mable's maternal great-grandfather, Stephen Johnson, who was married to the other Serena in Mable's family, found a way to keep his children close.[11] In 1872, he bought 12.5 acres for $100 in an area known as Quarlestown in Louisa County.[12] Eight years later his daughter Martha and her husband Thomas Hughes (Mable's grandparents) lived on the land.[13] By 1910 they had been joined by two of Thomas and Martha Hughes' married daughters. One was Lucy, who lived with her husband, Charles Winston, on the area of the property closest to her parents and grandparents. The other was Mable's mother, Dora, who lived in the next house over with her husband, Oscar Walls. The same year, Amanda Braxton, another of Stephen Johnson's daughters, who had been living with her husband some distance away, returned as a widow to the neighborhood. Now five families (representing three generations) lived close to one another: the Hugheses, the Johnsons, the Winstons, the Wallses, and the Braxtons. In 1920, the five families were still living in adjacent homes. Property records today show that the heirs of these families continue to hold pieces of the land on which these homes stood.

In 1904, Stephen Johnson sold 2 of the original 12.5 acres to his daughter Martha and her husband Thomas Hughes (Mable's grandparents) for thirty dollars.[14] Although it is unclear what happened to the remainder of Johnson's land, we know that sometime before 1918 Thomas Hughes acquired an additional two acres (for $15) from a J. R. Quarles, a member of the family for whom the area, presumably, was named.[15] Given the many relatives who lived near one another, it is possible some of the land was owned jointly as what was known as "heirs land." In that case, it could not later be willed to a single ancestor to create wealth.[16] Nevertheless, beginning in 1870 and continuing well into the next century, Stephen Johnson's descendants had a place to call home.

Like other rural, southern African Americans, Mable's forbears on both sides cared for and relied on an extensive kinship network. In 1880, Mable's paternal grandparents, Marshall and Harriet Walls, along with their two young children, provided a home for both a fourteen-year-old

TABLE 1 Adjacent family households in Quarlestown, Louisa County, 1870–1940

1870		Serena & Stephen Johnson (+ 7 children)				
1880	*Martha & Thomas Hughes (+ 2 children; Martha's uncle)	Peachy & Stephen Johnson (+ 9 children)				
1900	*Martha & Thomas Hughes (+ 9 children including Dora)	Peachy & Stephen Johnson (+ 1 child)				
1910	*Martha & Thomas Hughes (+ 6 children)	Peachy & Stephen Johnson (+ 2 children; 1 grandchild)	**Lucy & Charles Winston (+ 2 children)	**Dora & Oscar Walls (+ Oscar's grandmother, Serena Wood; Oscar's brother; 1 child, Mable)		*Amanda Braxton (+ 3 children; 1 grandchild)
1920	*Martha & Thomas Hughes (+ 2 children)	Peachy Johnson (+2 children)	**Lucy & Charles Winston (+ 6 children)	**Dora & Oscar Walls (+ 5 children including Mable)	**Maggie & Wilmat Jackson (+ 2 children)	
1930	Thomas Hughes (+ **daughter Lucy & son-in-law Watson Ellis)	Elizabeth & *Charles Johnson (+ Peachy Johnson; 1 adopted child)	*Winston family in Charlottesville*	*Walls family in Charlottesville*	**Maggie & Wilmat Jackson (+ 1 child)	
1940	**Mattie & Watson Ellis (+ Thomas Hughes; Mattie's uncle; 1 child)		**Lucy & Charles Winston (+ 1 adopted son; 2 grandchildren)	**Dora Walls (+ 2 children; 2 grandchildren, James and Thomas Jones; 1 "lodger")	**Maggie & Wilmat Jackson (+ 1 child)	

*Children of Stephen Johnson
**Grandchildren of Stephen Johnson

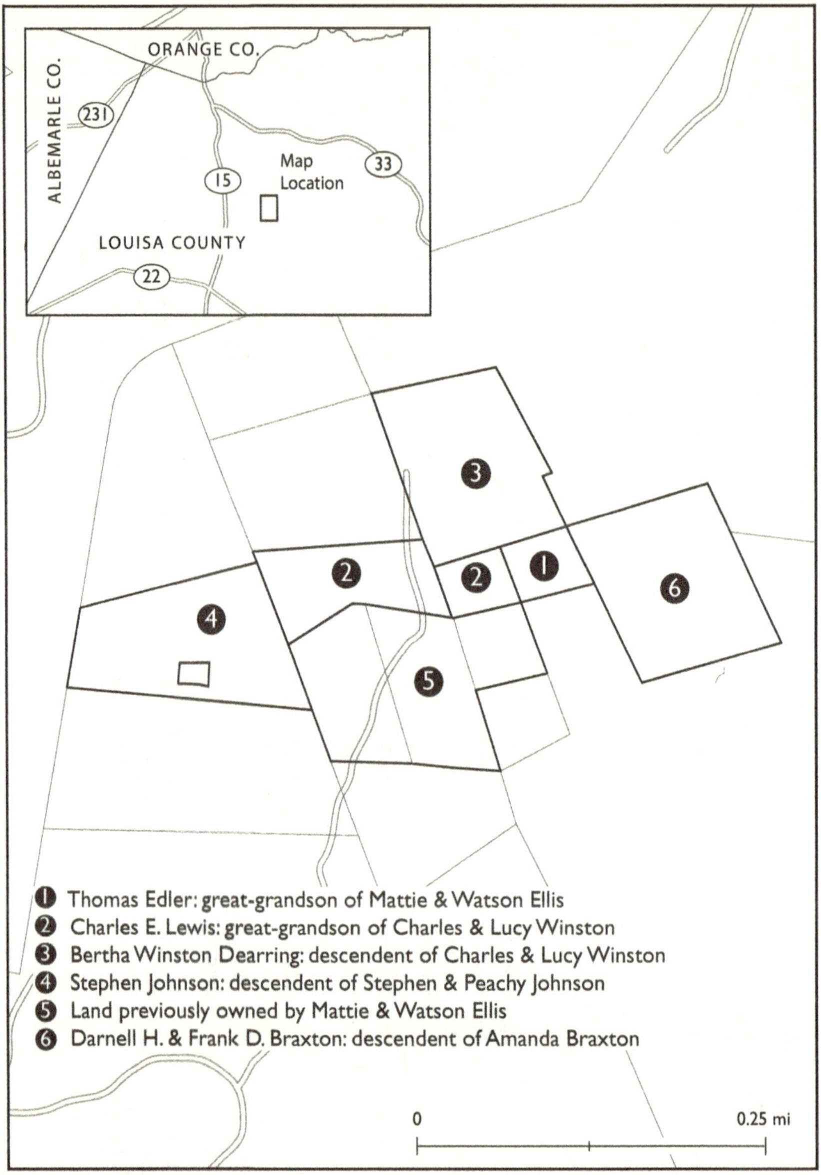

Location of land owned by Mable Jones's family in Louisa County, Virginia, in 2020

niece and Harriet's mother, Serena Wood, who was then approximately seventy.[17] In 1880, Mable's maternal grandparents, Martha and Thomas Hughes, who already had two children, offered refuge to an uncle.[18] When Serena Wood was in her nineties, she moved (or was moved) from the home of her daughter Harriet to that of her grandson Oscar Walls and his wife (Mable's parents), and as already noted, she was still living there along with one of Oscar's brothers when Mable was born in 1909.[19] Three decades later, in 1940, Mable's aunt Mattie Ellis cared for her father and uncle, who were then in their eighties, as well as her adopted child, Thelma; other family members were near enough to help.[20] These families also cared for their grandchildren and other children without resident parents. In 1940, Mable's two children (aged ten and nine) lived with Dora while Mable worked in Charlottesville. Dora's household also included a four-year-old girl; the census labeled this child, Constance Johnson, as a "lodger," but Dora subsequently referred to her as a daughter. Two of Dora's sister Lucy Winston's grandchildren from two different families (one was eight years old and one was five months old) lived with her and her husband without their parents. That household also included a three-year-old child born to the unmarried daughter of a preacher and a married businessman in Charlottesville; Lucy adopted this child, James Flanagan, at birth, and according to her grandson Charles (Chuck) Lewis, James was always her favorite.[21] Like other forms of interdependence, caregiving would be a prominent feature of Mable's life. She would care for her own relatives, the families of her White employers, and congregants in the churches where she worshiped.

Large families were the norm among African Americans in the rural South, and Mable's kin were no exception.[22] Mable's maternal grandfather, Thomas Hughes, was the third of eleven children born between 1845 and 1865; his wife, Martha Johnson Hughes, was the third of seventeen children born to Stephen Johnson with his two wives, first Serena and then Peachy. Thomas and Martha Hughes then had eleven children of their own, including Dora, Mable's mother. Mable's father, Oscar, was among the oldest of ten children. The 1910 census reveals that large families experienced many painful losses. At a time of high infant mortality, especially for Black people, many children did not live into adulthood.[23] Beginning in the 1870s, Peachy gave birth to ten children, of whom only four survived until 1910. Only nine of the twelve children of Dora's mother were alive in 1910. Dora's aunt, Amanda Johnson Braxton, lost three of her ten children. Only two of Dora's sister Lucy Winston's four children survived. In 1910, Dora was the only close family member who had not lost a child. Her first born, Mable, was one year old.

WORK IN LOUISA COUNTY

The men in Mable's extended family had two major occupations: railroad work and farm labor. In 1880, the railroad workers included her two grandfathers and a great-uncle. In 1910, the year after she was born, Mable's father, Oscar, also had a job on the railroad in Scottsville, Virginia, a town located at the border of the neighboring counties of Albemarle and Fluvanna.[24] In many ways this was considered good work: the wage was higher than in other occupations and was especially valued because it paid in cash rather than in scrip or as bills due. But the work was also difficult and dangerous. In her history of Atlanta, Tera Hunter described the kinds of positions Black men had: "As day workers, they groomed roads, distributed ballast, and shoveled snow off the tracks. As brakemen, they coupled and uncoupled stationary cars and ran along the roof of moving trains to apply the brakes, risking life and limb."[25] The fact that both Marshall Walls and Thomas Hughes had other kinds of employment in later years also might indicate that the work was grueling, better suited to young bodies. Mary Stark, born in 1922, the first of ten children, and raised in the Chestnut Grove neighborhood of Esmont, blamed her father's ill health on his working conditions. "At that time," she explained, "when they worked on the railroad, they had several of what you call motorcars, working from one end of rails to another, to be fixed you know. And they kept, if like wind was blowing in wintertime and the cold stuff, you still had to work. . . . So he was full of rheumatism and things." The family was very relieved when he "got a job at the station, keeping it clean." In many cases, railroad work also required men to leave home for long periods. Mary Stark's father worked for the railroad for forty-four years, much of the time in Kentucky; during her childhood "he'd come home maybe once a month."[26]

Farm labor was even more common. In one way, Mable's kin were fortunate. The soil of the Green Springs area where they toiled was unusually rich. As a result of a geological accident, the area was shaped like a basin, close to the water table.[27] Although most of Mable's relatives, like three-fourths of African American farmers in Louisa County in 1900, owned their own land, they encountered several difficulties.[28] Most plots were small.[29] One woman in the Esmont interviews noted that her family raised "cattle, pigs, horses, cows."[30] The farm probably provided some of the goods the family needed as well as income when crops were sold, but throughout much of the year they were cash poor. To make ends meet, some farmers hired themselves out as day laborers.

Life as a day laborer had its own indignities. Born in Esmont in 1927, William Rush worked on a farm as a young man, earning twenty-five cents a day. "Yeah," he said, "we used to work side by side with [the White workers]. You couldn't sit at a table and eat with them. . . . Because they eat, and there was another table in the corner, or sit at the door and eat. . . . I worked for [another farmer] some time, too, back when I was just a little lad. . . . He had a big stump. [White] people would come in the house and eat. We'd eat out there. . . . [He] put the food on the stump." When asked how he felt about that treatment, Rush was clear that anger was a luxury he could not afford: "If word got out, then you're a troublemaker. [They] can no longer use you. And you can't go to the next people, because when you get a job—'what happened when you worked for Mr. Dawson?' You done told why you left there, you know, and you can't get no job there. So, only way to keep a job like that—if you didn't like it you keep your mouth shut . . . and make what you can. . . . Maybe pray that God will bless you and times would get better."[31]

Only two men in Mable's family had other kinds of occupations. Stephen Johnson's son Charles was a carpenter for many years; he was probably well trained and highly sought after.[32] Another, an uncle by marriage, was an insurance agent. In 1940 he reported earning $625, the only income of any member of Mable's extended family living in Louisa County that year.[33] Whether or not the men in Mable's family were wage earners, they probably contributed to household survival by fishing, hunting, cultivating whatever land they owned, and raising animals. In the Esmont interviews, one man remembered that his father, who worked in a slate quarry, left home early in the morning, often when it was still dark outside. When he returned home at the end of the day, even before he "had a chance to bathe or to eat his dinner or anything, he would go out and get firewood in if enough wasn't in there."[34]

Domestic work was the primary paid occupation of Mable's female kin, as it was of African American women throughout the country. In 1870, two of Stephen and Serena Johnson's daughters held employment in "domestic service."[35] In 1900, Mable's mother Dora worked as a live-in "servant" for two White sisters, Virginia and Bette Crank, in Scottsville.[36] And in 1910, three of Dora's sisters were paid domestic workers, one as a cook in a private home and two in a boarding house as a chambermaid and a cook.[37] Perhaps it is from these women that Mable learned valuable lessons about how to conduct oneself as a domestic worker—what to do and, perhaps even more importantly, what not to do.

As far as we can tell, just one woman in this family had a higher-status job. The 1920 census identified Dora's sister, Edmonia, as a schoolteacher.[38] Although we assume her income was greater than that of domestic workers, it must have been much lower than that of White teachers. In the 1925–26 academic year, the average salary for a Louisa County elementary school teacher was $630 for a White man, $402 for a White woman, $415 for an African American man, and just $192 for an African American woman.[39]

It is possible that some women in Mable's family were the "chicken ladies" who sold their fried chicken at the Gordonsville station when the train stopped there.[40] In that case, their children would have helped cook, carry, or deliver the chickens.[41] One source suggests that family members who worked on the railroad tried to slow down the trains to give the women more time to complete their sales.[42]

Especially in the years immediately following emancipation, African American women tried to remain at home, if at all possible.[43] James Jordan, the tenth of twelve children in his Esmont family, remembered that his mother, who had previously been a schoolteacher, worked in the laundry room for the Van Cliefs, one of the wealthy White families in the area. Jordan's father did not like his wife working there because "Daddy just wasn't fond of anything that looked like it was kind of a slavery situation." The father might also have wished his wife could have an easier life. She worked twelve-hour days at the Van Cliefs, and when she returned home, she still had to complete the full round of cooking, cleaning, and caring for her children. Moreover, according to Jordan, the Van Cliefs took their staffs (their "help") when they traveled to Saratoga for horse racing for weeks or even months at a time.[44]

The census lists most of Mable's female relatives as "keeping house" or as "housekeepers." We learned from the Esmont interviews that domestic tasks filled their days, especially if they had many children, as Mable's relatives did. Women grew vegetables and preserved food for the winter months by pickling and canning; they sewed clothes, washed, and ironed them; they raised chickens and sold their eggs; they churned butter; and they cooked and cleaned. None of this was easy.[45] Contemporary pictures of the houses Mable's family lived in from the 1920s on as well as of other houses owned by African Americans in the area suggest they typically had four rooms: two on the first floor and two more on the second. Most of the households lacked indoor plumbing, cooked on woodstoves, and received light from kerosene lamps. In some cases, newspapers tacked onto the walls provided the only insulation. As late as 1950, just 17 percent of homes in Louisa County had hot water, private toilets, and private baths, compared to nearly 50 percent of those in the rest of Virginia. The great majority of Louisa County households still cooked with woodstoves.[46] Chuck Lewis, who lived with his grandmother, Dora's sister Lucy Winston, in Louisa County in the 1940s, wrote in his autobiography that it was his job to stoke the fire before going to sleep. Although he hoped the warmth would last until morning, "it never did" and brushing teeth "required breaking through the layer of ice that had formed in the water bucket."[47]

The women in these families also had responsibility for the health care of both kin and neighbors. "Communities in slavery nurtured a rich health culture," historian Sharla M. Fett writes, "a constellation of ideas and practices related to well-being, illness, healing, and death, that worked to counter the onslaught of daily medical abuse and racist scientific theories." Well into the 1930s and 1940s, African Americans relied on their own treatments and practitioners, cultivating an "ethic of self-reliance."[48] Florence C. Bryant, who grew up on a Virginia farm in the 1920s and 1930s, wrote that her mother was "the family's doctor. She used home remedies so effectively that licensed doctors were seldom called at our house to treat the family's illnesses." Bryant's brother told her that their grandmother, a midwife, "was as good a doctor as could be found anywhere."[49] Asked about the medical care they received as children, Esmont residents spoke first about home remedies. Ruth Brooks's mother put a hot flannel on her chest when she had a cold. Agnes Louise Rush would get turpentine with a couple of drops of sugar for a stomachache. "That would take the worms of your system. . . . Our stomachs would stop hurting, and we'd go on back to playing." Esmont residents also remembered older women who had been midwives. Ruth Brooks, born in 1928, said that one of her cousins was the midwife who came when her two younger brothers were born. Lorraine Paige reported that in the 1930s, the midwife would come to check on the new mother for a month after childbirth and that neighbors would then step in to help: "Most of the ladies were at home, you know, in that day. So, they were the ones that ran back and forth to see about their neighbors and see what they needed. But I remember hearing 'the month of care.'"[50] The persistence of healing traditions, from herbal remedies to the art of midwifery, had meaning and necessity for African Americans in that era.

In addition to sustaining their own families, some women, including Dora's Aunt Amanda Braxton, took in laundry, thus expanding the most difficult and dreaded household task. It involved making soap, carrying and heating gallons of water, lugging pails of wet clothes, scrubbing and rinsing each item, and hanging it on the line to dry. The process exposed women's hands to lye and other caustic soaps, and irons were heavy and dangerous, burning fingers.[51] Luella Swift-Gohaner, a Charlottesville resident, showed an interviewer the hands with which she had scrubbed other people's clothes on a washboard.[52] Historian Tera Hunter found that in late nineteenth-century Atlanta, "almost every white household" sent laundry out.[53] We assume White women in rural areas similarly handed over this chore to others whenever possible.

"To be productive," Florence C. Bryant wrote, her family's farm "required the cooperation and commitment of the whole family.... We children were assigned chores according to our sizes and ages."[54] The Esmont interviews similarly note that even young children had tasks. William Rush, for example, began working at the age of six. When Carlton Andrew Luck Sr. was about ten, he thinned corn, ten hours a day for a quarter. When he was a little older, he worked in the hay fields ("Oh, that was work, that was hard work"). Others fed animals, including hogs, chickens, horses, cows, and mules. In addition, children had domestic chores, hauling water from springs, finding wood for stoves, and helping wash, iron, and cook. James Jordan itemized some of those chores and the work they entailed:

> We had to make sure that there was enough firewood in the house. That might have meant going to the woodpile and actually cutting the wood.... We also had to bring water. We didn't have any water in the house, and the nearest spring [was down a hill].... We had chores like working in the garden.... And that meant going out there and chopping corn and tomatoes and whatever else was in that garden. We also had to gather the vegetables from the garden at times, like gathering beans and then preparing them so they could be cooked and so forth.... We kept our rooms straight. We made our own beds. We ironed our clothes.... And uh, really, I don't remember having to wash clothes, but we ironed our own... And we knew how to sweep the floors. We didn't have vacuum cleaners and things like that but we knew how to mop floors, how to wash dishes, practically everything around the house that had to be done.[55]

Even with multiple people working, these families were poor. Interdependence among households was essential for survival—another lesson Mable clearly received.

SCHOOL

"The schools for Colored Children were sparse," wrote local teacher Alice Fountain in 1949. "They were mostly log cabins, very small and poorly equipped. Seating capacity wasn't considered and the few seats they had were straight benches without backs or desks." Forty years earlier, another local teacher, Mrs. Verna Anderson, had been a student at Koontztown School, where we believe Mable began her education. According to Anderson, the enrollment was between sixteen and twenty students. The children walked to school and went home for lunch.[56]

When that school closed in 1920, the students transferred to the recently built Mechanicsville School.[57] Louisa County historians believe that, like many other schools for African Americans after the Civil War, Mechanicsville received some financial support from the Rosenwald Fund, endowed by Julius Rosenwald, president of Sears, Roebuck and Company. On average the fund contributed only about 15 percent of the total cost of running a school, leaving local Black communities the task of raising the bulk of the money through private donations and public taxes.[58] According to Robin Patton, local African Americans saved pennies to build schools in Louisa County. Mechanicsville had three rooms instead of one, electric

Mechanicsville School, ca. 1948. (Courtesy of Louisa County Historical Society)

lights, and an oil stove and a refrigerator purchased with the help of federal funds. Cooking occurred in a classroom.[59]

Verna Anderson noted that Black parents "were cooperative and took advantage of what they had by sending their children [to school] when they could."[60] Nevertheless, rural children often stayed home because they had to work, or the walk was too long or the weather too inclement. Although a bus was available to transport children to the Mechanicsville School, that amenity was unusual. William Rush, born in Esmont in 1927 recalled, "There was [a bus] for the white children, but we didn't have one. We had to, like, walk from here on over to the school every-year round—maybe four miles to school over here to get there, and when the . . . snow'd get bad, [the children] couldn't walk through the snow. Part time they were bare-feet anyway, so you couldn't get to school."[61]

RELIGION

Like approximately 60 percent of rural African Americans in the early twentieth century, Mable's family were Baptist. They attended the Oak Grove Baptist Church, founded in 1864 as "a brush harbor"—a secret meeting place enslaved people constructed beyond the boundaries of the plantation where they could worship without White surveillance.[62] After emancipation, the parishioners built a church. In 1977, Oak Grove merged with Bright Hope Baptist Church.[63] When we visited Louisa County in the summer of 2019, Robin helped us locate the site of the Oak Grove building. She drove us down a long dirt road surrounded by dense woods on either side, and because it was a hot day, we imagined a young Mable walking on a dusty lane with her family while the sun beat down. In a clearing we found the shell of the church, but it was in ruins.

We can gain some insight into the religiosity of Mable's maternal relatives from her cousin Chuck Lewis's autobiography. "From my earliest years," he recalled, "my grandmother [who was Dora's sister] would remind me that God was with us: 'God will fix it everytime,' she'd say. 'There's nothing He can't do. He heals the sick. He even raises the dead' . . .

Oak Grove Church, 2019. (Photo by Margaret K. Nelson)

Throughout the house, there were paintings of God—an old white man with a snowy beard—and Jesus, a young man with smooth brown hair and blue eyes. I would carry those images with me for years, reminders of the spiritual and moral discipline my grandmother instilled in us."[64] Dora's children and grandchildren may have had similar experiences.

LOOKING AHEAD

Even after moving her children to Charlottesville in 1925, Dora remained tightly bound to her family of origin. Two of her siblings lived near her in the city, and she returned with her children each summer to her home in Louisa County among her many relatives. In her oral interview, Mable recalled the summers she spent as a teenager in the country, where her mother had a garden. We will see that when the Great Depression affected Dora's livelihood, she moved back to her home in Louisa County with Mable's two sons.

2

"WHILE JIM CROW RULED THE SOUTH"

WHEN WE TOLD PEOPLE we were going to Charlottesville, they asked if we meant "*that* Charlottesville." We understood their incredulity. In August 2017, much of the nation had watched in horror as televisions displayed the Unite the Right rally in that city, when White supremacists spewed racist and anti-Semitic hatred and committed acts of violence. A car plowing into a group of protestors killed Heather Heyer and injured others. Visiting Charlottesville nearly two years later, we found a city still reeling from those events. The focus of the rally was a decision by the city council to remove two statues memorializing the Confederacy that had been erected in the early 1920s, just before Mable and her family arrived in Charlottesville.

The installation of the statues was not the city's first indication of the reign of Jim Crow. In 1898 a White mob lynched an African American man named John Henry James for allegedly raping a White woman.[1] In 1914 the Albemarle County Board of Supervisors razed a largely Black area called McKee Row, in deference to Whites who declared the buildings an "eyesore" and the inhabitants too "rowdy."[2] And then, soon after D. W. Griffith's enormously popular film *Birth of a Nation* opened in 1915, it was shown in Charlottesville. Depicting African Americans as lazy and stupid and Reconstruction as a savage period, the movie metaphorically united North and South in an Aryan civilization led by the Ku Klux Klan (KKK). The film propelled the resurgence of the KKK, launching a new reign of terror and violence.[3]

The two statues symbolized the regime of White supremacy. The first was unveiled in 1921, the year the KKK opened a Charlottesville chapter. Standing on land that had once been McKee Row, the statue depicted Thomas J. "Stonewall" Jackson astride his horse. Beneath the statue was a granite pedestal featuring two allegorical Aryans, one, a young man, with a sword and shield. The unveiling marked the culmination of three days of celebrations, including a grand gala reunion of Confederate veterans and a march of White elementary school students through the city.[4]

The second memorial, a large bronze equestrian statue of Robert E. Lee, appeared in 1924. Once again, the unveiling followed a series of galas and festivals. This time the celebrations lasted a week and included not only the opening of the organization of Confederate Veterans but also a nighttime KKK parade. Charlottesville's newspaper, the *Daily Progress,* reported that "thousands lined the sidewalks" to view the "march of the white robed figures."[5] At the inaugural ceremony of the statue, Edwin Alderman, president of the University of Virginia (UVA), declared that Lee "had done even more than his great prototype, Washington." He was "the embodiment of the best that there is in all the sincere and romantic history of the whole state. Its triumphs, its defeats, its joys, its sufferings, its rebirth. The pride and its patience center in him."[6] Alderman's remarks epitomized White sentiment in the city that greeted Mable when she moved there in 1925 with her mother and siblings.

THE UNIVERSITY

Before August 2017, Charlottesville was known primarily as the home of the University of Virginia, the institution designed and founded by Thomas Jefferson. In the past few years, several universities have begun to grapple with the place of slavery in their history. "At the University of Virginia," Maurice D. McInnis writes, "the role of slavery was . . . deeply entangled and . . . pervasive, shaping the lives of students, faculty, and the enslaved. In its very inception, even in Jefferson's own imagining of what the University could be, he understood it to be an institution with slavery at its core, both in how it operated and in its purpose."[7] Although early records remain fragmentary, it is clear that both skilled and unskilled enslaved laborers were essential to the construction of the institution. They cleared the land, cut down trees, hauled lumber, manufactured bricks, and cut and nailed timber.[8]

After UVA opened in 1825, it operated like a plantation, heavily dependent on the work of enslaved people. At any one time, the university, the faculty, and the hotelkeepers who boarded students (all of whom were men) enslaved a combined total of between 125 and 200 Black people.[9] As Jefferson had at Monticello, he designed the institution to carefully conceal their work, but the university could not function without them.[10] Those who worked in the boarding houses for students began the day by lighting fires in the bedrooms. They then cleaned, washed, prepared food, ran errands, and provided various other personal services for the students.[11] Although students were not allowed to bring people enslaved by their families, they were considered the masters of all enslaved people on campus. Students who committed brutal acts against them were punished erratically.[12] And proslavery thought pervaded UVA. At a July Fourth campus celebration in 1839, Robert M. T. Hunter, a UVA graduate and member of the US House of Representatives, declared that slavery "was the only relation in which the two races can co-exist in harmony and operate for the mutual benefit of both."[13] Harriet Beecher Stowe, the author of *Uncle Tom's Cabin,* was burned in effigy when her sister Catharine Beecher visited the university in 1855.[14]

After the Civil War, UVA continued to enshrine White supremacy. It was a major center for promulgating eugenics. In a 1900 speech, Paul Barringer, chair of the faculty, argued the abolition of slavery had disastrous consequences because "fifty centuries of savagery in the blood cannot be held down by two centuries of forced good behavior if the controlling influences which held down his savagery are withdrawn as they have been in this case."[15] In 1921, the school had a KKK chapter. The following year the student yearbook introduced the section on clubs and organizations with a display of White hooded figures on horses.[16] Numerous faculty members joined the Anglo Saxon Clubs of America, a racist organization founded by a UVA graduate. Its "fundamental purpose" was the "preservation and maintenance of Angle Saxon ideals in America."[17]

African Americans also continued to perform menial jobs in and around the university. Rebecca McGinness, a Charlottesville schoolteacher, told an interviewer that when she was growing up in the late nineteenth and early twentieth centuries, "most blacks made their living off of the University . . . or in a business near the University." Black men still "rose early and made fires for the students in the mornings." McGinness's grandmother, "a former slave," was "a seamstress, and in her spare time she took in student laundry." Other Black women "worked as domestics for the White people near the University who kept boarding houses for the students."[18] Interviewed in 1995, Lucille Woodfolk-Jones remembered her father going to the station to meet the trains so he could transport students' baggage to their rooms in his truck.[19]

Mable and her sons were among the many African Americans who worked at or near the campus. In 1950 Mable was a "maid" in the Brandon Apartments that now houses UVA students. Her son James H. Jones was a cook at the university, and her other son Thomas M. Jones was "a baker's second" in a cafeteria on Rugby Road, where many fraternities and sororities were located.[20] Although UVA enrolled its first African American student in 1950, it did not admit substantial numbers of African American undergraduates until the late 1960s, after most other southern universities had done so.[21] As far as we know, none of Mable's children or grandchildren were students there. Members of her extended family, however, continue to be employed by the university and its affiliates.[22]

THE CITY OF CHARLOTTESVILLE

If Charlottesville was distinctive in some ways, it also resembled many other cities throughout Virginia in the Jim Crow era. In the 1920s the General Assembly enacted two laws upholding White supremacy. The first, the Racial Integrity Act, was passed in 1924, the year the statue of Robert E. Lee was unveiled in Charlottesville and the year before Mable and her family arrived there. That act prohibited interracial marriage and stated that only a person "who has no trace whatsoever of any blood other than Caucasian" could be defined as White. Two years later, the General Assembly passed the Public Assemblages Act requiring segregation in all public places.[23]

Rebecca McGinness remembered playing with White children in her Charlottesville neighborhood. "But when Jim Crow laws were passed," she stated, "all of that changed. Jim Crow separated the races in everything."[24] African Americans encountered *Whites only* and *Colored only* signs everywhere, restricting them to the balcony of movie theaters, the back of buses, and special areas in bus stations. Ruth Ward, an Esmont resident, commented that in Charlottesville "the bathrooms [in bus stations] were segregated, too. And of course the quality of the black side naturally was not as good as the white side." Another Esmont resident, William Rush, recalled that when he wanted a sandwich in Charlottesville, "you couldn't go to a restaurant to buy you no food. You had to go to the window and buy it, pay for it there, and eat it on your way home. You couldn't go in there and sit down and eat it."[25]

Other Esmont and Charlottesville residents described buying clothes in the city. According to Jettie Gardner-Hardy, stores did not allow Black customers to "try on anything. We had to bring it home. If it didn't fit you, take it back, you know." She then amended her comment: actually, African Americans could not return anything. Ruth Brooks said that because there were no clothing stores in Esmont, her family went to Charlottesville to shop. Sometimes her parents "could go and buy the clothes for us, and if they were too small, if they got shoes for you and they were too small maybe you just had to wear them anyway."[26]

Residential segregation forced Black residents to live in the least desirable parts of town with the fewest city services, typically low-lying areas and near the railroad. Two sociology master's theses (later published by the University of Virginia as Phelps-Stokes Fellowship Papers) describe the lives of Blacks in Charlottesville in the early part of the twentieth century. Although racist comments mar both accounts, the theses provide some insight into the city's various African American sections. One area, known as South Sixth Street or "Old Scottsville Road," had a gulch that included two small factories as well as small homes. Marjorie Felice Irwin wrote, "The houses are merely two and three room shacks. They contain no conveniences and practically no furniture."[27] According to Helen Camp de Corse, the nearby "Cox's Row," where Mable's future husband's family lived in 1920, was similar.[28] It contained small houses lit by oil lamps, and a single outside hydrant provided water for the many families.

The area between Oak, Ridge, First, and Diggs was known as "Happy Hollow." Irwin reports that the name came "from the care-free attitude of the Negroes who used to live here."[29] That undoubtedly would have been a surprise to Mable's mother, whose son bought her a house on what was then an extension of Parrott Street (now Oakmont Street) in 1947. According to de Corse, the street was "little better than Scottsville Road in housing and social conditions." A 1929 map demonstrates that several businesses dotted the area, undoubtedly adding to the noise, dirt, and commotion.[30] The lack of modern conveniences must have meant that, far from enjoying carefree lives, Mable and her mother had to undertake extremely arduous household chores after completing the day's paid work.

De Corse had kinder words for another low-lying area, "a gradually sloping hollow, with a stream that carried refuse from the gas house and occasionally flooded the houses." Despite the stream, she reported that the houses were better than those in many other areas and most had vegetable gardens in the back. Most residents, de Corse added, worked "in the better white sections of the city."[31] The Black people de Corse deemed "successful" lived in three other areas with better homes and yards—"the west end of Preston Avenue, to Rugby Road," "the area from Fourth street N.W. reaching as far west as Thirteenth Street and along Page Street to Tenth Street," and "South of Main Street, in the section including Seventh, Oak and Ridge Street."[32] Mable and members of her family rented homes in these "better" areas when they first moved to Charlottesville.[33] The first home Mable's mother owned, however, was in one of the poorer sections.

De Corse was especially impressed by the Ridge Street area where, she noted, the living conditions "approximate those of middle class white homes with the same knick-knacks, finishing papers and magazines." "Indeed," she continued with what appears to be astonishment, "some of the literature is superior to that found in the average middle class white

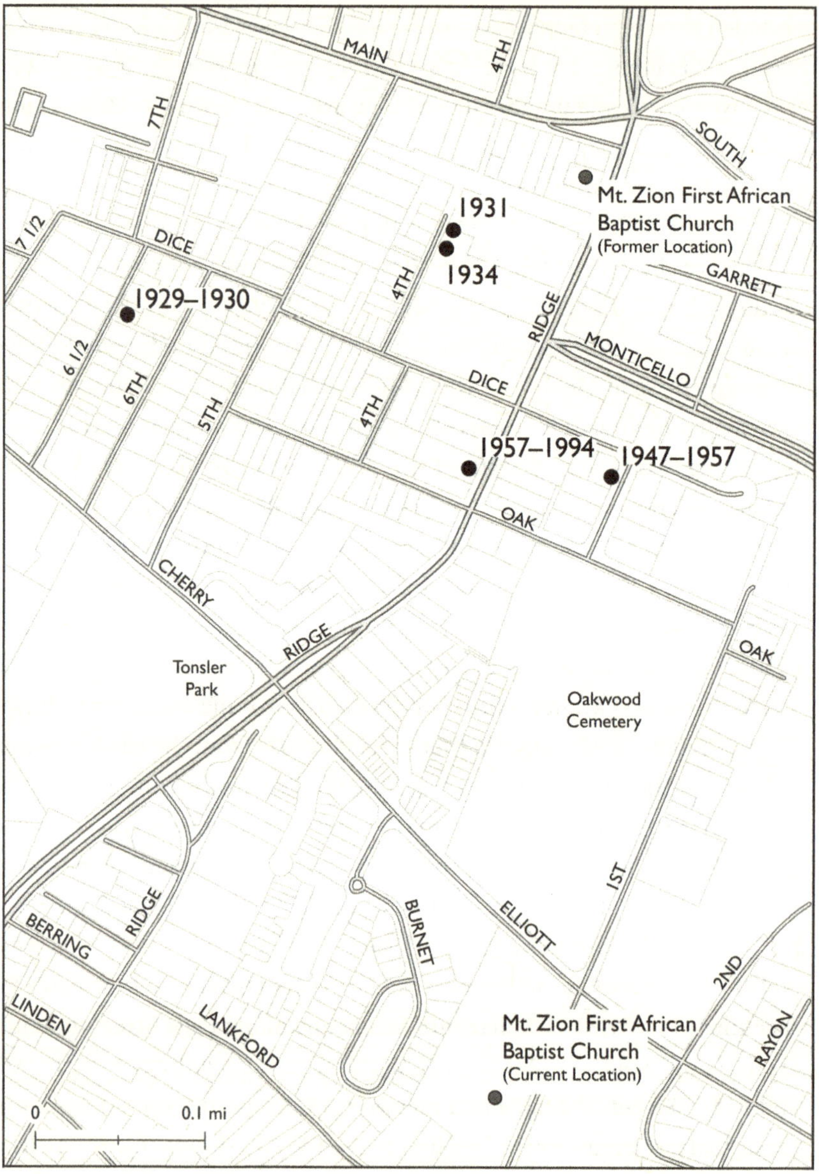

Location of Mable Jones's homes in Charlottesville

home."[34] As we will see, by the time Mable and her mother bought a house on Ridge Street in 1956, its reputation had begun to change.

As this survey of the various residential areas suggests, African Americans in Charlottesville, as elsewhere, were divided into distinct communities. Visits to and by Mable, her mother, and her sons were reported in the society columns of two African American newspapers, the *Reflector* (in the 1930s) and the *Charlottesville Tribune* (in the early 1950s). We assume, however, that they had relatively little interaction with the elite group of African American residents known as the "four hundred." According to historian John Hammond Moore, most members of that group were "businessmen, ministers, teachers and contractors, although their ranks also included a barber, doctor, cobbler and undertaker."[35]

EDUCATION

In her 1995 interview, Mable said that her mother brought her family to Charlottesville in 1925 because "the schools were better for the children."[36] If superior to the rural schools in Louisa County, Charlottesville African American public schools suffered in comparison with White ones. That year Virginia state and local governments spent nearly four times as much for each White school child as for each Black one ($40.27 versus $10.47).[37] The only school for Black students in Charlottesville at the time was the Jefferson Grade School, which continued through eighth grade. A teacher there from 1945 to 1960, Rebecca McGinness was able to provide especially helpful information. She noted that she had to buy supplies from her small salary, that the classrooms were so overcrowded that the school often operated on split sessions, and that she learned about the disparity in pay between White and Black teachers by accident. What she stressed, however, was her deep commitment to improving all aspects of her students' lives. "I tried to take care of both the children's physical and educational needs," she stated. "The teachers took turns preparing large pots of soup or oatmeal" to ensure that none of the children were hungry. She also conducted physical inspections and had a comb and brush ready for those who needed them. "The children did not think of this as meddling in their personal lives," McGinness insisted. "They took it as acts of love."

In addition, McGinness taught "character and morals building," not only the "three R's." Religious instruction was an important part of the day. "We tried to teach the students how to live. Some of them had no one other than the teacher to look up to."[38] We will see in chapter 6 that, when given the opportunity to transfer to previously segregated all-White schools, some students pointed to the dedication of teachers like McGinness to explain why they decided to stay where they were.

The year after Dora and her family arrived in Charlottesville, a high school for African American children finally opened. Until then, Black students who wished to continue their education had to go elsewhere, an expense only the most prosperous families could afford. "Many African Americans wanted to send their children to school above the eighth grade," McGinness noted, "but most could not afford to do so. It was not because they didn't want to, as many books would have us believe. A college education was as precious then as it is now."[39] McGinness was one of the fortunate ones. She was able to become a teacher because her parents sent her to the Hampton Agricultural and Normal Institute (now Hampton University), founded after the Civil War by Black and White leaders of the American Missionary Association to provide education to freedpeople.[40] The opening of the segregated Jefferson High School did not mean Black students had reached parity with Whites. Unlike the White high school, established in 1890, the segregated Jefferson High was initially just two years. A 2003 study by Elizabeth Moore, an architectural historian, examined the differences between that school and the "White" Venable Elementary School, which was built at the same time. Venable had two stories, a raised portico entrance, and dramatic white columns. According to Moore, that "civic-minded architecture [served as] a tool to teach students to be community leaders." By contrast, Jefferson's cheerless façade displayed "elements common in industrial architecture," demonstrating the social position its students were expected to occupy.[41] *The Negro in Virginia*, compiled by African American writers of the Work Projects Administration, reported that the cost of instruction for each student in the state in 1938 was $26.23 for Whites and $16.04 for African Americans.[42] Florence C. Bryant had taught in Black Charlottesville schools for eighteen years when she was transferred to Walker, a desegregated junior high in 1963. "Having been accustomed to shortages of materials and equipment at the segregated schools," she was "overwhelmed by the abundance of materials and equipment at Walker."[43]

Although it received less funding than its White counterpart did, Jefferson High School served its students and the surrounding community well. The school boasted a number of extra-curricular activities, including a band, a glee club, a debating society, and various sports teams. The school curriculum devoted weeks to special topics such as "music appreciation," "self appreciation," "a century of progress," and "patriotism." Course offerings included English, math, history, French, and science. Local groups, such as the "DeLuxe Glee Club," held premiers in the high school auditorium, and the senior class regularly performed its own play for large audiences. Moreover, the school was proud of the students' achievements. The African American newspaper, the *Reflector,* regularly reported on the honor roll and listed the names of students who graduated and were on their way to "Negro Colleges."[44]

Neither Mable nor most of her siblings appear to have benefited educationally from the move to the city. Mable was sixteen at the time and although she might have briefly attended Jefferson Elementary School, she said that she "quit" at the end of eighth grade. When the interviewer pointed out that her school did not extend further, Mable insisted the decision was hers. "I quit," she repeated. We lack information about the education of Beatrice, Mable's only sister. We know, however, her brother Lawrence, who was fourteen in 1925, did not continue his education past grammar school.[45] Thomas was twelve when the family came to Charlottesville, but it is unclear whether he attended school there. According to his draft card, he had poor eyesight.[46] The 1930 census indicates that he was living that year at the Virginia State School for Colored Deaf and Blind Children in Newport News, founded in 1909.[47] There he was one of approximately seventy-five students ranging in age from seven to twenty-eight.[48] Whatever education that school offered, it did not teach him to read and write; when Thomas signed up for the draft in 1940, he left a mark for his name.[49] Henry, seven at the time, appears to have been the only one who profited educationally from the family's move to Charlottesville. Among Mable's brothers, he alone graduated from high school.[50]

EMPLOYMENT

Mable said that her mother, Dora, also brought her family to Charlottesville because it provided more economic opportunities. Mable appears to have been proud of the dressmaking business her mother established there: "She used to make clothes for everybody *(chuckle)* in Charlottesville almost."[51] Dressmakers were considered "artisans" or "skilled tradespeople," and Dora must have been highly skilled.[52] Charles Jones, one of Mable's grandchildren, told us that Dora sewed wedding dresses, primarily for Whites, who could pay more than Black residents. Like other forms of homework, dressmaking enabled women to watch children during the day. But it often extended far into the night, made small houses even more cluttered, and increased the noise.[53]

Dora may have transmitted her skills to her two daughters, but they, like the great majority of African American women at the time, entered paid domestic work.[54] Charlottesville offered few other options. Like Mable and her sister, Ruth Ward moved to Charlottesville from the country. She then left for the North because "there were more opportunities. Here it was domestic only." As far as we can tell, domestic work in private homes and at the Brandon Apartments was the only kind of employment Mable ever had. A year before her death in 1995, when she was eighty-six, she said that the previous year she had ended over forty years of working "as a domestic" for her last employer.[55]

The 1962 memoir of Sarah Patton Boyle, a White woman who became a prominent civil rights activist in Charlottesville, helps us understand the attitudes of employers of private household workers during the early twentieth century. Born in 1906 in Albemarle County (the county surrounding Charlottesville), Boyle grew up assuming "that Negroes belonged to a lower order of man than we."[56] The only African Americans she knew were servants. "Nearly everyone above the 'poor white' class could afford a colored girl," she wrote. "You gave her a room, board, your cast-off clothes, and at most three or four dollars a month." The room "had a slave-quarters atmosphere." It was not "even plastered—just rib-like beams and rafters, with an occasional nail driven in an inch to serve as a clothes hook." The floor was "bare and unvarnished." Boyle's parents "had no consciousness of being less than kind in this" because "Negroes' own houses were worse still."[57]

Boyle carried those attitudes to Charlottesville when she married a young University of Virginia faculty member during the Depression. Because her husband's salary was small, they lived in a tiny one-room basement apartment. Boyle scrimped on food but "foregoing a maid entirely was one sacrifice to poverty which I didn't propose to make." She decided to hire a teenage girl who could stop by after school to clean the flat and wash the dishes. In exchange, Boyle would provide the girl with "the experience of her first job, my cast-off clothes and one dime an hour, or fifty cents a five-day week." Boyle's only requirements were "that the girl know her place, do her work quickly, and show appreciation of the opportunity I was offering by making a real effort to learn what nice people expected of their maids." "Unconscious of exploitation," Boyle felt "rather magnanimous."[58]

Boyle was unusual in her eventual criticism of her former attitudes. White Charlottesville residents interviewed twenty years later seemed unaware that anyone might have treated private household workers unfairly. Mrs. Dudley C. Smith, also the wife of a University of Virginia faculty member, remarked, "Everybody had a maid," before adding "mine lived in the basement."[59] Charlotte Yancey recalled that in the 1920s her family "had a black boy who lived in the attic at one time. He took care of the yard and the car."[60] Yancey was also one of the many respondents who took it for granted that, before the 1960s, Whites and African Americans interacted only as employer/employee: "Blacks lived further out. I've never really been exposed to minorities, but I've always accepted them. We had live-in servants that were black."[61] Josephine Boyke said, "Blacks and whites before never mixed socially. We really didn't see much of them.[62] Irene Valentine, who had married into a family that had lived in Charlottesville since 1838, accepted segregation as the way things were "the world over." She then added that "the 'colored' people were servants. I had a colored nanny."[63]

In addition, the respondents expressed stereotypical ideas about the devotion servants felt for their employers. Josephine Boyke insisted that she "loved [her nanny] and she loved me."[64] Irene Valentine could not understand why her servant refused to live in her employer's house in the better part of town: "Rosa, my maid has been with me 42 years, and she's the best friend I've got in the whole world. People still beg me not to take a Negro to board, but I'd take Rosa if she'd come. But she won't do it. She wants to live over 'across the tracks' with her friends."[65] From the perspective of Rosa and her peers, homes in the Black section of town allowed them to return to family and community each day and, perhaps most importantly, evade the gaze of their employers.

FIGHTING OPPRESSION

For all the virulent racism they encountered, African Americans were never simply victims of a brutal system. Studies of Black domestic workers in the South are filled with examples of various forms of resistance. James Jordan, an Esmont resident, noted that when his mother's employer withheld her pay, she asked, "Did the train not come? That's bringing the checks?" (Although her employers fired her on the spot, he rehired her the following day.)[66] Despite the difficulties of isolated workers engaging in collective action, washerwomen in Atlanta went on strike in 1881.[67] African American women in Houston formed the Women's Domestic Union in 1916. A year later, those in Norfolk established the Working Women's Union to "unite laboring women and bring about a closer relationship between them."[68]

Other forms of organized protest against Jim Crow occurred in Charlottesville. Rebecca McGinness remarked that "it took a long, hard struggle and a lot of agitation to finally get a high school for African Americans." The Reverend Clarence M. Long, the leader of the fight, "went to bat to help secure the basic rights for African American children in Charlottesville, when such carrying on was very unpopular. . . . He stirred up the white people so much that they thought it better to concede to the African American community's demand for a high school than to allow him to stir up the African American Community any further."[69] In 1921, a group of Black Charlottesville residents published a series of demands that included not only the creation of a four-year high school but also representation on the city council and school board, the abolition of Jim Crow streetcars, improved city facilities in African American neighborhoods, and teacher salaries that were not based on race.[70] Other African Americans protested oppression by voting with their feet. Despite considerable migration into the city from rural areas between 1900 and 1940, Charlottesville's African American population decreased as a percentage of the whole.[71] Like African Americans throughout the South, those living in Virginia headed North as part of what has been called the Great Migration.[72]

Moreover, as Rebecca McGinness noted, "While Jim Crow ruled the South . . . , African Americans created a vibrant, satisfying social life for themselves."[73] According to the *Reflector*, several people spent an evening "in dancing, revelry and feasting" to celebrate the eighteenth birthday of a woman living on Ridge Street on January 27, 1934. In February of the same year, "young people" in the city flirted at a Valentine Social.[74] Churches were at the center of much of the social life. "From the early days of slavery," historian Evelyn Brooks Higginbotham writes, "the black church had constituted the backbone of the black community. . . . As the 'invisible institution' of the slaves, the church had long promoted a sense of individual and collective worth and perpetuated a belief in human dignity that countered the racist preachings of the master class."[75] After emancipation, the church continued to support and nourish African American communities. Although men dominated leadership positions in the church, women made essential contributions to the various social service agencies associated with it.

By the early 1930s, Charlottesville boasted six African American Baptist churches.[76] During slavery, Black Baptists in Charlottesville had been able to worship only from the balcony of the White First Baptist Church. Soon after emancipation, they began to build their own church. McGinness's father was a carpenter, and "after working all day, he and other former slaves worked on the church in the evening. The women took meals to the workers at the church."[77] Built on the property of the Delevan Hotel, which had served as both a barracks and a hospital during the Civil War, the church was named the Delevan Baptist Church; later it became the First Baptist Church.

Mable and her family were members of the Mount Zion First African Baptist Church, established by members of the Delevan Baptist Church who refused to worship under a White pastor. In 1875 they constructed a wooden building at 105 Ridge Street. In 1883 the congregation razed that structure and replaced it a year later with a brick edifice designed by George Wallace Spooner.[78] After paying off its mortgage in 1905, the church gradually was able to construct a steeple and basement, add stained-glass windows, and install an organ.[79] "Standing like a mighty bulwark behind the religious life of Charlottesville," the African American newspaper the *Norfolk Journal and Guide* wrote in 1933, "the Mt. Zion Baptist Church . . . is still 'carrying on' in a highly commendable way the work which was initiated by the fathers in the early days of their freedom." The church had "been pastored by some of the race's most prominent preachers" and was still one of the largest in the city.[80] Chapter 7 discusses the central roles both Mable and her mother played there.

Although Mable and her family left behind some of their relatives in Louisa County, they lived near others in Charlottesville. The move also brought them close to a large Black community offering new opportunities for social engagement and political activism.

MARRIAGE AND CHILDREN

In 1929, Mable married James Henry Jones when she was twenty and he was twenty-two.[81] We do not know the details of how they met, but Charlottesville's thriving Black community provided plenty of opportunities for socializing. Born in Simeon, Virginia, to James Andrew and Louise Jones, James had three older sisters and younger twin siblings, a sister and a brother. By 1920, the parents were separated, and Louise had brought her children to Charlottesville, where they lived in Cox's Row. She supported the family by taking in laundry. It is likely that her children were also involved in that enterprise.[82] McGinness recalled that when her mother "washed and ironed for high-class white people," it "was a full-time job that we all had to help with. We children had to draw water into a big pot from a spigot in our backyard. We put the pot on top of the stove to heat. Then we brought in a supply of wood and coal. Those were our chores before and after school." McGinness's sister and brother delivered the clothes to their mother's customers.[83]

After they married, Mable and James lived first with Mable's mother.[84] Within a year they had a son, whom they named James Henry. Their second son, Thomas Marshall, arrived fourteen months later, and Mable and James moved into their own apartment with their two young children.[85] After each birth, Mable spent two weeks in the University of Virginia Hospital, the only Charlottesville hospital that admitted African Americans.[86] She probably did not have a happy experience there. Jettie Gardner-Hardy remembered that when her father broke his leg he was "in the basement where the black folks were. White folks upstairs." Another Esmont interviewee, Ruth Brooks, reported that when her father "had a lot of pain" after a serious accident at work and "suffered a lot," he, too, was put in the basement, "which wasn't very nice, but that's the way it was then."[87] What the sociology student James Wortham Barksdale called the "deplorable" aspects of the basement wards included a lack of ventilation and sunlight, overcrowding, rats, and dripping pipes. Although two Black doctors practiced in Charlottesville, neither had hospital privileges.[88] Barksdale noted that "patients on the Negro wards have been known to insist that they be allowed to return to their homes to die rather than suffer the inconvenience, discomfort, and exposure they often undergo during the course of their hospitalization."[89]

Historian Herbert Gutman has noted that the African American practice of naming children after beloved relatives, a custom that dates back to slavery, demonstrates the endurance of family ties despite the forces that threatened to destroy them.[90] Mable and James Jones adhered to that custom. Their first son, James Henry Jones, was named after his father who, in turn, had been named after his father.[91] The name might have had special significance for Mable as well: a James appears in Mable's family tree as an uncle (Mable's father's brother, James Harry Walls).[92] Mable's grandchildren told us that their father, James Henry, was often called Mickey, although they did not know (or reveal) the origin of that nickname.

The second son, Thomas, carried a name that goes back many generations in Mable's family. The family tree includes three Thomas Hugheses. One, born in 1833, was the brother of Mable's great-grandfather, and another born in 1852, the son of Mable's great-grandparents.[93] Because the second Thomas Hughes lived until 1940 and remained in Quarlestown,

Mable and her children came to know him well. A third Thomas Hughes (1872–1948) was Mable's uncle (Dora's brother) who also lived long enough to meet Mable and her children. Two other Thomases held the last name Walls (Mable's maiden name). Mable's brother and his son shared the same name as Senior and Junior; the older Thomas Walls, for some reason, had the nickname "Snap Goat."[94] Thomas Jones, Mable's son, had the middle name Marshall, which represented the paternal side of Mable's family: her father's father was Marshall Walls. Marshall was also the middle name of Mable's brother Lawrence.[95] When we visited Charlottesville, we learned that this name was used frequently to distinguish Mable's son Thomas from the many other Thomases in the family. Among those of Mable's friends and family we met, he was always called "Tom Marshall."

The arrival of James and Thomas begins to connect Mable's story with our own. We were aware from a young age that the care Mable bestowed on us represented an irreplaceable loss to her sons. As the next chapter demonstrates, Mable had been forced to surrender their day-to-day care even before she arrived at our house.

3

SURVIVING IN THE GREAT DEPRESSION AND WORLD WAR II

THE YEAR OF MABLE'S wedding was an inauspicious time to begin married life. The stock market crash on October 29, 1929, signaled the beginning of the Great Depression, which lasted twelve years. Although Virginia fared better than most other states, it too experienced rising unemployment, a sharp increase in the relief rolls, and drastic cuts in government spending. As elsewhere in the nation, in Virginia the disaster hit African Americans with special ferocity. The last to be hired, they were typically the first to be fired.[1]

New Deal programs provided little help to African Americans. The Social Security Act of 1935 excluded approximately half the workers in the American economy, including agricultural and domestic workers—a large percentage of whom were African Americans.[2] As a result, two-thirds of all Black workers had no coverage under the new act, compared with one-quarter of White workers.[3] Private household workers and farm laborers also were excluded from the 1938 Fair Labor Standards Act, which introduced the concept of the eight-hour day, forty-hour work week, established minimum wage and paid overtime, and forbade child labor. "Dear Madam," a cook wrote to Eleanor Roosevelt in 1938, "We the domestic find that we are not considered in the wage and hour bill and allso the social security act. I am writing you asking if you will please consider the domestic[;] after all we are essential we spend all of lives working in one place not getting enough to be able to save anything. So when we grow old we have nothing to go upon."[4]

Black workers also received paltry assistance from public works programs. The Work Projects Administration (WPA) relegated the relatively few African Americans it hired to the least desirable positions and paid them less than Whites for the same jobs.[5] Asked what her father did in the WPA, Mrs. Rush, who grew up in Esmont, just outside of Charlottesville, responded, "He did what most black persons do: cut bushes and dig ditches." More than half the women hired by the WPA worked on sewing projects. Some counties instituted tests that served to exclude many Black applicants. The requirement that local sponsors donate materials also worked to disadvantage African Americans.[6]

In addition, there is little evidence that the other major WPA program for women, "Household Training Centers," benefited many African Americans.[7] A letter addressed to Theodore Roosevelt, but clearly intended for his nephew, explained the impact of discrimination on impoverished lives: "I am writing you and askin you is it fair or not for the white woman to do all this WPA work in this county. Mr. Roosevelt I am a poor Negro widow woman and have 3 children to take care of and I don't have nothing to go upon. They told me that they diden no if they wood work enymore Negro woman on this WPA work. This is why I am writing to you . . . I wood like to no please sir Mr. Roosevelt is that right or wrong . . . We poor Negro is yours to. So plese turn us a helping hand by put us Negro woman to work on these WPA work." The writer identified herself as "a Negro woman here in Mt. Pleasant, Texas" who was "afraid" to attach her name to the letter.[8]

MABLE JONES'S WORK AND FAMILY DURING THE DEPRESSION

Although Mable must have experienced the arrival of her two sons as a great joy, she lost pay when she took time off for their births. Their births also compounded the difficulties of combining work with family responsibilities. Some employed women found ways to work at different times from their partners so they could share childcare. Some left even very young children home on their own or in the care of slightly older siblings. Some relied on relatives or neighbors, either paying them or drawing on their good will. Mable's granddaughter Theresa told us that Mable tried yet another strategy, taking the boys with her when she went to work. We are not sure, however, just how long that arrangement lasted, how old the children were, or how difficult it was for them to remain unobtrusive in someone else's home. Rosa Agee, a resident of Esmont, remembered that when her mother went to work in a private household "she used to have us to sit down . . . We had to sit a certain place and don't make any noise or anything, and when she'd finish she would let us go home." When asked why the mother took her children with her, Agee answered, "Because she have nobody else to keep us."[9]

Mable's husband James's family probably was in no position to help. By 1930, his mother, Louise Jones, had moved the family from Cox's Row to Fourth Street SW, where she continued working as a laundress.[10] Louise's daughter Eva was living with her and able to assist her mother. They may have had less paid work. One historian notes that by the early 1920s, many White Virginia families had "mechanical devices in their homes" and thus were less dependent on Black domestic workers.[11] In addition, the need to economize must have forced many White families to dispense with such assistance in the Depression. The paid workload of James's mother and sister may have diminished, but they now had a new caregiving responsibility. The census reports that another daughter, Lillie, was living at home with a one-year-old son. Because she was identified as a "maid" in a hospital, we assume she left the baby with her mother and sister when she worked. Other children were no longer living nearby.[12]

But even had James's family been able to offer assistance, Mable probably would have turned to her own mother, Dora. The two women had always had a close bond and had lived together except for a few years after Mable's marriage. Thus, when Mable accepted employment as a live-in domestic worker for the Paxson family in Ivy, a rural town adjacent to Charlottesville, she sent her sons James and Thomas to her mother.[13]

Since the 1920s, growing numbers of private household workers had begun to reject jobs that did not allow them to return to their own households at night; women with children were especially adamant about refusing live-in work.[14] Day jobs had other advantages as well. With clearly defined hours and tasks, day workers did not remain "on call" at all times. Traveling to and from their jobs like other workers enhanced self-esteem. And workers with several different employers were less beholden to one.[15] City directories and censuses indicate that both Mable's sister Beatrice and her sister-in-law Beulah (married to Mable's brother Thomas) worked as "maids" for many years; however, neither appears to have held a job requiring her to live in her employer's home.[16] Mable must have felt she had no choice. On various documents during the 1930s and early 1940s, including the census, city directories, and both his selective service registration and enlistment record, Mable's husband, James, described himself as an auto mechanic.[17] Those records revealed that he changed employers at least once but provided no information about either his wages or whether or not he experienced periods of unemployment. We do know, however, that the rate of joblessness of Black men in Charlottesville was extremely high throughout the Depression.[18] It also is possible that the marriage had broken down by this time. Mable later reported that James deserted her in 1944. But perhaps she already knew that she could not count on him and that the full burden of supporting the household fell on her.

Mable also may have accepted a live-in job because she had difficulty finding other employment. "The plight of Negro domestics is an exceedingly serious one," wrote Mary Anderson, head of the Women's Bureau in the Department of Labor, in 1936.[19] Whites who had been accustomed to hiring domestic help dismissed some or all when incomes fell. African American household workers also faced increasing competition from Whites who would have spurned such work in better times. In May 1934, the Norfolk Housewives League was reported to be giving instruction in techniques of domestic service to unemployed White women.[20] African American women who secured employment often found that their wages had dropped while the workload had increased. In 1937, the educator and activist Nannie Burroughs noted that the exclusion of domestic workers from the Social Security Act had left them at "greater prey to exploiters who themselves are protected by the act."[21] As we will see in chapter 5, African American newspapers were replete with stories of unscrupulous employers of domestic workers.

In that context, Mable's job at the Paxsons' might have seemed like a very good one. Unlike most day jobs, it meant full-time work. In 1940, Mable's employers reported her salary as $416, well above the average of $354 for live-in domestic workers in that local area.[22] The Paxsons could afford to pay well. Although C. Armonde Paxson's income is not listed in the census, we know he was an attorney with an office on Court Square in Charlottesville.[23] Mable's job with the Paxsons was the first among three (that we know of) with wealthy, if not prominent, families. Whites, such as the Paxsons, may have seen Mable as a desirable employee for several reasons. One possibility is that because Mable had been brought up in a rural area, she was viewed as a particularly desirable candidate: the White women Susan Tucker interviewed for her book, *Telling Memories among Southern Women: Domestic Workers and Their Employers in the Segregated South,* believed "country-bred blacks were more docile and trustworthy than city-bred blacks."[24] Perhaps Dora Walls's reputation as a dressmaker paved the way for Mable. In addition, Mable was a respected member of her church and, as we know from our own experience, presented herself as extremely warm and competent.

This new job changed Dora's life. By the time she assumed charge of James and Thomas, she was once again living in Louisa County. On December 16, 1933, the African American weekly newspaper, *The Reflector,* reported that several women, "motored to Gordonsville where they were guests of Mrs. Dora Walls, formerly of this city." Three weeks later, readers of *The Reflector* learned that Dora's daughter Beatrice had joined her in Gordonsville.[25] In all likelihood, desperation drove Dora back to Louisa County. We assume her dressmaking clientele dwindled as Whites cut back on nonessential services. In Louisa County, she had a house and garden as well as the support of relatives, including two sisters who had remained there with their families. After Dora's sister, Lucy Winston, and her husband also decided (or were compelled) to bring their two grandchildren and their adopted son from Charlottesville back to their home in Louisa County, four sisters lived in adjacent houses.[26]

In leaving her children with her mother in order to accept better employment, Mable was following a common practice.[27] But the arrangement could not have been easy for anyone in the family. The autobiography of Chuck Lewis, the grandson of Dora's sister Lucy Winston, helps us imagine how James and Thomas may have experienced the separation. Lewis's mother, too, worked in Charlottesville while he lived with his grandparents. "Sometimes I wished she wouldn't come," he wrote. He was "always so glad when she came, but so sad to see her leave." She arrived by bus every Saturday to "spend the night, offering up some little treat, just being the sweet, loving woman that she was. Then she'd climb back on the bus again Sunday and head away on the dusty Virginia roads that led to Charlottesville, twenty miles and an hour or two of tears from her little boy."[28]

The limited testimony we have of other children suggests that Lewis's feelings were widely shared. For example, Irene Williams, who grew up in Louisiana in the 1930s and 1940s deeply mourned her mother's absences:

> My mother—they called her a live-in maid because she stayed with the white folks. She left us with our grandmother so she could go off to work. And I remember her coming home, and I was so glad to see my mother. She stayed with us Saturday and Sunday, and she told me, she said, 'Baby, Mamma got to leave again.' And I would cry. I didn't want my mother to leave, but she did. And my grandmother took me into the kitchen as she didn't want my mother to see me crying and feel sorry because she had to leave . . . I wanted my mother there with me then. But she couldn't take care of me; she had to work.[29]

If James and Thomas ever accompanied their mother to the Paxsons', the boys' responses might have resembled those of Lewis when his mother took him to "the comfortable homes of the 'white folk' who employed her." Lewis's eyes "grew wide as I saw how well they lived. I didn't feel deprived, just amazed by all that I saw. Everything seemed to sparkle. They had wooden floors that were waxed and shiny, fine antiques, beautiful china and crystal. I remember more than once getting on a little area rug and pulling myself through the house while my mother cleaned. Those houses were like a wonderland."[30]

Lewis's autobiography enables us to glimpse other aspects of James and Thomas's lives in Louisa County. Lewis (and we assume James and Thomas) lived in "a four-room house in a little speck on the map called Quarlestown." Because their little community was entirely Black, they encountered little racial prejudice. They had "a country life, heating with wood, growing our own food, drawing water from the well, heading for the outhouse when nature called. Like most kids growing up then, you would look at the kid next door, figure he had the same type of life that you did and think things must be okay." And despite the poverty, "there were good times, with lots of kids in the neighborhood, with baseball games and general mischief everywhere." Moreover, the village was "close-knit; people worked together, helping each other." Every fall, "they would gather at hog-killing time, salting the meat to use over the winter, which seemed much longer and colder in those days." One of his first memories was of his mother trying to hold a hog for slaughter. "The hog turned and kicked her in the leg. Until she died, there was a mark there, where the blood vessels had burst from the force of the blow."[31]

Although Lewis's family worked hard all week, the weekends were different: then "you drink, you scream and yell, and you fight." That was especially true of Lewis's father: "There were times that my father drank too much. There were times that his anger and frustration came out in ways that were wrong, times when he would beat my mother." Lewis could not approve of that behavior, but he gradually began to understand his father's point of view. His father, Lewis said, resented his wife's close attachment to her parents, whom she supported and with whom she spent every weekend. "He wanted to build a better life, and he did not want his family separated. But because he couldn't get his life together in a way that made sense to him, he let it get out of control with anger and alcohol."[32] Although we know little about Mable's husband James, we learned that he was an alcoholic, and it is possible that he had similar feelings.[33]

Historian Jacqueline Jones writes that during the Depression "nine out of every ten black households lived on the thin edge between subsistence and complete economic disaster."[34] Dora's and Lucy's households may well have been included in that number. According to the 1940 census, neither reported any cash income. Only one man in the four families living side by side reported receiving wages the previous year.[35] Like many other rural African Americans, they might have found it more difficult than they had in the past to find jobs for supplemental income.[36] Although we cannot know whether James contributed to his children's support, it is clear that Dora relied heavily on Mable's earnings.

TRANSITIONS DURING WORLD WAR II

At some point shortly before or during World War II, Mable left Charlottesville for Washington, DC. We do not know exactly what precipitated that move; nor do we know whether she moved alone or with her husband. Perhaps the Paxsons had let her go. Perhaps some aspect of her employment conditions had become intolerable to her. Or perhaps she (and possibly James), like many others, believed they could earn more farther north. "Washington DC was transformed during World War II," writes Elliot Carter, "as the population swelled and defense dollars were pumped into the economy. The 1930 census records 468,869 District residents, by 1950 that number had nearly doubled to 802,178."[37] The Black population grew from 132,068 in 1930 to 284,313 in 1950.[38]

Pernella Ross, a domestic worker, recalled her astonishment upon her arrival at Washington's Union Station for the first time in the early twentieth century: "When you looked up at the ceiling, you knew you were North! I remember looking up, the ceiling so tall and beautiful with gold all over it. I just knew that gold was going to fall into my hands!"[39] But despite Ross's first impressions in 1940, Washington was still very much a southern city. John Darnton, a journalist who worked for the *New York Times* for nearly forty years, remembered that when his mother accepted a job in the War Department, the African American woman who had cared for him and his brother in Connecticut moved with them to Washington, "but soon the city's racism chased her back north."[40] Northern African Americans were not the only ones to condemn the discrimination they encountered. Rebecca McGinness commented on her first experience there as a young woman: "In Washington, I went into a drugstore to get a drink and the lady passed it to me in a paper cup. Another person received a nice big glass, and I looked at it and said, 'Why don't I get that?' She said,

'We don't serve you people with a glass.' That did something to me and I got up and walked out. I said, 'Well is there a difference in the money?'"[41]

In Washington, as in Charlottesville, White and Black residents lived far apart. African Americans clustered in inner urban zones while Whites settled in racially homogenous neighborhoods in the outer urban districts and nearby suburbs. By 1947, approximately two-thirds of all African Americans in DC lived within a 2¼ mile radius downtown.[42] Since the antebellum period, many African Americans lived in dwellings in alleys between streets. A 1980 study of alley life between 1850 and 1970 noted that, as the newest migrants, alley dwellers were among the poorest residents in the city and were often viewed as a "separate class" at the bottom of society. Nevertheless, these migrants "used their primary groups and folk experiences to create strategies which enabled them to survive the often harsh and difficult urban experience."[43]

The war also brought our parents, Miriam and Milton Klein, to Washington. In 1942, our father left his law firm job in New York City to work for the Office of Price Administration, established in 1941 by President Roosevelt to control prices and rents. He was drafted into the Navy two years after the move to Washington, in January 1944. Our mother found her first job at the Works Project Administration and continued working until our father returned from overseas in November 1945, becoming one of the more than 6.5 million women who joined the labor force during the war.[44] Our parents arrived in Washington with our older sister. During the time the family lived there, Emily was born in 1942 and Peggy in 1944. A month after Peggy's birth in December of that year, our father left for Guam; he returned home ten months later. Our mother always spoke of those months as some of the most difficult in her life. Growing up we heard stories of broken furnaces, repeated bouts of boils, and worries about a husband at war. Our father's correspondence with the Navy suggests the threat of an eviction precipitated by an inability to make ends meet. Although her parents were wealthy, our father insisted she not turn to them for support.

And she had three children under the age of five. Although she could use the war nursery for the two-year-old and send the four-year-old to a preschool, the infant needed another kind of care.[45] We do not know how our mother and Mable came into contact with each other. But our mother must have been greatly relieved when Mable agreed to come to the house every weekday to care for Peggy. A headline in the *Washington Post* in August 1943 read, "It's an Employe's [*sic*] Market Today with Quality Down and Wages Up You Have Maid Trouble." The reporter wrote, "Despite the Capital's large Negro population, the number of efficient maids was not adequate even in prewar years. But now in this bulging city the problem has reached a crisis as domestic workers desert brooms and wash tubs for more alluring private and Government jobs."[46] John Darnton noted that after his mother's servant fled the racism in Washington, DC, his mother had, in the language of the day, "problems finding dependable help."[47] For women like Mable, the demand for domestic workers may have offered the opportunity for higher wages than they could earn at home.

Of course, Mable did much more than solve a childcare crisis. Although she did not live with us, she probably both cleaned and cooked while our mother was at her work. Moreover, as we all became deeply attached to her, our mother began to wonder if Mable would be willing to follow us north, should this war ever end. Historian Premilla Nadasen notes that "families became dependent upon individual workers because of the emotional ties and bonds of trust that had been forged, and because their personality seemed well suited to the job. Some children saw caretakers as 'second mothers,' and some employers relied on housekeepers to ensure the smooth function of the home." Nadasen provides examples of household workers who were able to "use this power of loyalty to win demands from their employers."[48] We do not know to what extent, if at all, Mable used her power to negotiate good terms. Nevertheless, our mother's reliance on Mable, her belief that Mable was the best person to care for us, and her sense that their personalities, though very different, somehow meshed, meant that our mother had a vested interest in offering better working conditions than Mable could find anywhere else and in acceding to any demand she might have made.

While Mable continued her employment as a domestic worker, the men in her family went to war—or at least waited to do so. Mable's husband, James, and her three brothers signed up for the draft in 1940, when the Selective Service Training Act went into effect. Their enlistment dates came some years later. According to historian George Q. Flynn, "thousands of blacks were passed over by the draft" in order to keep their presence in the military at the same level as their percentage in the population at large.[49] As a result, Black men had to wait to receive the wages the military offered. The base pay, approximately $50 a month, "would scale out to a net annual pay of about $3,600 'civilian' dollars'" and thus more than what was earned by 80 percent of all single workers in the United States at that time.[50] With a wife and two young children, James could have made as much as $100 a month, at about the time when Mable had been earning less than $35 a month in Charlottesville.

James was drafted on June 30, 1942, Mable's brother Lawrence on January 19, 1943, and her brother Henry on August 5, 1943.[51] (Her brother Thomas, with poor eyesight, did not enter the military). If the three enlisted men sent money to Mable's and Dora's households, they could have helped enormously, but it is unclear how much any of them did. We have noted that we have no way of knowing whether Mable's husband, James, still supported his family. Among her brothers, both Lawrence and Henry already had other dependents.

Mable said little about her years in Washington in her interview, and we could not find information about them. Although her siblings were either in the military or still in Virginia, she probably lived close to or with members of her extended family and attended a Baptist Church, as she had in Charlottesville. Following the war, Mable and James never lived together again, and, as far as we know, he never again contributed financially to the family. Now the sole breadwinner, Mable returned to Charlottesville, where Jim Crow remained in full force. Although she could not escape employment as a domestic worker or reunite with her sons if she accepted our mother's invitation, traveling north may have seemed to promise a brighter future than any other option.

4

"THE SOCIAL PARADOX IN THE NORTH"

MABLE AND HER FAMILY have no place in the postwar story Americans hear most often. According to that narrative, massive numbers of people moved to the suburbs, where growing prosperity and government programs enabled them to buy single-family homes and fill them with new consumer goods. Heeding government propaganda celebrating domesticity, suburban women left the work force. In 1953, when 27 percent of women throughout the nation worked outside the home, just 9 percent of suburban women did.[1] The birth rate soared. Between 1946 and 1964, nearly 72.5 million children were born in the United States.[2] And *White* became a more capacious term. Suburbanites who previously might have been considered Italians, Poles, Greeks, or Jews increasingly identified themselves as White as they ruptured ties to the older generation left behind in the cities.[3]

Our family was representative of that White story in many ways. Shortly after our father returned from overseas, he resumed his New York law practice. We settled in Larchmont, a Westchester County suburb twenty miles from New York City, where our grandparents lived. Although our mother began a successful career as a writer (eventually publishing a total of seventeen mystery novels), she did not work outside the home again for many years. She also contributed to the baby boom, adding two sons to the three daughters she already had.

We never doubted we were White. Although most of our friends and all our parents' friends were Jewish, we practiced a very diluted form of religion. Our grandparents went to the synagogue every Saturday, observed all the holidays, and prayed in Hebrew. One grandmother kept Kosher and one grandfather seriously considered becoming a rabbi after retirement. Our mother, who was both sentimental and conflicted about Judaism, took her three daughters to High Holiday services but not to any others. Our father stayed home, as did our brothers. Judaism was what he had most wanted to flee when he left his immigrant parents' house to pursue the higher education that would catapult him into the upper-middle class. The Reform facility that hosted the services we attended sought assimilation with the mainstream. It called itself a temple, not a synagogue, and offered confirmations at sixteen, not bar or bat mitzvahs at thirteen. Located on a street with two Christian churches, it sought to blend in with its neighbors. A 1951 fund-raising appeal stressed that the "two-story Georgian Colonial design" had been "planned to integrate architecturally with the surrounding community."[4]

And anti-Semitism was not a major factor in our lives. True, like most other Westchester yacht clubs, the Larchmont ones in our neighborhood did not accept Jews. When he graduated from Columbia Law School, our father had had no option but to enter a Jewish law firm. Nevertheless, he enjoyed all the privileges of other corporate lawyers. He earned enough to buy a large house in a wealthy town, where we were surrounded by plush, manicured lawns and had access to excellent public schools. Our parents assumed their children would get into top colleges, the boys would become doctors or lawyers, and the girls would marry professionals.

Mable's experience in the postwar period, by contrast, was sharply at odds with the reigning narrative. In Charlottesville, she lived in an extended family, not a nuclear one. Rather than moving to the suburbs, she remained in the same predominantly Black area of the city where the family had lived for many years. Nor could she retreat into domesticity. Far from sharing in the postwar prosperity, she faced severe economic hardship created and compounded by the constraints on African Americans in what was still the Jim Crow South. Her husband had left.[5] In order to support her sons and various other family members who depended on her, she had to work not only outside the home but also hundreds of miles away from it. She could not send her children to good schools, much less dream of their entering the professions.

The one sibling who could share Mable's burden was Henry, her youngest brother. (Her brother Thomas was a laborer, her brother Lawrence a truck driver, and her sister Beatrice a "maid.") In 1947, Henry bought his mother the house at 609 Parrott Street in Charlottesville. Mable said Henry used the money he had saved from his military service. It is likely that he also could afford the house because he had married Mary Evelyn Johnson, the descendant and only heir of a White real estate agent and his African American housekeeper.[6] Henry probably did not take out a mortgage. Local banks were loath to lend to African Americans.[7] Since its creation in 1934, the Federal Housing Administration (FHA), responsible for the federal mortgage insurance program, had denied mortgages to most African Americans who applied. As a veteran, Henry should have been eligible for a mortgage guarantee under the Servicemen's Readjustment Act of 1944 (better known as the GI Bill of Rights), but the VA program established by that legislation followed FHA guidelines and provided most of its help to Whites.[8]

The house Henry bought must have been especially significant at a time when the government exhorted all Americans to purchase single-family homes. It also was a great economic boon for Dora, who could move back to Charlottesville free from the worries of rent. We can assume, however, that she did not acquire much equity in the house. It was located in a segregated neighborhood. According to Eugene Williams, who had grown up nearby, Parrott Street was unpaved and so narrow that his mother referred to it as an alley; a 1929 map shows Dora's house located on an extension of Parrott Street rather than on the main portion of the road.[9] Some of the houses had just three rooms—two small ones on the first floor and a larger one on the second. Although Dora's brick house was one of the more substantial ones, the neighborhood diminished its market value.

When Mable agreed to go to Larchmont to work in 1946, she probably traveled with people who were leaving the South for good. Between 1916 and 1970, six million African Americans joined what historians call the Great Migration.[10] Unlike Mable, most would come to regard the North as their permanent home, even if they returned to the South for visits. Interviews conducted by Fordham University and the Hudson River Museum about migrants to Westchester Country reveal other ways their experiences differed from Mable's.[11] Several of the interviewees chose specific areas because the communities had Black populations that included their relatives. Although Alberta Wren was only seventeen when she traveled by herself from Fairfax, Virginia, to Yonkers, New York, in 1924, she was not afraid "because I had a sister here" and "I moved in with her." Eva Lillian Goode Jones in 1955 "had two brothers in New Rochelle already, Iron and Willie," who took her "under their wings." A year later, she encouraged her sister to join them. Calvin O'Neal in the mid-1960s "had three brothers already living in Yonkers, so this way I have somebody to guide me."[12] In contrast, Mable moved into an entirely White neighborhood and, we assume, knew no one apart from our family.

Many women in the Great Migration who had left children behind in the South sent for them after finding employment and housing. Eva Lillian Goode Jones had not wanted her ex-husband to leave their small son with his grandmother back in South Carolina. Once the boy was gone, however, Eva realized "it was a blessing in disguise." Life as a single mother with a low-paid job had become increasingly difficult:

> I called, and I talked to her, and I says mom, I called her mom, I said mom, your son took the baby without my permission. But I know that you've been saying and the sisters have been asking why didn't I let the child go and stay with his grandmother and it would help me out a lot because I wouldn't have to be getting to the baby sitter and all that and I could work. I said, let me ask you, would you mind keeping him for a while? And she said, oh yes, I'd love to keep him. So I accepted that and then I went out and got a second job. And she kept him for two or three years and then somehow I just sensed that he should be with me.[13]

After Eva went to South Carolina for a wedding, she returned with the boy. Mable, however, had no intention of settling permanently in the North. We learned from the African American newspapers *The Charlottesville-Albemarle Tribune* and *The Norfolk Journal and Guide* that her mother visited her at least twice in Larchmont.[14] But Dora's home, like that of Mable's sons and the rest of her extensive kinship network, remained in the South.

When we visited Charlottesville for the first time, we realized that Larchmont might not have seemed as alien to Mable as we had assumed. Charlottesville looked more like a town than a city and was very green in the summer. As we drove around, we saw houses in more affluent areas in Colonial Revival style that bore a remarkable similarity to our own, with the same red-brick exteriors, rectangular floor plans, symmetrical façades, and two-story porticos.[15] On our second trip, in December, we were surprised by how cold it was. Nevertheless, the relentlessness of a northern winter must have been a shock.

Regardless of how long people expected to remain in the North, they had to travel at least part of the way on segregated trains. The case at the heart of the notorious *Plessy v. Ferguson* decision had involved a Black man who refused to vacate his seat in the White section of a train. In 1896, the US Supreme Court ruled that "separate but equal" railroad cars were constitutional in interstate travel. Soon afterwards, southern states began passing laws mandating separate cars for Black and White riders (though ignoring the requirement of equal treatment). Virginia was the last southern state to do so. According to *The Negro in Virginia*, compiled by writers in the Work Projects Administration, the governor decided to act after traveling overnight to Atlanta, Georgia, in 1899. Waking up in his sleeping compartment, he found "a negro opposite him, above him, and in front of him."[16] Within three months he had signed an "Act to Require Railroad Companies to Provide Separate Cars for White and Colored Passengers." Passengers who refused to occupy the assigned seat could be removed from the train.[17]

In 1946, the year Mable began traveling between New York and Charlottesville, the Supreme Court invalidated the Virginia law on the grounds that it violated the interstate commerce clause. Nevertheless, segregation continued on southern railroads well into the 1960s. Washington, DC, was the dividing point. George Swanson Starling was an African American conductor on trains that crossed the city. The historian Isabel Wilkerson notes that "during the run between New York and Alabama," he was "responsible for moving the colored passengers from their seats in the White section and into the Jim Crow Car before crossing from Washington into the segregated state of Virginia."[18] Essie Mae Washington-Williams, the "secret" daughter of Strom Thurmond, remembered this transfer when she traveled south in the early 1940s:

> I soon came to wonder about Lincoln's legacy when we changed trains at Union Station. After the fancy parlor car we had started in, our new accommodations, to which we were herded, felt more like a cattle car. There were only blacks in these tattered seats. Half the windows wouldn't open, and the fans didn't work. It smelled awful. I was hungry and wanted a snack, but [my Mother] held me back. "This is a southern train," she said, meaning that blacks were segregated in the worst cars and weren't allowed in the dining car. Eventually, a black porter came through with a cart selling soft drinks and sandwiches, which we ate in our hot seats.[19]

In the oral history collection of Charlottesville residents, *From Porch Swings to Patios,* Rebecca McGinness also recalled that moment while traveling in the other direction: "We had Jim Crow laws on trains, yet when you passed into Washington, you could sit anywhere you wanted. And it changed something in you—it created something in you—I know, and I'm not a violent person."[20]

Mable's trips between Charlottesville and New York took approximately seven hours on the Southern Railway. In Charlottesville, she would have had to sit in a segregated car until the train reached Washington, DC. There she would have been free to sit wherever she wanted, although she might not have found the train personnel in the integrated car welcoming.[21] After arriving at New York's Pennsylvania Station, Mable would have had to take the subway to Grand Central, where she boarded a train on the New Haven Line for the forty-minute trip to Larchmont. In her interview, Mable remarked that her brother once told her that she could have bought the Pennsylvania Railroad because she used to ride the train "all the time."[22] Although that company did not operate trains in segregated states, its agents sold tickets to passengers on southern railway trips originating in New York. In the mid-1940s, civil rights groups protested that Pennsylvania Railroad agents booked African American passengers in segregated cars throughout the entire trip, not just after reaching Washington. Company officials claimed the practice was for the "convenience" of African American passengers, eliminating the need to switch seats in Washington.[23] In 1949, the company yielded to "vigorous" pressure from the New York State Commission against Discrimination and the New York City Mayor's Committee on Unity and agreed to sell tickets on through trains from New York to the South "to all passengers, negro and white alike, in any part of the train."[24] For her trips south from then on, Mable could have ridden in an integrated car until Washington, DC, when she would have been forced to change to a segregated one.

Jim Crow cars received more cinders and ash from the engines than other cars. Interviewed in 2001, Mary Lewis later remembered how "grimy" she felt after arriving in New York City from Fayetteville, North Carolina, in 1945.[25] The Smithsonian's National Museum of African American History and Culture displays a restored Southern Railway passenger car. Calling the exhibit "a visceral reminder of the Jim Crow days," the museum notes that "visitors will see there are no luggage racks in the 'colored' section, requiring travelers to cram their suitcases around their feet, and that the 'colored' bathroom is smaller and lacks the amenities of the 'whites' bathroom."[26] If Mable rode in a similar car, the lack of a luggage rack must been a special burden. Because she stayed in both Larchmont and Charlottesville for extended periods before traveling to the other location, we can assume she did not pack lightly.

Segregation did not end once she reached Penn Station. In 1944, two years before Mable arrived for the first time, Gunnar Myrdal wrote, "The social paradox in the North is exactly this, that almost everybody is against discrimination in general, but, at the same time, almost everybody practices discrimination in his own personal affairs."[27] Mable had come to a land with its own racist history and practices. Because Larchmont was inextricably connected to New York City, we begin there.

NEW YORK CITY

A discovery in the summer of 1991 forced New Yorkers to acknowledge that US slavery had never been confined to the South. Workers excavating land in lower Manhattan in preparation for building a federal office building found the remains of 419 Africans, half of them children. Archeologists now believe as many as 10,000 African people may be buried nearby.[28] "For nearly three hundred years," historians Ira Berlin and Leslie M. Harris write, "slavery was an intimate part of the lives of all New Yorkers, black and white, insinuating itself into every nook and cranny of New York history."[29] Throughout much of the seventeenth and eighteenth centuries, enslaved men and women represented approximately one-quarter of the city's labor force. Most of the founding fathers from New York enslaved people. New York was one of the last northern states to abolish slavery, and even after the passage of the first emancipation legislation in 1799, the institution lingered for many decades. Moreover, as the number of enslaved people slowly declined, New York's economic dependence on slavery deepened. After the War of 1812, New York City became the primary port for transporting raw cotton from the slave states to European textile mills. White New Yorkers financed the cotton plantations and manufactured many of the goods they used.[30]

In addition, recent studies have revealed that slavery was entangled with one of New York's premier universities, not only with those in the South.[31] Learning about Columbia's past represented a special shock to us. Our father graduated from Columbia College and Columbia Law School and never let us forget his rank at the top of his classes at both despite the prejudice against Jews he encountered. He met our mother when she was in her last year at Barnard, the women's college. We both did graduate work at Columbia, and both of our husbands graduated from the law school. The connection continued into the third generation, when two of our nephews attended Columbia College.

To be sure, Columbia was very different from the University of Virginia. Enslaved people did not build the institution or serve students and faculty for decades. Nevertheless, slavery figured prominently in Columbia's past. Half of the ten first presidents of both King's College (Columbia's predecessor) and Columbia College enslaved people, as did all the treasurers before the Civil War. Those schools depended heavily on funding from wealthy merchants who participated in the slave trade. Faculty members who supported the abolition movement believed that emancipation should be gradual and that all African Americans be removed from the country. And like professors at the University of Virginia, some at the College of Physicians and Surgeons (the forerunner of Columbia's medical school) disseminated the tenets of scientific racism. John Augustine Smith, a faculty member between 1808 and 1820 and president of the school between 1831 and 1843, argued that the "Caucasian . . . might justly be said to stand at the head of all races of the earth," while "blacks' mental powers are upon an inferior scale." Some measurements he taught his students placed "the Ethiopian race" much closer to orangutans than to Caucasians.[32]

Discrimination and segregation persisted in New York long after the end of the Civil War. By the last decades of the nineteenth century, prominent New Yorkers had begun to seek rapprochement with Southern plantation owners by embracing "many of their 'romanticized' notions of a mythic South before the war."[33] When the influx of African Americans during the Great Migration intensified racial hostility, *Whites only* signs appeared on a growing number of New York restaurants, bars, shops, theaters, and swimming pools. We tend to assume that the worst instances of poor treatment of domestic workers were in the South, but the North had its own horror stories. The most publicized occurred at what became known as "slave markets," where African American women waited on street corners for daily work during the 1930s. Although approximately two hundred markets existed throughout New York City, those in the Bronx received the most attention.[34] A 1935 article by civil rights workers Ella Baker and Marvel Cooke in the NAACP journal *Crisis* helped to memorialize one at 167th Street and Jerome Avenue and another at Simpson and Westchester Avenues. "Rain or shine, cold or hot," Baker and Cooke wrote, "you will find them there—Negro women, old and young—sometimes bedraggled, sometimes neatly dressed—but with the invariable paper bundle, waiting expectantly for Bronx housewives to buy their strength and energy for an hour, two hours, or even for a day at the munificent rate of fifteen, twenty, twenty-five, or, if luck be with them, thirty cents an hour. If not the wives themselves, maybe their husbands, their sons, or their brothers, under the subterfuge of work, offer worldly-wise girls higher bids for their time."[35] One woman, interviewed by the sociologist Bonnie Thornton Dill in the 1970s, remembered her experience when she first came to the North in 1937: "You would go to the Bronx and there was certain corners that you would sit on. So some people had a box they would sit on, some lean up against a store or wall. . . . And they would come and just pick out a nice clean girl they thought they could trust. And you worked, thirty-five cents an hour or a quarter, or when you finished they give you what they thought—which was good in times like that."[36] Dill notes that "one of the most striking aspects" of a description like that was that "while the women present themselves as selling their labor on street corners, . . . their entire person was evaluated as part of the sale. They had to look trustworthy, reliable, strong, and clean in order to be selected for a day of heavy housework."[37]

The African American newspaper, the *New York Amsterdam News,* repeatedly condemned the trafficking of domestic workers during the Depression. "Slavery Laid to Jerseyites" read the title of one article, which noted that a group of household workers in New Jersey urged the Board of Health to "take the trouble to investigate the importation of Negroes from the South to work in the homes of some of the wealthy families in Englewood at starvation wages." The group also charged that the women had to work as long as fifteen hours a day.[38] Although the markets disappeared at the end of the Depression, the trafficking by employment agencies of Black women as domestic workers from the South to the New York area persisted after World War II.[39] As we will see in chapter 5, domestic laborers continued to receive miserly pay and work in substandard conditions.

WESTCHESTER

Designated as a county as early as 1683, Westchester was one of the first areas in the world to develop into a suburb.[40] The railroad greatly abetted that transformation. As different lines emerged in the mid-nineteenth century, some of the wealthiest New Yorkers converted agricultural land into country estates. When Grand Central Terminal opened in 1871, the editor of the *Westchester News* wrote, "Great improvements are being made to utilize the splendid physical and commercial resources of Westchester County by making its unsurpassed harbors available for commercial purposes and its excellent sites for . . . suburban homes accessible to settlers. The reasons for these enterprises are the inevitable certainty that Manhattan Island, upon which is located the New York City, will soon be entirely inadequate to provide homes for its increasing population."[41] Not only was the city becoming crowded, but it seemed to be filled with growing numbers of poor people, immigrants, and people of color. Businessmen and executives anxious to escape New York's dirt and the disease they associated with it found Westchester's more salubrious air, waterfront properties, and wooded areas increasingly attractive. Seeking to boost ridership by increasing the county's population, the railroads offered discount fares on certain Sundays to passengers who met with real estate agents.[42] As some of the first estates were subdivided and year-round residents joined those with summer and weekend homes, the population grew quickly, doubling between 1850 and 1870, doubling again between 1870 and 1890, and doubling yet again between 1890 and 1910, by which time the county was home to 283,000 people.[43] Today the county includes large numbers of blue-collar workers and people of color in some areas, but it is still best known for its affluent communities, including Scarsdale, Bronxville, Rye, and Larchmont.[44]

The uproar surrounding an interracial marriage in the mid-1920s demonstrated that Westchester residents, like southerners, adhered to the one-drop rule. In 1924, a scandal broke out when a local Westchester paper announced that Leonard Kip Rhinelander, the scion of one of New York's oldest and wealthiest families, had married Alice Beatrice Jones, the daughter of a Black cab driver and a White domestic worker. Under pressure from his family, Rhinelander sought an annulment. The widely publicized trial that ensued focused on whether Jones had deceived her husband by not revealing her "colored blood." At one particularly humiliating point, she was forced to partially strip in an attempt to reveal her "true" racial identity.[45]

The Hudson River Museum interviews reveal how racial discrimination circumscribed the lives of migrants from the South who settled in

Westchester. Several women who had come north hoping for new employment opportunities found themselves relegated to the kinds of jobs they had had in the South. There were, of course, exceptions. Louisa Haines's mother was one. In Roanoke, Virginia, the mother boarded Louisa with a family "because my mother worked in service and she lived where she worked and she had off, I think, Thursdays, and maybe Sunday." In Westchester, Louisa's mother "could work in a factory as opposed to domestic work" and Louisa could see her "every day." Many other women were not so fortunate. Mary Lewis "had to get a sleep-in job." She went to "different places on sleep-in jobs." Some migrants who avoided domestic work provided other kinds of personal service. Sarah Green worked in a laundry for thirty-five years. Eula Ellington found employment in a hospital "cleaning floors, cleaning the beds, that kind of stuff . . . You didn't work any other job, no office job, no other skilled job. Just working as a maintenance person was basically what I did." After doing days' work when she first came to Westchester, Eva Lillian Goode Jones was hired by a dry cleaning company. And even domestic service jobs could be hard to find. "There were people who didn't want colored help," Alberta Wren recalled. "They'll say, I want help but I don't want colored. I want all white. . . . They were almost like the South."[46]

Mable's experience was different. She was not seeking a new kind of employment or even new employers when she traveled to the North. She came to work for and live with people she already knew. But moving into our parents' home left her isolated from other African Americans who could neither rent nor own homes in the neighborhood. "You take up here in Scarsdale," Addie Fields commented. "Colored people have a hard time living up there. They almost as bad as the people down South. Down South they used to burn crosses. They called them the Ku Klux. Well, there's a lot of Ku Klux in New York. They break down people's windows, they break down people's doors, throw garbage and stuff in the yard. . . . Take one lady up on I think it's McLean Avenue. They took her fence away. Things like that because they didn't want 'em in the neighborhood."[47] A survey of housing developments in Westchester between 1935 and 1947 supports Fields's contention that Whites did not want African Americans "in the neighborhood": 53 percent of the developments had racially restrictive covenants, and that figure was even higher—85 percent—for the larger ones.[48] In a 1960 speech to an interracial New York City audience, the Reverend Dr. Martin Luther King Jr. declared, "There is a pressing need for a liberalism which is truly liberal." He called for a liberalism that not only "rises up with righteous indignation when a Negro is lynched in Mississippi, but will be equally incensed when a Negro is denied the right to live in his neighborhood."[49]

Despite her mother's success finding a job in a factory, Louisa Haines doubted the move to Westchester had improved their lives in every way. "The only thing I noticed when I came here was that when you got on the bus, you didn't have to go to the back of the bus. You could sit anywhere.... What we did not see was the sign saying, 'Colored go in the back,' or when you go in the restaurants, you couldn't sit at the counter; you had to go to the back. That we didn't see when we got here." "But," she continued, "that didn't mean that we left the segregation behind. Because it was here. It was here."[50] The northern version of segregation was more subtle, and southerners like Mable had to learn how to navigate among a myriad of unwritten rules. She might have discovered, as Louisa Haines did, that although she could sit anywhere when riding on public transportation, Whites moved away whenever she sat close to them. And she might well have had repeated experiences of being denied both respect and the rights that were formally hers. As Isabel Wilkerson explains, drawing on her conversation with George Swanson Starling, "You never knew when perfect strangers would remind you that, as far as they were concerned, you weren't equal and might never be. It was just the prerogative of whoever happened to be in a position to keep you from getting what the law said you had a right to, because nobody was going to enforce it anyway."[51]

The largest Black community in Westchester in the 1940s was in New Rochelle, a bus ride away from our house. It boasted two African American Baptist churches. When interviewed, Mable said that she attended one of them and met several "nice people" there. It is likely that most of the women were also domestic workers. "If you worked in New Rochelle," Henrietta Mills told an interviewer in 1966, "you did domestic work."[52] By the late 1940s, most domestic workers returned to their own households at night and over weekends, but they typically had the same days off as live-in workers like Mable: half of Thursday and all day Sunday. Willie Carrington recalled, "Since most of the people [in New Rochelle] were domestics and off on Thursday, there was always something going on in the churches, including dinners . . . They spent most of the day cooking and serving it to each other and they enjoyed it. It was a social outlet too."[53] As the historian Andrew Wiese comments, "Like payday in the mill towns, 'maids' day off' was a shaping feature of African American social life" in suburbs like New Rochelle.[54]

When Mable attended a Black church in New Rochelle, she might have heard about a fight about school desegregation much like the one she would see in Charlottesville several years later. As Whites increasingly fled New Rochelle's inner-city in the 1930s and 1940s, the student body of Lincoln Elementary School had grown from one-quarter Black to virtually all Black. Following the practice of other northern school boards, New Rochelle allowed White students in the Lincoln school district to transfer to other, predominantly White schools.[55] White parents in the North as in the South responded with outrage to the notion that their children attend Black-majority schools and were happy to transfer them out. Interviewed in 1987, Pauline Billups Flippin explained she became involved in the movement to desegregate Lincoln "because I was surprised to find when I graduated from college that I was living in a segregated community with a segregated school. It was just something I could not accept . . . Certainly not here in New Rochelle." She initially assumed it would be "a fait accompli," that the Board of Education immediately would desegregate Lincoln School "and that would be the end of it." But "lo and behold, we were confronted with a steadfast barrier that lasted [until] 1961, when the school was actually desegregated."[56]

LARCHMONT

Occupying a square mile along the Long Island Sound, Larchmont is one of the affluent communities that give Westchester County its distinctive character. It was incorporated as a separate village within the town of Mamaroneck in 1891. At that time, it was largely a summer retreat for wealthy New Yorkers, who traveled on the New Haven Railroad from the city. With the arrival of automobiles, it gradually became a commuter community. "I Know a Village," Phyllis McGinley's poem, published in the August 4, 1951, issue of the *New Yorker*, captured the self-satisfaction that pervaded the village in the postwar years. The poem portrayed Larchmont as a bucolic enclave; the one phrase that occurred three times was "all the streets are named for trees."

The poem also epitomizes what Elaine Pagels calls "the smugness of suburban America that keeps the suffering of others at a distance."[57] Here families enjoyed the good life, safely removed from the problems afflicting urban environments and the anxieties of the atomic age. Children were especially prized after the terrible loss of life in World War II, and Larchmont was filled with them. In the poem, they sled down hills, rode bicycles, and screeched with joy when let out of school. A reference to weddings reminded readers that the parents were all married, heterosexual couples.

The sense of security and serenity McGinley lauded derived partly from the virtual absence of people of color. One widely publicized incident in the 1930s demonstrates the extent to which residents were willing to go to preserve the community as an all-White enclave. Adelaide Hall was a well-known African American musical comedy actress in the Harlem Renaissance in August 1932 when she attempted to buy a house on Kilmer Avenue, which the *New York Amsterdam News* called "the most pretentious and fashionable thoroughfare of Westchester's 'ritziest' community." The paper described the house as "an imposing edifice, a seven-room brownstone brick building, set off in front by expansive green lawns, and intersected by gravel walks and driveways."[58] The newly formed "Kilmer Road Association" protested in various ways, appealing to the mayor, attempting to raise enough money to purchase the property, boycotting the markets where Hall shopped, threatening to commit violence and blackball her career, and filing an injunction against her. But Hall remained undeterred, and, a few weeks later, she and her husband moved in. After she won the court case in December, the *New York Amsterdam News* exulted, "The snooty white Larchmont neighbors of Adelaide Hall have taken it on the chin again." Hall declared, "I will continue to live in Larchmont because it is the nicest place I know."[59] Two years later, however, new threats of violence weakened Hall's resolve, and she and her husband fled to Europe.[60]

As children in the 1940s and 1950s, we heard nothing about either Adelaide Hall or the various public and private measures that kept our community almost entirely White. We were aware that African Americans (like Jews) were not allowed to join the Larchmont Yacht Club and the Shore Club and that the Manor Beach, where we went every day in the summer, practiced discrimination. African American domestic workers who accompanied their charges to the beach were not allowed to join them on the sand. We remember the row of seated African American women in uniforms looking down at us from their platform above. Whether because we somehow intuited that interracial bathing raised special anxieties or because so much discrimination was hidden from us, we viewed the Manor Beach as an exception.[61] We took pride in the (now debunked) stories we heard about the Underground Railroad station in the basement of the oldest house in Larchmont. In school we learned about the evils of Communism and the legacy of slavery in the segregation and discrimination in the South, but nothing about the racist forces that undergirded our virtually all-White community. The next chapter shows how those forces also pervaded our home when Mable arrived in 1946.

5

"WOULD YOU COME UP FOR SIX MONTHS OR A YEAR?"

IN HER 1995 ORAL history interview, Mable remarked about coming to New York for our family, "Where I worked in New York, she was a writer, and if she would write and call and say, would you come up for six months or a year or what, take care of the children while I write, and I'm gone [from Charlottesville]."[1] We don't know the precise dates of these calls. We moved to Larchmont in 1946; we believe Mable stopped working for us sometime after October 1953, when she needed to care for her aging mother back home. Our mother published her first mystery, *A Corpse in Diplomacy,* in 1949, and the second, *Ring and Walk In,* appeared in 1952.

It is perhaps unsurprising that our mother sought a domestic arrangement that so clearly clashed with her leftist political beliefs. Her parents were wealthy, and the grandparents with whom she spent some portion of her teenage years were exceedingly so. Because both households employed live-in domestic workers throughout her childhood, she was accustomed to having non-family members wait on her at home. According to sociologist Judith Rollins, women are more likely to employ household workers if they have had them as children.[2]

Moreover, middle- and upper-class families in the New York area commonly hired household workers after the war. In *New Jersey Dreaming*, anthropologist Sherry B. Ortner describes the experiences of her Newark high school class of 1958. Among the indicators of racism her classmates recalled was the practice of compelling "maids" to drink from separate glasses.[3] Private household help was especially prominent in elite suburbs. When we visited our friends in Larchmont, we encountered domestic workers more often than not. Our parents' siblings also employed household workers. Even our mother's sister, who had joined the Communist Party, hired a woman who lived in her Scarsdale house. She and our mother were hardly the first examples of women whose politics and practices conflicted. Historian Vanessa May demonstrates that many Progressive-era women reformers who campaigned for better conditions for factory workers resisted attempts to improve the lots of the men and women they employed in their homes. As May writes, "Domestic service posed a problem for those who believed the private home to be a world apart from the public realm of work, labor conflict, and public politics."[4]

In addition, our mother had limited options if she wanted to pursue a career. Because middle- and upper-class White women were not expected to work, few formal services were available for those who did. Most nurseries that had been available during World War II had closed. Aside from Cub Scouts (Boy Scouts) for boys and Bluebirds (Camp Fire Girls) and Brownies (Girl Scouts) for girls, almost no programs had emerged to provide afterschool activities for children. If middle-class parents wanted to provide enrichment, they had to do it themselves. Having moved away from our grandparents, our mother could not turn to them for assistance. As far as we could tell, neighbors felt little obligation to help each other with childcare. And our mother already knew and trusted Mable.

We don't know whether or how our mother knew that Mable would be available to come north. Nor do we know precisely what Mable did for her own employment in the intervals between those trips, although a Charlottesville city directory from 1950 indicates that she was working as a "maid" in the Brandon Apartments near the University of Virginia.[5] In all likelihood, responding to our mother's summons would have meant the possibility of earning more money than she could in Charlottesville. However, we can also conjecture that doing so would have entailed an enormous sacrifice. Before then, Mable periodically had left her mother and her sons for months at a time, but she could regularly travel home, especially during those years she worked in or around Charlottesville and probably even when she worked in Washington, DC. Now hundreds of miles away, she could not visit them as frequently as she previously had.[6] By the time she returned to Charlottesville permanently, James and Thomas, then twenty-three and twenty-two, were young adults. And if our mother had few options, Mable had many fewer. Despite Mable's brother Henry's generous contribution that had enabled Dora to purchase a home, the family might have needed the higher wage Mable could obtain in the North.

There she joined an occupation that had undergone three major transformations. The first stemmed from the dispersion of household technologies. As washing machines and vacuum cleaners reached more and more homes, employers found that they could either dispense with household workers entirely or hire one in place of the large staffs who previously had divided tasks among themselves. As a result, domestic service became a lonelier endeavor.[7]

The second shift was in the racial composition of the labor force. Paid domestic work had historically been an exclusively Black job in the South. In the Northeast, however, a high proportion of domestic workers at the turn of the twentieth century were immigrants from northern Europe (Scandinavia, Germany, and Ireland). Most were young women in their teens and early twenties, who quit their jobs as soon as they married.[8] As increasing numbers of people joined the Great Migration, African American women represented a growing proportion of household workers throughout the North. They tended to be older than the immigrants they replaced and continued work for pay after marriage.[9] Developments during World War II and its immediate aftermath further encouraged the shift to a predominantly Black work force. In 1945 the Department of Labor announced that 400,000 White women had abandoned domestic service for factory jobs between 1941 and 1944 while the number of African American domestic workers had increased by 50,000.[10] During the demobilization period, historian Jacqueline Jones writes, "All of the mechanisms that employers and union leaders used to deprive female war defense workers of their jobs were used with a vengeance against black women." One result, she concludes, was that "the chances were greater in 1950 than in 1940 that the maid would be black."[11]

The third change in domestic work was related to the second. Because many African American domestic workers had families, they wanted jobs that allowed them to return to their own households at night. Thus, in the North, as in the South, growing numbers of women refused to accept live-in work.[12] In 1935, Heywood Broun, a liberal journalist who founded the American Newspaper Guild (later the Newspaper Guild and then the NewsGuild-CWA), noted that private household workers in New York were "loth to 'live in.' In spite of Harlem's high rents they are generally insistent upon going home when the day's work is done."[13] Six years later, the *Afro-American* reported that "securing servants who will 'live in' is actually difficult."[14] As an African American woman who had come from the South, had children, and was the only household worker in her employer's household, Mable could be considered typical of domestic workers in the North. As a woman who lived in, however, she belonged to a group that was slowly contracting.

We analyzed the 1940 enumeration census to obtain more specific information about private household workers in Larchmont.[15] Although Mable did not arrive for another six years, this is the most relevant detailed census we have; the data help us place her experience in context. We recorded the information about live-in domestic workers for every tenth house in each of the five separate census districts in Larchmont. Among the 161 homes we studied, 25 percent had at least one live-in household worker and many had more than one (the average was 1.3). Although White domestic workers outnumbered Black ones, the difference was small: 54 percent as opposed to 46 percent. Most live-in domestic workers were women (77 percent). The proportion of women was higher among White workers (87 percent) than among Black workers (65 percent).[16]

In Larchmont (based on the 10 percent sample), the majority of Black male domestic workers were butlers (67 percent) or some combination of butler and chauffeur (22 percent); another 11 percent were simply listed as "servants." The majority of Black women were listed as maid (76 percent) or some combination of "cook-maid" (18 percent). White household workers held somewhat different positions than Black workers: more White men than Black men were chauffeurs (75 percent) and more White women than Black women held positions such as "child nurse," "chambermaid," "parlormaid" and "housekeeper." Annual wages differed as well: on average Black men earned $565 and Black women earned $548; on average White men earned $800 and White women earned $699. (That year, as a live-in domestic worker near Charlottesville, Mable earned approximately $130 less than she would have received in Larchmont.)

Although the majority of White women domestic workers were single (65 percent), most Black women were either currently married (47 percent) or widowed (23 percent). Among the men, all the White household workers were married, as were the majority of Black ones. Black workers were also more likely than White workers to be hired as a couple (38 percent versus 13 percent). (Often the wages for the men and women in these couples were listed as being identical. For example, in one household the census recorded the earnings of both the butler and maid as $600. We do not know whether the couple received two separate wage packets or whether they were given just a single one to divide between themselves.)

Without the detailed census, the data for 1950 are much sparser. Nevertheless, we can discern some trends. In 1950, 50 "nonwhite" men and ninety-two "nonwhite" women lived in Larchmont. We assume that the great majority were live-in, paid household workers. (Racial covenants barred virtually all Black people from owning houses in Larchmont, although we knew of one Black family whose children went to school with us.) This means there were only about half as many live-in Black domestic workers in Larchmont (a total of 135) as there were a decade before (about 270). We cannot calculate the number of White live-in private household workers because they are "invisible" in the total population count. The census does not indicate how many families hired day workers. Altogether the census lists 19 male and 202 female residents of Larchmont whose occupation was "private household worker." However, the census records neither their race nor whether they had live-in or day jobs.

WHITE PERSPECTIVES

Personal accounts of experiences of people living in homes with domestic employees in the 1940s and 1950s add depth to these numbers. Scouring our bookshelves and Amazon lists for memoirs that mentioned household workers, we found two by women who had employed private household workers themselves and another fifteen by people who had been children in households with such workers.[17] We also watched the documentary *Martha and Ethel,* produced by two women who discussed their memories of the women who had cared for them as children.[18] And we interviewed six friends and acquaintances about their memories of the men and women who worked in their childhood homes. In order to obtain a sizable number of accounts, we extended our search beyond Larchmont to the entire New York City area. In what follows, we refer to the memoir authors, the two women who appeared in the documentary, and the people we interviewed as informants. They all present as White. (We provide the names of the authors and film producers but pseudonyms for the people we interviewed.)

Among our various sources, fifteen of the households hired only African American domestic workers; six had both White and Black workers; and three had only White workers. The accounts reflect our finding from the 1940s census that White and Black domestic workers occasionally had different roles. In the households with workers of both races, White domestic workers typically were nannies or governesses, while African Americans performed more menial work. The three households with only White workers were among the wealthiest in our study: all three employed large staffs. Perhaps because people were most likely to remember servants who lived in their homes, our sample recalled only six domestic workers who did day work.

Many of the informants confessed they knew little about domestic workers' lives. Much of what they did learn (typically from a rare visit to the workers' homes or attendance at their funerals) upset them. Richard Lempert, a law professor, recalled Mame, the African American woman who cleaned his family's apartment and watched him and his sister after school: "One day, so she could give her son, who was about my age, a birthday party, my mother told Mame that after school she could take me to her home. The apartment was a flat, one floor up, perhaps above a store, and dimly lit. . . . My family had little money, but even as a six- or seven-year-old I sense that Mame's family was far worse off."[19] Cathy Wilkerson, a member of the Weathermen, wrote that she learned about a domestic worker's living accommodations from her mother: "One day my mother drove Catherine home after she had missed the last bus . . . When my mother returned, she commented with some dismay that although Catherine lived in a torn-up tenement, she had to pay approximately the same amount of money in rent that we paid in mortgage payments for our wonderful home in the woods. As she turned her attention to fixing our dinner, I mulled over her words. Like most children, I had a fierce belief in fairness, and this didn't seem fair."[20]

Several informants were amazed to discover how little they had known about the workers' lives. Judy Sternberg, a social worker, remarked, "It hurts me that I didn't think of her [a live-in worker] outside the family. There was a wall. We know how she was to us, but how were we to her?" Three others had been unaware that the care they and their family members received had been at the expense of the workers' own children. A significant event in the life of the anthropologist Arthur Kleinman was "when our maid Hatty, the . . . African American woman who had raised me from age four, told me when I was fifteen that every day she had spent with me represented a day she had failed to spend with her own son and daughter. That was the first and only time she didn't laugh when she picked up after me, but broke down in angry tears. And although I truly believed I had always loved her, it was the first time I had heard the tone of her pain and saw through the cruel fiction of her being 'a member of the family.'"[21] Lempert realized "only in retrospect" that Mame "was leaving her own children to earn money caring for me."[22] The woman who cared for Adam Hochschild's mother for many years was "a young widow with three small children." Now he wondered who had taken care of them. "I never thought to ask her," he acknowledged.[23]

But the informants also occasionally learned that the workers' lives were much fuller than had been assumed. "Clara Peterson was our cleaning lady," wrote Dorien Grunbaum, who taught English as a second language, "but her real business was making hats. . . . Her house in the Negro part of Mt. Vernon was also her office, and the show room was in the dining room where an array of ladies' felt hats decorated with colored beads, silk flowers, long feathers, and costume jewelry populated the table, each sitting on top of its spindly stand. It was easy to imagine the elbow-length gloves and high heels that completed the outfits."[24] A college professor, Michael Adelson similarly discovered that domestic service was a minor part of the of the identity of Sarah Burdge, a day worker in his Westport, Connecticut home. When she died, he attended the funeral with his mother and two siblings. The service was an "eye opener." They had known that the church was important to her (they had always given old clothes to her "for the church"), but not the extent of its importance and what a central figure Burdge had been. Here was someone who ironed and cleaned for his nonworking mother, and it turned out that she was "a revered person," a "pillar of the Church."[25]

We were struck by how many of these childhood memories echoed stereotypical description of enslaved people as exceptionally large and strong. Michael Adelson, for example, remembered Sarah Burdge as an "imposing presence."[26] Cathy Wilkerson referred to Catherine as "a large black woman."[27] Arthur Kleinman viewed Hatty as "tall" and "unflappable."[28] Allen Shawn, the writer and composer, wrote that because "Bessie [the domestic worker in his house] was physically sturdy," she could hold his sister when she was upset, although "no one else could." In a few cases such descriptors seemed to suggest that the worker was an interloper in the household. Laura Furman, a high school student when her mother died, wrote about the terrible period that followed: "In my mother's place at the kitchen table when I came home each day was a large black woman."[29]

The emphasis on size and strength also could indicate that Whites thought domestic workers easily could perform even the most arduous tasks. Christopher Lukas, a writer and television producer, described Proctor as a "tall, sturdy African-American" who "served as occasional chauffeur, as well as a man of all trades, fixing the lawn mower, the sump pump, the kitchen sink."[30] Elsie was one of the many men and women employed by the grandmother of writer Reeve Lindbergh. According to Lindbergh, she "had brown curly hair, a pale, smiling face, strong arms, and a knack for catching and cooking fish. When not making meals or supervising her kitchen, Elsie would put on a sun hat on summer afternoons, take a fishing rod and a can of bait, and go down to the rocky beach, where she would get in the rowboat that was left hauled up on the shore, and row out to fish for flounder."[31] We are left with the impression from Lindbergh that Elsie's job was far less strenuous than the activity she chose on her time off. Of course, this perspective both minimizes domestic labor and ignores the possibility that Elsie fished to feed herself and her family.

In her book of interviews with household workers in the South, Susan Tucker provides a useful perspective on such comments. She notes that "the black domestic in literature is . . . frequently shown as physically strong and robust, particularly by White authors." Maum Hannah in Julia Peterkin's *Green Thursday*, for example, is an old woman, but she can still "wield an ax . . . and the fire in her open fireplace was never allowed to go out." Black authors, by contrast, show more of the toll domestic service work exacted. Toni Morrison describes Ondine in *Tar Baby* as exhausted. She often soaks her feet. Another character remarks, "Her feet are killing her, killing her."[32] Law professor Mario L. Barnes made a similar point about the day he accompanied his grandmother to her job cleaning houses: "At the end of the day I remember sitting at a bus stop with my grandmother very upset about how tired she looked and how hard she had worked. I am not sure at the time I appreciated that she was in her 60s and suffering from diabetes, but I did understand that this brand of physically demanding labor was not good for her."[33] None of our informants, however, commented on the onerous nature of private household employment.

Devotion was another quality White employers and their children attributed to household workers in the North, as in the South. "Our nanny was warm and generous and devoted to us," Christopher Lukas wrote. In a photograph of her with Christopher and his brother, she "looks with great love upon the scene," suggesting there was no place else she would rather have been.[34] Allen Shawn wrote that because Bessie was childless, she "directed her maternal feelings toward us." Marie Killilea, a Larchmont author, wrote two books about her daughter Karen who had been disabled from cerebral palsy. In the second volume, Marie describes Rose Hurley as "the dark-skinned angel who was 'mother' to my children when

I had to be away."[35] Other passages suggest that Hurley's interests were so completely aligned with those of the Killilea family that she happily took on extra work. When Marie, her husband, and Karen returned home after Karen underwent a serious operation in Pennsylvania, the oldest daughter, also named Marie,

> came and sat beside me. "I think you should know what your good Baptist friends, Rose and John Hurley, did for Karen." She took my hand. "Rose came down the day of the surgery and when I got home from school she had the washing and ironing all done. She got our dinner and stayed the evening, knowing we'd be missing you and Daddy." Marie's eyes were wide. "She and John not only prayed, Mommy, they *fasted!* For two days they took nothing but water. I tried to get Rose to take a cup of tea, at least, but she said that when they asked God for something so big, they felt they should make some small sacrifice.[36]

When Killilea's adopted daughter was married, "Rose Hurley, her dear dark face shining with happiness, came to take over the kitchen for the day."[37] In the 1995 film *Martha and Ethel,* Barbara Ettinger depicts her nanny Ethel as a faithful employee who provides unconditional love to her charges and happily relinquishes her own needs. She is portrayed as being enormously grateful when Ettinger takes her to visit her home in South Carolina and does not seem to mind that before then she had never once returned in the sixty-four years since she left. At the end of the film, Ethel describes Ettinger's mother as her best friend although they clearly remain in an employer/employee relationship; Ethel wears a uniform and serves the tea the women drink together.[38]

Although only four informants credited domestic workers with special devotion, several others emphasized what they wanted to believe was reciprocity: the exchange of what felt like tenderness received with their own deep affection for the workers who cared for them. For example, Rose Lambert, a nurse, referred to her relationship with Lillian Payne, the woman who lived in her childhood home, as a "heart connection."[39] Alexandra Styron was the daughter of the author William Styron and Rose Styron, who was deeply involved in human rights work. Because her father was "tempestuous and scary" and her mother began to travel "constantly" when Alexandra was five, she viewed the couple who arrived at the house every morning as the "rock foundation of the family." Her sense of connection to the man was especially strong: "Along with the feel of his flannel shirt against my check, the aroma of Terry's shed was the essence of comfort and permanence."[40]

A few informants were shocked to learn that the tender care bestowed on them derived as much from economics as from love. Believing that Ethel was a regular member of the family, Barbara Ettinger felt "betrayed" when she heard Ethel received a salary. One day, John Darnton received "the sad news that Inell had gone." In order to "ease the transition," Darnton's mother arranged for the boys to have dinner at the home of Inell Jones's new employer. Now Darnton discovered the limits of Jones's dedication. He and his brother "wanted only to visit with Inell in the kitchen, while she was scurrying about nervously trying to put on a feast that would please her new boss. She made it clear that we were 'underfoot.' The dinner conversation was awkward. As Inell served us, I kept looking to her for some sign that she missed us as much as we missed her." None, apparently, was forthcoming.[41]

In other cases, bonds of affection did persist long after the economic relationship ended. In 1968, when John Rosenthal's mother sold the family house in New Rochelle and moved to the city, a woman named Eva Brown stopped working for her. Nevertheless, the two women had what Rosenthal described as "deep" phone conversations every morning until his mother died in 1996.[42] Many years after Lillian Payne had worked for Rose Lambert's parents, Lambert sent tickets so Payne could visit her, first in her country house in the Catskills and then in San Francisco. Each time, Lambert recalled, they had "a blast." Later, Lambert and her brother traveled to Payne's home in South Carolina.[43]

But our informants did not recall their relationships with the workers as uniformly warm and loving. The woman Laura Furman found in her mother's kitchen "didn't like us very much, and I became aware for the first time of the need to be liked in order to get food and clean clothes."[44] In contrast to Barbara Ettinger, who depicts Ethel as invariably affectionate, Jyll Johnston, the other narrator in the film *Martha and Ethel,* portrays her nanny as cold and rigid. A German immigrant, Martha never smiles and Johnston acknowledges she sometimes "hated" Martha.[45] Like family members, domestic workers probably had favorites. Rose Lambert believes that the woman who showered her with love was mean to her older sister.[46] Sarah Paine Stuart, a novelist, was a baby when her mother stayed in a psychiatric hospital for eighteen months. Her brothers were much older. Sarah is confident that Margaret, the woman who cared for them in their mother's absence, "loved me and held me and gave me my chance for happiness." But, she adds, "Margaret gave my brothers no indication that she loved them, nor did they love her." When Margaret told one of the boys that their grandmother had died, he "turned away and walked down the stairs to the chalkboard. Margaret followed him. This is the only time he remembers her putting her arms around him."[47]

Whether or not they now acknowledge their privilege, our informants were far more critical of their parents' relationships with domestic workers than they were of their own. The vast political and social changes that had occurred since the 1940s and 1950s undoubtedly affected the memories of those who had been children in households with domestic workers in that era. If they seemed unaware of the harm the labor may have inflicted on workers' bodies, most now recognized the class and race dynamics that shaped the employer/employee relationship. According to various accounts, parents ignored the families of household workers, paid them too little, demanded that they wear uniforms, provided live-in workers with grossly inadequate living spaces, and kept day workers after hours. The harshest condemnation came from those who had grown up with large staffs. The writer Adam Hochschild, half asleep while he waited at his son's babysitter's home, remembered the "sounds of other people laboring to make the place run for my benefit." He realized that when the "extra help" hired for the summer worked outside, he "did not even know their names."[48] He also castigated the common practice of referring to household workers with "a possessive pronoun and first name, as in 'Do you still have your marvelous Ellen?'"[49] Above all, his critique focused on his father, who gave gifts instead of decent pay and repeatedly demanded that Adam serve the beer while "the maids watched." After handing out drinks to the guests, Adam "sat down again, feeling humiliated . . . Looking back at it now, I think that this feeling came not from having to do a menial task—for I hated having servants and, later, once I moved away from home, took pride in cooking and cleaning for myself—but rather from the fact that Getting the Beer was a ritual denial that we *were* employers of servants."[50]

AFRICAN AMERICAN PERSPECTIVES

While many White observers simultaneously minimized the grueling nature of domestic labor and exaggerated the bonds of affection that developed, Black household workers painted a very different picture. They did not need social movements to understand the exploitative aspects of their employment and the race and class issues involved. As we noted in chapter 2, studies of workers in the South emphasize the various forms of resistance in which they engaged, including quitting, chicanery, and rejecting live-in work. Although domestic workers in the North have received less scholarly attention, evidence suggests that they took similar actions.[51]

By the 1940s, many workers in New York also had participated in organized resistance. A major target were ordinances passed in various cities and towns in the New York area requiring household workers to undergo medical exams before securing employment. Whites throughout the country had long assumed that poor people, immigrants, and people of color spread disease. Because domestic workers were believed to bring germs directly into White homes, Whites especially feared them. During the 1916 New York polio epidemic, health officials viewed immigrants as disease carriers despite epidemiological reports showing that it affected affluent communities most severely. When a doctor's child was diagnosed with polio, officials assumed that the child's nurse rather than the father had brought the infection into the home.[52] The health officer of Newark, New Jersey, clearly viewed himself as responsible for protecting the well-being of White, middle-class families only. Discussing medical examinations of domestic workers in that city, he told an audience of the American Public Health Association that the goal was "the exclusion from the homes of our people of those with contagious diseases."[53]

News of proposals to mandate health exams for domestic workers frequently provoked resistance from African Americans. In New Rochelle, that resistance achieved success. The New Rochelle city councilors may have assumed that their ordinance requiring medical exams in 1937 was uncontroversial because it had the support of numerous civic groups. The *New York Amsterdam News* reported that the city clerk received a list of "twenty-eight organizations which had gone on record favoring the legislation, including all the prominent women's organizations and the Board of Education."[54] Domestic workers, however, responded with fury, arguing that because they washed their employers' laundry and cleaned their bathrooms, they were the ones most likely to be exposed to new germs. One woman wrote to the editor of a local newspaper, "A maid's life and health is just as important to her, as the lives of the family are to the employers." Another considered it "too bad and that well-meaning organizations should spread through the newspapers that domestics are disease-ridden."[55] Workers and their supporters thronged the council chambers the night of the hearing on the ordinance. Dr. Carver McClendon pointed out that employers would have to be included in any measure mandating health inspections: "Every physician knows that you don't know where you get tuberculosis. It is just as possible for a domestic to get it from a child as for a child to get it from a domestic." Because syphilis aroused special concern in the 1930s, McClendon addressed that disease as well stating, "It has been my experience that there have been very few cases of syphilis contracted except by intimate contact. And after a certain time they are perfectly safe, despite the fact that the Department of Health in this city will not allow four-plus syphilitics to work as food handlers." And Dr. Toothaker reminded the councilors that "what's sauce for the goose is applesauce for the gander. There's as many people in the upper crust have syphilis as in the lower element." Soon after that meeting, the council voted against the ordinance.[56]

The 1930s also witnessed one of the first efforts to organize household workers in New York City. The Domestic Workers Union, led by Dora Jones and affiliated with the Building Service Union, had 350 members by 1937, three-fourths of whom were African American. Visiting the office in 1939, a member of the Federal Writers Project reported she met "a group of unceasing workers who delegate their lives to providing ways and means of lifting the level of the shamefully neglected domestic workers." The union had drafted a petition, "the gist of which was a plea to the members of the state assembly to limit the domestic workers to a ten hour day—a sixty hour week," establish a minimum wage of $3.50 an hour, and agitate for the "inclusion of domestic workers in the Social Security Act." The visitor also praised Jones's attempts to solicit the help of local clergy in the campaign to eradicate the "slave markets" in various areas of the city.[57]

The Black press frequently alerted their readers to the abuses domestic workers experienced. We have noted the outcry in African American newspapers about the "slave markets." The papers were replete with stories about other unscrupulous employers as well. Over and over articles ridiculed the value system that placed wealthy, lazy Whites above hard-working Black people. Reporters applauded instances of resistance. A full-page article by civil rights activist Marvel Cooke in the *New York Amsterdam News* featured Bessie Brown, a maid who had been "kicked and beaten brutally" by a "wealthy white couple in their beautiful Mt. Vernon mansion" because she "courageously fought for her rights." Like many other household workers, she had been "ill paid, overworked and mistreated at the hands of their employers who, drunk with the power money stimulates, have no regard for humanity."[58] Another issue of the *New York Amsterdam News* praised a magistrate who heard the case of a "schoolteacher-lawyer who brazenly made indecent advances to a woman on a subway." The legal system was stacked against African Americans but, surprisingly, in this case, "justice was done, although the complainant was a poor Negro woman domestic worker and the defendant a well-educated professional man."[59] An article in the *Pittsburgh Courier* noted that domestic workers deserved greater respect because their "important" work, "nobly performed," requires "a high degree of intelligence and judgment" and "rises to the level of dignified labor."[60]

Two other African American newspapers, first Paul Robeson's *Freedom* and then the *Baltimore Afro-American,* published stories by Alice Childress. In 1956, the stories were collected in a book titled *Like One of the Family: Conversations from a Domestic's Life*.[61] Each episode consisted of a conversation "Mildred," a day worker from the South now living in New York City, has with her neighbor "Marge," another domestic worker. Mildred does virtually all the talking. It is clear from the beginning that she has a rich and full life outside her work. She has friends, shows visitors around New York, goes to dancing parties, has a love life, entertains the children in her building and teaches them "Negro history," and drinks endless cups of coffee and tea with Marge. Most of her monologues expose the indignities of private household work. The first story, also titled "Like One of the Family," sets the tone. Overhearing an employer use that phrase to describe her, Mildred explodes in rage: "I am *not* just like one of the family at all! The family eats in the dining room and I eat in the kitchen. Your mama borrows your lace tablecloth for her company and your son entertains his friends in your parlor, your daughter takes her afternoon nap on the living room couch and the puppy sleeps on your satin spread. . . . So you can see I am not *just* like one of the family."[62] She is proud of her work, demands raises, sees through attempts to trick her out of money, and informs employers when they are condescending or hypocritical. She also finds fault with the children she encounters at work. Although their parents insist that Mildred "loves them," she prefers more "inhibited" behavior.[63]

Mildred lives in an ideal world in one respect. She constantly rebukes her employers, but in her case, unlike that of Bessie Brown, there is no retribution. No one beats or even admonishes her. When she leaves a job, it is because she has had enough, not because she has been fired. Mrs. C., who made the mistake of calling Mildred one of the family "*apologized* and said she'd talk to her husband about a raise."[64] When Mildred explains to another employer why a worker who does the family laundry should not have to present a card testifying to her good health, the woman turns "green" and agrees the card is unnecessary.[65] The many readers who identified with Mildred and appreciated her depiction of household work must have delighted in her inevitable triumphs.[66]

Interviews conducted by sociologist Bonnie Thornton Dill raise many of the same issues. Dill spoke with twenty-three African American women over the age of sixty who were still working in Philadelphia and New York in the 1970s. Most of the women had worked in the occupation for at least ten years, and all had migrated from the South between 1922 and 1955.[67] Like the fictional Mildred, several emphasized the rich social lives they enjoyed outside their working hours. Jewell Prieleau had labored and lived in the home of one family for thirty years. "In the late '40s and '50s," she commented, "domestic girls used to get together and have clubs, social clubs. . . . We would meet every Thursday night."[68] Several women also demonstrated what Dill refers to as a "defensive" pride in their work, rejecting what they understood to be the social stigma attached to domestic labor. One stated, "So many people have gotten their education by it, and it isn't any disgrace. . . . I wasn't embarrassed that I'd done that work because I knew I was prepared for something else. I did it because it was something I could do to help my husband out. . . . I think I should be proud and want to work. Domestic work is nothing to be ashamed of, but it's an art, just like anything else. You just have to learn how to do it."[69]

Women who had not succeeded in negotiating what they considered acceptable work arrangements found ways to resist. Oneida Harris learned from her aunt (probably also a domestic worker) that resistance was sometimes necessary to maintain self-respect. One day Harris's employer accused her of having neglected to wash the floor, which was damp from children's feet, and then of lying about it. "That was unpleasant," Harris said. "The thing I had to learn was not to let it get to me, and to call her a liar back. My aunt says, 'Listen, you've got to learn when you work for people, to treat them as they treat you. If they're nice and sweet you can be that too. But if they use bad words to you, you gotta use 'em back.' That's what I had to learn to do. I had to learn not to cry 'bout it, but to find some kind of way to get back at her. And that way I survived."[70]

Bea Rivers confronted her employer to preserve her pride. She described the time she had refused to work over the weekend. When she returned Monday morning, the employer remarked, "Well, one thing about you, Bea, nobody could ever say anybody took advantage of you." Rivers responded, "Well maybe they can't say it, but you certainly have tried. The only difference is you didn't succeed because this job here is *your job*. This job is not the type of job that I have to live with the rest of my life. I lived before I ever came here and I could leave here and go back to the city and find another job. Don't you ever feel that this is the only job. When I came here I didn't sign any contract. I work here and I do enjoy it, but if there comes a time when things can be so unpleasant that I no longer enjoy it. . . ." The threat—that she could quit at any time—remained implicit.[71]

What was perhaps most striking about Dill's interviews was the absence of any comments about love and devotion. Although our White informants occasionally implied that the workers were bound to them by ties of affection, at least one worker made it clear that she accepted the job because she had no other option. "I didn't really want to do [this work]," Pearl Runner said, "but I didn't have no choice because I didn't have the education to do what I like to do. My husband and I were struggling and I had to help him some way. So I made myself satisfied, let's put it that way. I made myself satisfied."[72] To these women, good employers were not necessarily the ones they liked but rather those who paid decent salaries and provided good benefits. As a result, the women preferred employers with high social status who were more experienced in supervising household workers and more likely to offer generous terms.[73]

MABLE JONES AND OUR FAMILY

As we reflect on our mother's relationship with Mable, we consider how both their different positions in the hierarchies of class and race and their distinctive personalities may have influenced their interactions. "The story of the suburbs is largely a story of how communities are formed around the desire to live among like-minded people," writes Michael Botwinick.[74] But our mother set herself apart. Chafing at the codes for suburban women in the 1950s, she underdressed for the part: wrap-around denim skirts, blue shirts, sneakers (or comfortable shoes), no makeup except lipstick, a bobby pin in her hair. She walked when everyone else drove, earning, to her children's chagrin, the sobriquet of "the Larchmont walker." (She also rode a bike until her teenage daughters begged her not to.) She wrote books when other mothers shopped, sat around pools, and indulged in leisurely lunches. The daughter and granddaughter of great wealth and privilege, she enacted that privilege in part by refusing to conform to expectations. She was fiercely political—to the left of what was deemed appropriate for that time and place. She refused to greet neighbors who supported Senator Joseph McCarthy and barely acknowledged acquaintances who sent money to Israel. She didn't bake, volunteer for the PTA, or join any club for that matter. She loved her father, tolerated her mother, fought with one sister, and adored the other sister. She was loyal to the (relatively few) family and friends she liked. But she was not either warm or cuddly; her children do not recall signs of affection (in fact, quite the reverse) although at least some say they know they were loved. Watching the tender concern Emily's daughter and son-in-law expressed toward their daughter when she broke her arm, Emily remembered how furious our mother became when she "fussed" after breaking her wrist while ice skating.

Our mother neither wasted time nor sought out pleasures. She did not watch television, listen to music, or even read unless it was the *I. F. Stone Weekly,* the *New Yorker* or Henry James. She was volatile and occasionally vengeful, raging when someone crossed some spoken (or unspoken) family norm. We all bear scars. Peggy remembers the first time she did not do what the voice on her GPS instructed. Instead of going into a fit of anger as our mother did when she considered us disobedient, the voice simply said, "recalculating" and found an alternative route. Maybe out of fear—maybe out of desire—we all conformed to our mother's expectations that we would marry and give her grandchildren. Along the way we took advantage of our privileges to accomplish a great deal.

Mable was, in many ways, the converse. If she chafed at the bonds of domestic service, that chafing was invisible to us. She was invariably respectful. And, in an odd counterpart of our mother's attire, Mable was beautifully dressed and coiffed, with carefully tailored clothes and elegant shoes and not a hair out of place. In the picture we treasure from our family album, three of us—the daughters—are slouching, legs spread, clothes awry; Mable is sitting erect, legs carefully crossed, with our baby brother perched on her knee. Whatever the motivation—likely a combination of the politics of respectability, the church, and the constraints in general of Black womanhood—she was the one displaying dignity and self-possession. We wonder now if one reason our mother respected Mable so much was because she seemed very strong, not someone our mother easily could overwhelm.

Mable was also the one who knew how to have fun. We watched *I Love Lucy, Arthur Godfrey's Talent Show,* the *Jackie Gleason Show,* and Perry Como with her. And she was the secure rock. Peggy remembers weeping when she came home with a bag full of hair a neighbor child cut off while

Mable Jones and four Klein children, Emily, Peggy, Jimmy (*on lap*), and Liz, 1949. (Courtesy of the Klein family)

they were playing beauty parlor and being consoled when she showed it to Mable. Emily felt much safer when Mable was in the house. We were both heartbroken when she left for the last time.

If their personalities differed sharply, Mable and our mother shared a commitment to hard work. In addition to writing mystery novels, our mother shopped, cooked, shortened our clothes, and sewed on buttons. She also weeded the garden, mowed the lawn, pruned the hedges, and maintained a compost heap. Mable shared the cooking, sometimes side by side with our mother, sometimes on her own. She also did some of the childcare, most of the cleaning, and all the ironing, both for us and for herself. Our father, like many men of his generation, did no housework at all. Outside he kept a small vegetable garden (for a few years) and took charge of the charcoal grill.

Only three letters from Mable to our family survive. In 1954, just one year after Mable left, she wrote to our sister Elizabeth that she had been in the hospital for some months and would "write a long letter" when she went home. She added that her mother and sons were well. Two years later, we met her in Washington, DC, and had a meal together. After that she wrote to our sister Elizabeth again and said, "I enjoyed seeing you and just think you are all grown and I wasn't there when it happened." She was miffed that our youngest brother, just two years old when she left, had not recognized her. And then she said, "I don't worry though as long as I can see you every two or three years we won't forget each other."

When our mother died in 1992, we wrote to Mable, who responded that she always felt "like one of the family," the phrase Whites so often used to describe the status of Black houseworkers. It was a lovely thing to write but we doubt it was any more apt in her case than it was in that of others. True, she did not wear a uniform or serve us at the table, and our mother was proud when she removed a bell in one house that previously had been used to summon servants. But Mable did not eat with us. Everyone in the family used her first name. And although Mable did not use "Miss" or "Master" when talking to the children, we believe she called our father "Mr. Klein" and our mother "Mrs. Klein." We also believe that she slept in a small, unfinished attic room in our first Larchmont house. We remember clearly that when we moved down the block in 1952, she had a much larger and nicer room with her own bathroom, but still away from the rest of the family in a finished attic.

Mable's letter continued that our mother was "the best friend I have ever had and she went through a lot bad of times with [me]." Mable then listed some of the "nice things" our mother did for her including "writing schools to get James and Thomas in—when [I was] going through the divorce and when Thomas was wounded in [the war in] Korea how she stood by me and when he came home she gave us tickets to the [Broadway play] South Pacific."

Some of this, we know from numerous other accounts, were quite routine practices—especially the giving of gifts.[75] But most gifts mentioned involved food and used household goods and clothing, all of which preserved the status differential. Our mother gave a gift that allowed Mable and her son to do what more privileged people did: get dressed up (as one did in those days) and go to a Broadway play. Our mother may have known that both Mable and Thomas enjoyed singing. Nevertheless, with its tense racial dynamics, South Pacific seems like a particularly odd gift.

The issue of the schools Mable mentions might have been enrolling Thomas in the Christiansburg Institute. Thomas would have had few alternatives for attaining a high school education, especially when he was living with his grandmother in Louisa County. However, although our mother might not have known it at the time, the Christiansburg Institute, which followed the Hampton-Tuskegee model of education advocated by Booker T. Washington, would at best have set Thomas on the road to trades, not higher education.

Thomas's wound during his time in Korea was extremely serious, and we recall the terrible anxiety it engendered as well as the recording he sent his mother assuring her that he would recover. He was transported first to a hospital in Japan and then to a convalescent facility, presumably Goldwater Hospital, in New York, where Mable could visit him frequently. Our family album included a picture from the Larchmont daily paper of Thomas in the hospital in Japan with a pipe from a voluntary organization.

It is unclear exactly how our mother helped Mable with her divorce. As we have noted, Mable married James Henry Jones in 1929 and had two sons soon afterwards. James listed her as next of kin when he registered

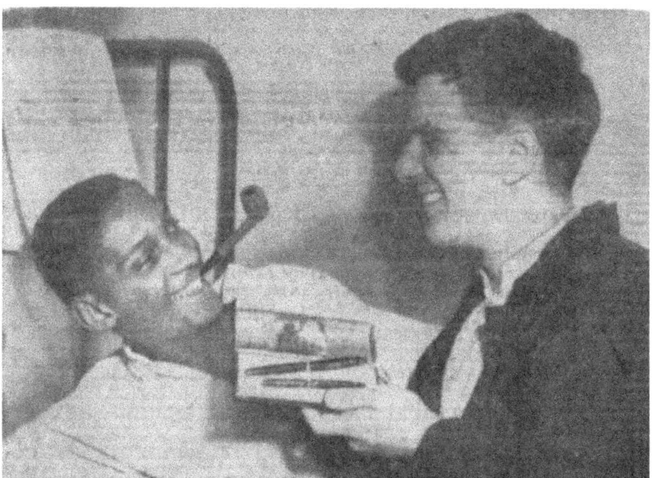

THE JAUNTY ANGLE on that pipe exemplified the Christmas happiness of Pvt. Thomas Jones, 20, of 24 Locust ave., Larchmont, N. Y., comparing his Stateside holiday greeting with Pvt. Maurice Drangel, 22, of 287 Division ave., Brooklyn, at Tokyo Army Hospital. Despite shrapnel wounds in the leg, thigh and wrist, Jones is a great organizer of quartets to entertain his wounded buddies. These two gifts came from Bernadette Brennan, of 226 Mt. Hope pl., Bronx, and Margie Budell, 626 Hillcrest ave., Westfield, N. J.

Thomas Jones in the hospital, ca. December 1952. (Courtesy of the Klein family)

for the draft in 1940.[76] When they divorced in 1957, she was living in Charlottesville, and James was in Washington, DC; our parents were in Larchmont. On the divorce decree she listed the separation date as September 16, 1944, two years after James enlisted in the army (and around the time she began to work for our mother in Washington, DC).[77] One possibility is that our mother offered Mable emotional support when she and her husband were first separated. The other possibility is that Mable asked our parents for help in 1957 either in applying for the divorce or in paying the associated fees.[78] Kellie Carter Jackson, a professor at Wellesley College, has written about her grandmother, who had been a domestic worker in the 1950s. When asked why she had not gotten a divorce until 1959, many years after she had separated from her husband, the grandmother "responded by saying it was too expensive." When asked how much it cost, Jackson's grandmother sighed, "Oh, about fifty dollars."[79]

In her final letter to us, Mable addressed Peggy directly, reminding her of the day she brought a "black girl home for lunch. . . . [who] wanted to know if I was the maid [and] your mother said she is my cousin." We wrote about this episode in the Introduction. We wonder even now what it meant that Mable chose to retell it while honoring our mother. As far as we can recall, this was the only time Mable ever addressed the issue of race with us.

We can never know what Mable really thought of us. A common theme in accounts of African American domestic workers is that, while they attend to the most intimate aspects of their employers' lives, the employers know little about them. Through that asymmetry workers can hide many parts of their lives. But employers also use that concealment to turn workers into stereotypes, devoid of consciousness and voice. We have noted that as a child, Mable endured terrible poverty and segregation and had responsibility for many arduous chores. How did she feel taking care of children who were free of chores, lived luxuriously, and seemed unaware of their many privileges? How did she make sense of and respond to our mother's behavior? We experienced Mable as calm and warm. We do not know whether she was naturally so, or her job permitted her to display only a limited range of emotions. By contrast, our mother's periodic explosions of rage terrified us, our siblings, and our father. What did Mable think about our father? In one generation he had left his immigrant background behind and launched himself and his children into the upper-middle class. Although Jewish, he could claim Whiteness. As an African American man, Mable's husband—a man of the same generation—faced far greater barriers. He disappeared from Mable's life when her boys were young; her children and grandchildren grew up in poverty. What was it like for her to live in such a secular household? Susan Tucker interviewed one worker who found her employer's family "lacking in a rich spiritual life."[80] Did Mable view our lives as similarly impoverished? Although numerous sources enabled us to unearth a great deal of information about Mable's life, we could find none that helped us answer these questions.

6

"WE MARCHED FROM DOWNTOWN . . . UP UNTIL MT. ZION CHURCH"

WHEN MABLE LEFT OUR house for Charlottesville for the last time in 1953, she returned to a city that closely resembled the one she had first encountered three decades earlier. African Americans still attended segregated schools, lived in segregated areas, and performed the most menial jobs. They could not eat at lunch counters at local diners or sit in either the front of buses or the orchestra section of movie theaters. In May 1951, the *Charlottesville-Albemarle Tribune,* a weekly African American newspaper, called attention to "the glaring differences in the physical conditions of the Negro and white public and private wards," including the presence of "huge rats" that "frequently saunter about" on "C-Ward for colored women" in the University of Virginia Hospital.[1] But a burgeoning civil rights movement already had begun to transform the city.

CIVIL RIGHTS MOVEMENT

Eugene Williams grew up around the corner from Mable. Like her, he moved away from Charlottesville for several years and returned in 1953. "Just about instantly," he later stated, "I got the feeling most of the black people, and a few white people were tired of Charlottesville's racial segregation and discrimination from the founding date of 1762."[2] In 1945, local activists had established a branch of the National Association for the Advancement of Colored People (NAACP), which Williams subsequently led and which spearheaded many of Charlottesville's most important civil rights campaigns. One of the first was promoting the candidacy of Gregory Swanson to become the first African American student at the University of Virginia. Swanson first applied to the law school in 1949. Although he had received the unanimous support of the law school faculty, he was rejected on the grounds that he was "a colored man." A suit brought by the NAACP the following year succeeded in reversing that decision. On September 22, 1950, the *Charlottesville-Albemarle Tribune* announced, "A dignified looking young man stepped into the lobby of the University of Virginia Law School building last Friday afternoon and ended the all-white tradition which has been followed at this famous institution of learning since Thomas Jefferson founded it back in 1819." After registering, Swanson "told school officials and reporters that he expected to concentrate on insurance and corporate law." He then completed the "numerous formalities with the other students."[3] But Swanson's victory was only partial. Although permitted to enroll in classes, he was prohibited from living on campus and attending dances. He left at the end of the first year.[4]

Mable might have learned about Swanson when he spoke at her church soon after he enrolled in the law school, but she probably was far more interested in the battle about elementary and high school education that raged for fourteen years, galvanized the African American community, and directly affected her grandchildren.[5] Mable's pastor told us that one of her primary causes was children's education. When we mentioned that we knew she had taught in the Sunday School, he responded that her interests were much broader than religious education. Having left school at a young age, she knew what a limited education meant for a person's life chances. She was also undoubtedly acutely aware of the deficiencies of the segregated schools she and her siblings, as well as her two sons, had attended in both Louisa County and Charlottesville. We can only imagine how she felt when she witnessed the lengths White people in her city would go to deprive Black children of a good education.

In 1950, Charlottesville had one all-White high school (Lane) and three all-White elementary schools (Clark, McGuffey, and Venable). Two buildings housed the only schools for Black students—Jefferson Primary School (for grades 1–4), Jefferson Elementary School (grades 5–8), and Jefferson High School. In 1950, the White primary and elementary classrooms were filled to capacity, but those for African Americans were "drastically overcrowded." Moreover, the facilities at Lane were far superior to those at Jefferson High School.[6] The next four years witnessed major changes. In 1951, the Jackson B. Burley High School, consolidating the Albemarle Training School and Jefferson High School and operated jointly by the city and county, was established for Black students. The school remedied some of the inequities. Florence C. Bryant, who had been a teacher at Jefferson, transferred with the rest of the staff to Burley. "Inspired by the beautiful new facilities," she later wrote, "the faculty put forth a special effort to design an exciting new, vital, and dynamic education program."[7] In 1954, two new elementary schools (Johnson and Burnley-Moran) opened for Whites. And then, that year, the Supreme Court decision of *Brown v. Board of Education,* declared "separate but equal" unconstitutional.

Having waged a decade-long campaign culminating in that decision, the NAACP immediately took the lead in its implementation. Acknowledging that voluntary compliance was unlikely, the Virginia state office urged local branches to file petitions for the admission of Black students in White schools, beginning with those in urban areas.[8] In 1956, the Charlottesville branch acted on behalf of forty-five Black students. According to George Ferguson, the president of that chapter, their request inaugurated "a long, drawn out process. It didn't just happen here, here, here. We had these hearings in court. Then the city, I believe, spent a million dollars fighting or more."[9] Some opponents of integration also engaged in violence. Three cross burnings occurred between 1955 and 1956—one on the lawn of a White family's home because the father had worked with a civil rights activist, another outside a Unitarian church that supported school integration, and the third on the lawn of Sarah Patton Boyle, a White woman who worked closely with the civil rights movement.[10] Watching from an open window, Boyle saw the flames "six feet tall and not a slipper's toss from the house . . . The soft hiss and crackle was a fitting voice for live malice, and the odor of burning, oil-soaked rags a fitting miasma of human moral degradation."[11]

In 1956, US Senator Harry F. Byrd Sr., who wielded enormous influence over Virginia politics, called for a policy of White massive resistance. "This is when those people in authority, the governor on down, said that they would resist and encourage the people to resist any integration," explained Sherman White, a Black student who was one of the plaintiffs in the suit to desegregate Charlottesville schools. "The leaders of the state were saying, telling the citizens to willfully disobey the law."[12] Thus, after Judge John Paul Jr. of the United States District Court for the Western District of Virginia ordered the integration of Venable Elementary School and Lane High School in August 1956, Governor J. Lindsay Almond Jr. seized control of the schools and demanded their closure. "Fortunately," White added, "because the NAACP at that time was very strong and very well organized, it was able to bring a lot of pressure to bear legally and turn the things around."[13] The White community was divided. The Parents' Committee for Emergency Schooling (PCES) offered the NAACP limited support. Like many Charlottesville Whites, that group did not want desegregation but believed that compared with school closure, it represented the lesser evil.[14] Other parents, however, established private academies for White students who would have enrolled in either Venable or Lane. Those students received financial support from the state.[15]

On January 19, 1959 (ironically, Robert E. Lee's birthday) both federal and state courts invalidated the school closing laws.[16] Soon afterwards, the school board adopted what it called a "plan of desegregation." In fact, Boyle later wrote, it was actually a plan "of 'containment.' This meant that a few Negroes would be accepted in White schools, but—by various devious means—the number would be kept to a minimum."[17] The plan divided the city into six elementary school districts closely aligned with residential segregation. The few exceptions benefited Whites alone. White students who lived in the district assigned to Jefferson Elementary School were transferred to one of the other schools. Black students in "White" zones were assigned to Jefferson; if they wished to transfer, they had to apply. The two existing high schools continued to serve different populations. All African American students were assigned to Burley, all White students to

Lane. A Black student could attend Lane, but only after satisfying certain residential and academic requirements not applied to Whites.[18]

On September 8, 1959, nine Black students began their lonely walk up the stairs to Venable. Another three entered Lane. Like Black student pioneers throughout the state, they encountered harassment and sometimes violence.[19] John Martin, the oldest of the "Charlottesville Twelve," later reported that "he was physically attacked by his peers [at Lane], barred from playing on the football team and ignored by every teacher except for his Spanish instructor."[20] Florence C. Bryant recalled that the Black students there "became objects of hate and derision. They had to determine for themselves how to cope in a hostile environment."[21] The number of Black students in previously all-White schools crept up very slowly. There were eighteen in 1961–62 and thirty-five the following year.[22] Eugene Williams proudly noted that one was his daughter Scheryl, who entered Johnson Elementary School under police escort.[23] Williams also went door-to-door, encouraging other African American parents to enroll their children in Johnson. Theresa Woodfolk remembered that he convinced her mother to try to send her younger children there.[24]

Mable's grandchildren Charles and Theresa, however, decided to remain in the school their mother had attended. Segregated schools had some benefits. Although expert testimony about the harmful effects of segregation on African American children played an important role in *Brown v. Board of Education,* two of Mable's Ridge Street neighbors later emphasized the special sense of community all-Black schools had provided. "At Burley," Joan Woodfolk commented, "the teachers were your extended family, . . . and they cared about you."[25] Luella Gohaner-Lyles had decided to stay where she was "because in those years and right today I still believe there is an incredible impact between an African American teacher teaching an African American Child. . . . It's an incredible chemistry there." Gohaner-Lyles pointed as an example to "Alisha Lugo," who "was energized to teach you because you were African American. It makes sense to me. I mean all of her experience and all of her knowledge she gave to us. And there's a big difference today [in integrated schools]."[26] Interviewed in 2017, Patricia Edwards, another longtime Charlottesville resident, noted she had been disappointed when her parents refused to allow her to apply to a White school. Later, she was glad they had done so because students in segregated Black schools were "very much nurtured, and protected and cared for." Moreover, the "teachers were . . . very proud, and really believed in education as a way for us to live different lives, and we were told frequently that we could do anything that anybody else could do and when you were told [that] frequently, you believed it." She reiterated that she grew up "in a very nurturing community."[27]

Another reason Mable's grandchildren may have decided to stay in segregated schools was to avoid the kind of humiliation and violence John Martin experienced. According to Paul M. Gaston, a historian at the University of Virginia, "Arch segregationists warned that there would be fights, knifings, and riots."[28] Parents as well as children faced intimidation. Melvin Hamilton, another Ridge Street homeowner, told an interviewer that after he and his wife, Gertrude, announced their decision to send their children to a formerly White school, groups of men approached them at their places of work. Gertrude Hamilton worked for Miss Fowler, who informed her one day that three White men had come to speak to her. Gertrude Hamilton recognized one as a banker but knew nothing about the other two. "And so," Melvin Hamilton recalled, "they had my wife in the room with these three white men" who "told her what they wanted to see her about [was] about her children getting hurt going to integrated schools." Gertrude Hamilton let them talk but declined to accept their advice. Melvin Hamilton worked as a janitor when the assistant fire chief arrived to tell him that three White men wanted to talk to him:

> So I went on out to see what they want. And I backed up against the flower box, big old flower box out there . . . and I said what's this all about. [They] said Mr. Hamilton you know your children are going to be hurt going to integrated schools and so and so and so and so and so. I would advise you to try to don't put them in integrated schools. . . . And I said, that's all you all got to say? Yes. And I stood up and dust off my hands and I said I got something to tell you men. You know, I appreciate you all coming to see me, but I said they're going, and if anything happens to my children the white folks are going to answer to me. And everybody look and never bothered me no more.[29]

What George Ferguson called "a long, drawn out process" finally ended in the second half of the 1960s. In fall of 1965, two new desegregated junior high schools (Walker and Buford) opened. Jefferson Elementary School became a sixth grade center and McGuffey a special education center. New attendance lines were drawn for grades 1–5 in the remaining elementary schools (Greenbrier, Venable, Burnley-Moran, Johnson, and Clark). Because those boundaries stretched into the center of the city, each school could serve Black students. And then, in 1967–68, Lane High School enrolled all high school students, regardless of race. Now, at long last, Charlottesville's schools were formally desegregated.[30]

But desegregation did not mean integration. Hundreds of White students remained in the two segregated academies.[31] And, as elsewhere in the state, Black and White students had different experiences even within the officially desegregated public schools.[32] "From the beginning," Florence C. Bryant wrote, "the black students were concentrated in the low-level classes and the whites, in the average and above-average classes, creating somewhat of a de facto segregated situation."[33] Although Bryant's three children were assigned to accelerated classes, "they learned quickly that they were not expected to excel in those classes." When her son received a perfect score on a geometry class, the "teacher was so sure he had cheated that she required him to retake the test."[34] All three children chose predominantly Black colleges because "they were fed up with the feeling of nonidentity they had been subject to in the desegregated schools."[35]

Mable was not part of the Black elite, which consisted largely of professionals and businessmen, who led the fight for school integration.[36] Nevertheless, she could follow the major events in the *Charlottesville-Albemarle Tribune,* which covered the struggle in enormous detail. In a book about the desegregation campaign in Virginia's Prince Edward County, journalist Kristen Green wrote that her grandmother's domestic worker Elsie had been forced to send her daughter north for an education after the schools closed. Although the grandmother made an insensitive comment to Elsie, she "went about her work as if nothing was wrong."[37] Although we cannot know how Mable's employers felt about school desegregation, we can speculate that she practiced "cultural dissemblance" there as she had elsewhere and said little or nothing at work about the controversy and the impact of its resolution on her grandchildren.[38]

The school desegregation fight may have captured the most attention, but civil rights activists focused on other areas as well. Raymond Bell, the owner of the city's Black funeral home, described the campaign to integrate the University of Virginia Hospital. We have noted that although that facility admitted African Americans, it restricted them to the basement. In 1960, Bell and a few others threatened to sue if the hospital refused to reverse that policy. "They were able to desegregate the black ward in one day," Bell stated. "They moved all the black patients up to the wards." But victory was not achieved so quickly or so easily. "Although the administrators and policy makers made the policy," Bell continued, "we ran into the problem of people who were ward nurses who wanted to maintain segregation. They would put blacks with blacks. They wouldn't integrate the wards. So, we had to go back and threaten them with a lawsuit." As a result, the administration circulated a memorandum warning that staff members who refused to comply with the policy of integration would be fired. Nevertheless, resistance continued. "You had to fight all the time," Bell remarked. He reserved a private room with a bath for his wife when she gave birth to their second son, but "they wanted to stick her in some little nondescript room without a bath." Bell then used his contacts with the Black staff to learn what private room remained vacant and demanded that the hospital director move her there. "You had to do all those kinds of things," he commented. "We were going to sue them, and they knew it. We meant business."[39]

Inspired by the example of civil rights activities throughout the South, African Americans, supported by some Whites, engaged in various additional forms of protest in Charlottesville.[40] In February 1961 students and others picketed the University Theater, operated by the Paramount Corporation, for three days. Because it had no balcony, the theater refused admission to African Americans. In May 1963, Reverend Henry Floyd Johnson, president of the local NAACP, and Reverend William Johnson led an interracial group on a sit-in at Buddy's Restaurant, a popular establishment which refused not only to serve African Americans but also to speak to civil rights leaders. Paul M. Gaston later recalled that before he left for the demonstration, he comforted his wife by saying "something like, 'This is Charlottesville, not Mississippi: nobody is going to attack us here.'" He was wrong: "On the fourth day, Memorial Day, violence erupted."[41] The most severely hurt was Floyd Johnson, who spent two nights in the hospital. Nevertheless, Gaston concluded that the Buddy's sit-in "was a major turning point in Charlottesville's history. We had been negotiating with local restaurants, motels, hotels, and theaters, with almost no success. Our sit-in movement accomplished what negotiation did not. About ten restaurants agreed to desegregate; so did two of the three theaters in town, including the University Theater, the object of our boycott two years earlier."[42]

It is unclear to what extent Mable and her family members participated in any of these events. In her interview she said that she "used to go to some of [the Civil Rights] meetings." We also know that her church, along with other Black Charlottesville churches, took part in in many civil rights activities, and that Mable went on at least one protest march with other congregants.[43]

On the day the 1964 Civil Rights Act banning discrimination on the basis of race, gender, religion and nationality was passed, an editorial in the *Daily Progress* offered lukewarm support, noting that President Johnson "appealed to the American people for their voluntary compliance." Thus, even those who opposed the legislation had an "obligation to obey it." The editors also urged civil rights advocates to "refrain from activities that would provoke resistance and endanger public order, and to leave such violations as may occur to be dealt with by the orderly processes of law."[44] The same day Buddy Glover, the owner of the eponymous restaurant, closed it rather than comply with the law. "The Civil Rights Act," he argued, "leaves me no control over how my business is to be operated."[45]

But the act spurred positive changes in Charlottesville as it did throughout the South. When Connie Brooks left Charlottesville in the early sixties to attend high school in New York, she "couldn't think of ever sitting down, even to have a Coke," in a drugstore. She remembered the day she went with her sister and two nephews "just to get . . . sodas. They wouldn't serve us." When she returned in 1964, she was "shocked" to see "these black people sitting in the Five & Ten." She asked her friend what was happening. "'Oh, you can sit down there now,'" the friend replied.[46]

VINEGAR HILL

If Mable applauded the civil rights movement, as evidenced by her participation in at least one march, she likely watched urban renewal with shock and sorrow. The 1949 Housing Act launched urban renewal projects throughout the United States. By 1965, nearly eight hundred American cities were engaged in such projects.[47] Most involved the destruction of African American communities. As policy analyst Richard Rothstein writes, public officials "shifted African American populations away from downtown business districts so that white commuters, shoppers, and business elites would not be exposed to Black people."[48]

In Charlottesville, the major target was Vinegar Hill, a triangular, twenty-acre parcel of land in the downtown area that was not only home to many African Americans but also a vital center for Black commerce and culture. To Thomas Inge, a grocery store owner, "the greatest thing" about Vinegar Hill was "all that business there." He listed some of the most prominent ones: "There was the undertaker, Mr. Bell. J. F. Bell started his place on Vinegar Hill. My grandmother had a boarding house on Vinegar Hill. Another man, Mr. Joe Watson, had a shoe cobbler's shop—a shoe repairing shop they call it now on Vinegar Hill. Mr. George Jones had a restaurant on Vinegar Hill. There were cleaning pressing establishments—two of them—on Vinegar Hill. There was our store, which was on Vinegar Hill."[49] In this segregated society, many African Americans depended heavily on the goods and services available to them in this small area.

Others focused on the entertainment they found. Esmont resident Agnes Louise Rush remembered The Hilltop, where she and her husband could drink beer, listen to records on the jukebox, and dance.[50] Raymond Bell commented that because the Black fraternal organizations (the Odd Fellows, the Elks, the Masons, and Eastern Star) met either on Vinegar Hill or adjacent to it, that "was where the blacks were concentrated in in terms of entertainment. . . . When I was coming along in the '30s and '40s, all the black dances were held at the Odd Fellows Hall. . . . That was the only place we had that black folk could have a dance."[51] George Ferguson remembered that "men would congregate in the barbershops and discuss politics, discuss all the phases of life, whether it was safe to ride in an automobile, and who [wasn't going] to ride in an automobile." What "fascinated" Thomas Johnson as a boy were the many festivals and parades he saw.[52]

Former residents of Vinegar Hill reminisced about a tight-knit community. "They were very nice people," Alies Jones commented. "I used to cross from my yard to somebody else's, and somebody'd holler across their yard to me. And we'd borrow wood and coal and stuff like that from each other."[53] When Sadie Mason was a small child, "Friends looked out for us."[54] Connie Brooks added that "because of segregation," "people were more helpful to each other at that time . . . We would go every morning and knock at every door and see how everyone was."[55] Historian Robin D. G. Kelley writes, "African-American communities often created an alternative culture emphasizing collectivist values, mutuality, and fellowship." Kelley is careful to avoid idealization: "There were vicious, exploitative relationships within southern black communities, particularly across class and gender lines, and the tentacles of Jim Crow touched even black institutions." Nevertheless, he concludes, "The social and cultural institutions and ideologies that ultimately informed black opposition placed more emphasis on communal values and collective uplift than the prevailing class-conscious, individualist ideology of the white ruling class."[56] Evidence suggests that Vinegar Hill represented such a community.

Mable and her family lived within walking distance of Vinegar Hill, and it is likely they went there regularly. An Esmont resident told an interviewer that although he had never lived on Vinegar Hill, he spent "all [his] childhood in that area." He "used to go to the movies and to the restaurants and to the pool hall, and to the barbershop." "Oh yes," he concluded, "I was there quite a bit."[57] Another neighbor remembered "a lot of little grocery stores, family grocery stores," and a fish market. "We shopped there every day," she stated.[58]

In Charlottesville, as elsewhere in the nation, the rationale for urban renewal was slum clearance. Although Vinegar Hill contained many substantial dwellings, it was not difficult to point to substandard houses that lacked indoor plumbing and electricity. Listing the advantages of the project, the *Daily Progress* noted, "Urban Renewal will eliminate slums where neighborhood conditions and dwellings have become detrimental to health, safety, and morals, and where the social and economic liabilities so greatly outweigh the assets that rehabilitation is neither practical or feasible."[59] The paper also summarized the views of Lindsey B. Mount, a candidate for the city council: urban renewal "means we can get rid of unsanitary conditions which seriously menace the health, not only of the people living in the area, but all with whom they come in contact; and it will remove a potential fire hazard which endangers large areas of valuable property nearby."[60] Mable would have recognized the name of this city council candidate. Mount was the stepson of Mable's previous employer, C. Armonde Paxson and had been a teenager when Mable worked at the Paxson house in 1940.[61]

Mount expressed a view that was common in the United States but also widely criticized. "Slum clearance has not been for the benefit of slum residents," wrote Harvard law professor Derrick Bell, "nor has slum rehabilitation benefited families of low and modest incomes . . . Urban renewal has hurt and scattered the poor and Negroes, while subsidizing the right of the more affluent to replace them."[62] More succinctly, "Urban renewal means Negro removal."[63] In 1963, the city of Charlottesville destroyed twenty-nine businesses in Vinegar Hill and uprooted more than six hundred people.[64]

Many displaced residents were relocated to Westhaven, a 126-unit public housing project that opened in 1963. Some commentators contended that many people appreciated their new accommodations which were more structurally sound than their former dwellings and provided indoor toilets, running water, and electricity.[65] Many others, however, argued that modern conveniences could not compensate for the loss of a vibrant community. Laura Franklin had two elderly aunts who were slated to move. One "didn't want to move, and [said] she would rather die than to move, and she did. The Lord took her. But she was 82." The other "didn't die, but she worried all the time . . . She always wanted to walk around there and see it. It was terrible that she had to move."[66] Raymond Bell knew an elderly woman who moved to Westhaven "and all she talked about was not having a place to plant little flowers or plant little gardens. She couldn't do that in the projects."[67] Nearly twenty years after the destruction of Vinegar Hill, Rebecca McGinness commented, "Some of the people forced out of their homes never got over it. Even today it's a sore topic to talk about."[68]

Former residents were not the only ones to mourn the loss of the community. Newspaper editor Sherman White noted that urban renewal "removed a symbol. While it wasn't much, it was all that we had. It took away the image of blacks in business, the importance of blacks in decision-making positions. Not just because they're black, but because there are other blacks looking at them. And my kids coming up, if they never see their father do anything but janitorial work—I'm not saying there's anything wrong with janitorial work—but if that's all they ever see me do, that's all they may ever aspire to."[69] Joan Woodfolk "missed things that connect you" to Charlottesville. She remembered "seeing all these businesses" owned by African Americans when she and her sister went to Vinegar Hill on Sundays and then stopped into stores to "buy comic books and things like that." As children they had not understood what they had. As adults they "see what is not here. There's nothing that really says that we even exist here. What is there, now? . . . Woodfolk Lane is named after our family, you know, but where's the community? Where's the sense of anything? There's nothing that you can just visibly put your hands on . . . What is there physically that you can see? . . . There's nothing but a hill of buildings."[70] A documentary about Vinegar Hill was titled "That World Is Gone."[71]

Root Shock, by Mindy Thomas Fullilove, a professor of urban planning and public health, helps us understand why the consequences of urban renewal were so devastating. After studying the destruction of African American communities in cities throughout the United States, she concludes that many individuals experienced "root shock," which she defines as "the traumatic stress reaction to the destruction of all or part of one's emotional ecosystem." Just as an injured person must struggle "to restore the body's internal balance," so people also must maintain an external balance between themselves and the environment. Fullilove asks us to imagine victims "of an earthquake, a hurricane, a flood, or a terrorist attack." They, too, experience a shock as they look "at the twisted remains of the known universe, searching for the road to the supermarket, which used to be there, but is now a pile of rubble." Emergency assistance can provide immediate help, but the consequences often linger for generations.[72]

Outrage over the destruction of Vinegar Hill intensified when the land remained vacant for more than twenty years. The first building, an Omni Hotel, opened on May 1, 1985. Today a large Staples Office Supply Store stands opposite. The area that was once Vinegar Hill feeds into the tony Downtown Mall. Like public housing projects in other cities, Westhaven gradually deteriorated. By 1986, the president of the residents' association commented that it was "beginning to look like a slum." Some apartments lacked heat; others had inoperable controls. A 2007 report by University of Virginia researchers pointed to the "degradation of the interiors and exteriors of the buildings" that had occurred over time. "Playground and other recreational facilities [were] in disrepair." The apartments were dark and damp.[73]

A NEW HOME

Mable's daily life changed little in the years of the desegregation battle and destruction of Vinegar Hill. But her living conditions improved immensely. In 1957, she and her mother moved from their small house at 609 Parrott Street to a much larger and grander one at 409 Ridge Street. Built in 1840, the house was reputed to be the oldest one on the street. Mable proudly described it as "a beautiful home. . . . It had, I guess, fourteen rooms in all. . . . Lots of closets, hardwood floors and everything. It was beautiful! . . . Inside we had a fireplace in the hall, a fireplace upstairs, and we had, I think we had about three fireplaces, but I never used them. . . . Mantelpieces, beautiful mantelpieces in the hall and the living room, and in [an] upstairs bedroom."[74] Behind the house was a small building that had originally been a kitchen and later became a place for household workers to live; Mable's neighbor Elizabeth Dawson, described it as a "charming brick cottage . . . which had lovely hardwood floors, a living room, bedroom, kitchen, and bath."[75]

Ironically, two events that had a deleterious effect on many African Americans enabled Dora to buy this new property. The first was urban renewal. Even before the devastation of Vinegar Hill, the city demolished the segregated area around Parrott Street, which had been home to Mable's family since they first came to Charlottesville. Although we do not know whether Dora received the market value for her house, the compensation enabled her to buy the new one without a mortgage: "Momma put the money from the house that she sold on [the] Ridge Street [house].[76]

The second event was White flight, which made the property affordable. We have noted that in the late nineteenth and early twentieth centuries the northern section of Ridge Street had been famous as the major residence of wealthy White families. Many had built houses that still are considered architecturally significant. (Thirty-two houses on four blocks now constitute the Ridge Street Historic District, which was listed on the National Register in 1981 and in the Virginia Landmarks Association the following year.[77]) African Americans lived on the southern end of the street, which was unpaved and had many fewer city services. The only African Americans

Picture of 409 Ridge Street taken many years before Mable Jones and Dora Walls moved in. (Courtesy of the Albemarle-Charlottesville Historical Society)

living in the north end of the street were domestic workers. John Frederick Harlan told an interviewer that he was raised by his "maid," Sinie Payne, who "lived rent free in a house in the back of the lot" and who "would start the fire . . . and bake biscuits every morning."[78] As Whites increasingly left for the suburbs and African Americans moved into their part of Ridge Street, housing prices fell. When Eugene Williams looked for a home for himself, his wife, and his two small children, many of the properties he saw were in poor condition. One day, the realtor showed him a place on Ridge Street, known as the Michtoms' house. As he later commented, "The opportunity came for us to buy this house because of white flight."[79]

In the following years, many of the new owners of the largest houses either tore them down or converted them into apartments. Rather than divide her house into rental units, Dora filled it with family members, including not only Mable but also at various times Mable's sister Beatrice, Beatrice's husband James John Frye, and their daughter Mary Anna (who lived in the cottage in the back); Constance Johnson (the child Dora adopted sometime in the 1930s); both of her grandsons; and occasionally great grandchildren.

Longtime Black residents of Ridge Street who were interviewed in 1995 stated that the conversion of houses into rental apartments and the placement of low-income housing there in the 1970s changed the neighborhood from a tight-knit community into an area where people barely knew each other. Luella Gohaner-Lyles talked about the "dramatic change" that had occurred since all the children "played together" and "knew each other." Moreover, "the whole street raised you up": if she did something wrong, a neighbor would call her mother and before she "got home, momma knew." Now, she said, "you don't dare interfere with somebody else's children." Other older residents listed by name the many neighbors with whom they had associated over the years; they knew little about newer arrivals.[80]

Along with increased rentals, actions by the city council transformed Ridge Street. In 1957, the year Dora and her family moved in, the city sought to rezone the street to allow businesses as well as residences.[81] The departure of Whites also led the city to reduce the number of services it provided. Joan Woodfolk remembered "street sweepers and the man that used to pick up this street, the trash in the street." But now "the street sweeper doesn't . . . come to this area any more."[82] Between 1959 and 1960, two houses on Ridge Street were demolished to make way for the extension of Cherry Avenue. And then in 1973, an additional eleven houses were destroyed during a realignment of Ridge and Fifth Streets. As the "Supplement to the Survey of the Ridge Street Historic District" reports, the "loss of these old and architecturally significant dwellings, accompanied by the new traffic pattern, fundamentally altered the Ridge Street neighborhood's residential character."[83] The new roads also destroyed much of the beauty of the street. Joan Woodfolk remembered as a child "walking home from school and, especially in the spring time of the year when the trees were budding, flowers blooming and stuff and the grass was green. It was almost like looking through a kaleidoscope. I mean that's how pretty it was. And I just enjoyed this street." But after "they cut up the street, they pushed us back in a hole." And, she noted bitterly, those changes were not for the Black residents of Ridge Street but rather "for the good of the city." Her once beloved street was now simply a thoroughfare for people "to use . . . to go other places."[84]

Although Ridge Street no longer had all the amenities those residents remembered, it still boasted a number of grand homes. Mable cherished hers at number 409, where she lived for many years. Its destruction by a falling tree shortly before her death represented a horrendous loss.

7

"NOBODY LEFT BUT MABLE"

A GREAT ADVANTAGE OF the Ridge Street house where Mable and Dora lived for many years was that it was a short walk to the Mount Zion First African Baptist Church, which they had joined as soon as they moved to Charlottesville. The *Norfolk Journal and Guide* enables us to glimpse some of Dora's activities. For example, in July 1950, she attended the Baptists General Meeting in Richmond.[1] In the Jim Crow South, where African American communities struggled to survive in the face of White cruelty and brutality, Black churches were social service organizations as well as spiritual ones. Dora played central roles in two benevolent societies, the Missionary Society, which raised money for people in need in both Africa and the local community, and the Industrial Club, which sought to "aid the Church . . . and contribute to the sick, distressed and bereaved members of our group."[2] In December 1956, she was elected treasurer of the Industrial Club at a meeting at her house.[3] She spoke on the topic "Is Your Life Bearing Fruit for God" at a Missionary Society meeting in July 1957 and led devotionals at the group's meeting the following December.[4]

GROWING OLD IN CHARLOTTESVILLE

Church

Mable's grandchildren described Mable as deeply religious (even more so, they said, than her mother) and they believed she went to church every day. Mable noted that she taught Sunday School and sang in the choir. Choir practice was scheduled for Thursday evening, Mable's night off. Like Dora, she was active in both the Missionary Society and Industrial Club. In addition, she belonged to the Daughters of Ruth, which supported women's role in charitable work and church affairs. A lifelong caregiver at home and at work, she was also, she remarked in her interview, "busy" at church.

Mable appears in two pictures in the 1992 Mount Zion First African Baptist Church Yearbook, celebrating its 125th anniversary. In one, she sits among the nine women of the Industrial Club, wearing a hat on her head, large round glasses (she had glaucoma), and a long strand of pearls around her neck.

Work

Mable had returned to Charlottesville in 1953 to take care of her mother. Dora, seventy-two at that time, had spent much of her life caring for children and other family members. Although large numbers of African American migrants to the North left their children with grandparents, most sent for those relatives after finding work and housing.[5] But Mable's family had always remained in and around Charlottesville. To reunite with them, she had to return.

Once back, she continued her employment as a domestic worker, still a common occupation for Black women there. In 1960, 42 percent of "nonwhite" women in the labor force in Charlottesville were domestic workers.[6] But she now lived in her own home. She identified her employer of four decades (until 1994) as "Mrs. Claude Jessup." Mable assumed everyone knew the Jessup family. Claude Ambrose Jessup (1904–1986) was one of six children of Samuel Ambrose Jessup who owned a Pepsi-Cola bottling plant, a dairy and ice cream plant, a bus company, an insurance business, a laundry, a beer franchise, and a cigar company.[7] Claude, the first son, became president and general manager of that bus company as

Industrial Club, Mount Zion First African Baptist Church, 1992. Mable Jones is second from left in the front row. (1992 Yearbook, courtesy of Mount Zion First African Baptist Church)

well as another he started. For many years he also owned a cemetery. He lived with his family in Farmington, described in 2019 as "an upscale, private community located just outside of the Charlottesville City limits."[8]

In the years Mable worked there, controversy swirled around the Farmington Country Club. Located on 275 acres of land with views of the Blue Ridge Mountains, gardens, manicured lawns, a golf course, and a building designed by Thomas Jefferson, the Farmington Country Club advertises itself today as upholding the tradition of southern hospitality and graciousness.[9] For many years one of those traditions was excluding African Americans as both guests and members. Thus, in 1974, when the University of Virginia student newspaper reported that large numbers of faculty members and administrators (including the president, seventeen department chairs, and seven deans) were members of this all-White club, members of the campus community expressed outrage.[10] In 1976, the club managers polled the 3,867 members about the club's policy. Ignoring the issue of membership, the questionnaire asked only if the club should admit African Americans as guests. By a two-to-one vote, the members voted no. Publicity about the questionnaire led to new demands that the university president, Frank L. Hereford, resign, which he did only as a result of student protests.[11] Whatever comments Mable may have heard from her employers and their guests about the country club, she would have likely kept her views to herself.

Mable mentioned that the day before her 1995 interview had been the first anniversary of Mamie Jessup's death and that she had gone to the cemetery to put flowers on her grave. When the interviewer remarked that she must have been "pretty good friends" with Mrs. Jessup, Mable replied, "very close. Very close."[12] The Jessups had one daughter, Claudia, who wrote that because her mother and Mable were of the same generation, they were "very similar, in basic aspects. Different colored skin, different backgrounds and upbringings, but like my mother, Mable did not disclose anything personal. Never any significant facts." Of course, Mable's emphasis on privacy may have derived not only from her personality and age but also from the need to engage in the cultural dissemblance we discussed in a previous chapter. Claudia was "certain that my mother and Mable were friends, even good friends, for forty years, but Southern society and protocol prevented them from acknowledging that fact openly, even to each other. Was there affection between them? Yes, I believe so, though I never observed it in person." Claudia added that her mother's health went downhill rapidly during her last six months of life and that "Mable came to the house a few times a week and sat with my mother while whichever 'ad hoc' nurse who was on duty took a break." Although Claudia's "mother was pretty much out of it then, with occasional lucid moments," Claudia "felt that she could still intuit Mable's presence, even if she couldn't acknowledge it verbally."[13]

Before those last years of Mamie Jessup's life, Mable was one of several domestic workers in the household. Because there was a "cleaning lady," her primary job was to cook. Claudia was ten when Mable first came to the house, and she remembers sitting at the table doing her homework while Mable cooked: "I sometimes performed *sous chef* duties for her, stringing beans & shucking corn while she fried tomatoes and oysters and chicken and whipped up potato salad and the whole Southern repertoire of overcooked vegetables. Mable never consulted a recipe, except occasionally when she decided to try something new. She was an instinctive cook, though my mother generally laid out the menu earlier in the day and did the grocery shopping." Through these long afternoons, they "talked about many things," although the proscription about sharing personal information meant those conversations were "all chitchat." Like us, Claudia remembered Mable as a "calm, capable, and loving presence, . . . a kind person, and always *there* for me."[14]

Over the years, Claudia told us, Mable's job gradually became easier. Claudia left home in 1961, Claude Jessup died in 1986, and Mamie Jessup was in poor health in the years before her death in 1994. Mable brought her a sandwich at lunch and reminded her to take her medications, but she no longer cooked large dinners unless Claudia and her family were coming home for a visit. Then, Claudia said, "she'd gear up" and "we'd have that fabulous fried chicken & potato salad waiting for us when we arrived."[15]

Friends

When we returned from our visit to Charlottesville in July 2019, one of our brothers asked if we were surprised by what we had learned. The answer was, not really. We had heard about a woman who had been deeply loved by many people. We had read in the interview that she and her close friend and neighbor "Mrs. Dawson" had visited each other so frequently that they had "beaten" a path between their houses. In Charlottesville, Pastor Alvin Edwards introduced us to Violet Price, who had been a secretary at the church. Now in her nineties and living in a nursing home, she spoke of the love and fun she and Mable had shared. When pressed for details, she mentioned that they had played dominoes together and that Mable had been an "excellent cook" and skilled seamstress. We were not surprised when she told us Mable had a beautiful voice because we remember her singing to us—"Swing Low, Sweet Chariot," an old spiritual; "Goodnight Irene," which Huddie "Lead Belly" Ledbetter recorded in 1933; and "A Bushel and a Peck," the song by Frank Loeser that first appeared on the radio in 1950 and was popularized in his musical *Guys and Dolls*. In church, she sang hymns and was occasionally the soloist. As we left, we told Price our next stop was the cemetery to put flowers on Mable's grave. "Please give her a message," Price asked. "Tell her I'll be with her soon."

From her grandchildren we also learned that she had a friend whom they knew well enough to call "Uncle Marshall" and that he joined them at

Christmas and other family gatherings. It was "Uncle Marshall," they told us, who drove Mable to and from her work for the Jessups in Farmington.

Memories

Thomas Edler, the grandson of Dora's sister Mattie Ellis, was born in 1958 and grew up in Washington DC; he now works as a dentist for the Veteran's Administration there. Every summer, he said, his family would return to Virginia, and he remembered many visits to the Ridge Street house. He loved sitting on the porch with Dora, whom he described as being "quiet, low-key, soft-spoken," and the "sweetest old lady." Mable's grandchildren also told us they loved to visit the house where they were welcomed by their Grandma Dora before her death in 1978 and for many years after by their Grandma Mable (though they wished she hadn't kissed them on the mouth). They described Dora for us much as Thomas Edler had: meek, mild, happy, churchgoing (albeit not as much as her daughter), and a seamstress who made wedding dresses. In turn, they described Mable as kind, taking care of everyone, proud of everyone, and a good cook who always had homemade cookies for them when they arrived.

Just as we were about to leave our get-together with Mable's grandchildren in 2019, after having shared so many stories about Mable's warmth and generosity, Emily pointed out that she could be witty and sharp as well. Emily told two stories: One was that Mable teased her relentlessly about wearing her favorite t-shirt day after day and warned that if she didn't change, she would find herself walking down the aisle in it. The other occurred after a close family friend showed us her infant in our backyard, and we all dutifully oohed and aahed. When Emily went inside, Mable remarked that that was the "ugliest baby" she had ever seen. Charles, Theresa, and Walter laughed. "Yes," they agreed, "That's Grandma Mable."

MABLE JONES'S SONS: JAMES AND THOMAS

We learned that like their mother, Mable's sons James Henry Jones and Thomas Marshall Jones were beautiful singers and they came in second in an amateur music contest at the Radio City Music Hall in New York. More regularly, the brothers, with two others, sang in a quartet called

“The Desirable Four,” which performed at Madison Hall at the University of Virginia and on the local radio stations WUVA and WINA.[16] Another quartet, the “Southern Harmoneers,” included their Uncle Henry and performed at various benefit events in Staunton and Charlottesville.[17]

But we were also told that drinking clouded the lives of both men. Mable’s grandchildren spoke openly about this and offered several explanations. One was the role of genetics. James’s son Charles noted that their grandfather, Mable’s husband James was also an alcoholic. Moreover, he was rarely around. He did not move with his children to Louisa County and they seldom saw him after he and Mable separated in 1944; Mable believed he moved to New York. The grandchildren remembered meeting him only once and suggested that perhaps he had modeled drinking as a way of life to his sons. Another grandson, Walter, pointed out that both James and Thomas served in the Korean War. Many soldiers who

The Southern Harmoneers. (Courtesy of Piedmont Preservation)

returned from Korea had had harrowing experiences and suffered from post-traumatic stress disorder.

We have to acknowledge that, like many other domestic workers, Mable often was absent when her sons were young. Providing for them frequently meant putting the needs of her employers' children, like us, ahead of her own. Of course, James and Thomas were first Black boys and then Black men facing daily humiliations in the Jim Crow South. After serving in integrated units in Korea and, in Thomas's case, suffering a grave injury while fighting for his country, the indignities of segregation must have been felt especially keenly.[18] Moreover, James and Thomas had few employment opportunities when they were released from the army. The University of Virginia hired African American men primarily as cooks, busboys, porters, and janitors. Other White-owned businesses and industries in Charlottesville similarly restricted Black men to low-paying, unskilled jobs with little or no chance of advancement. One ad in the *Daily Progress* in the early 1950s read: "Colored man, able-bodied and sober, for coal work." Another asked for a "Colored man for janitor work. Job seekers should apply to the Monticello Hotel."[19] Some White-owned businesses outright refused to hire any African Americans.[20] And neither James nor Thomas had either the training or financial resources to become part of the thriving Black community that owned businesses on Vinegar Hill and offered professional services to their peers.

Whatever the reason, both James and Thomas had irregular work lives.[21] James left school after the eighth grade. He never earned enough to support his family, and his children told us that they experienced great poverty when they were growing up. He depended heavily on his Uncle Henry (Mable's brother who already had purchased a house for their mother). For many years James was employed at the car repair shop Henry owned in Staunton. James's children remember that although their father often did not show up for work, Henry always brought their mother the weekly paycheck.

From city directories and the information Thomas provided at his mother's interview, we can piece together a list of his many jobs. At various times he was a cook at both a University of Virginia cafeteria and a nursing home, drove a sanitation truck, was a janitor at the University of

Virginia, and worked at both a plant nursery and E. C. Ferron, a construction company.[22] It is possible that he, too, relied on the extended family. Mable's brother Thomas Walls Sr. and his son Thomas Walls Jr. worked for many years at the E. C. Ferron company and may have helped Thomas find employment there.[23]

The family lives of the two men were equally rocky. James married Helen Mae Vest in 1951 when she was already the mother of two children. Together they had another eleven children, one of whom died from an accidental poisoning at the age of two and another of whom was given up for adoption.[24] In 1965, James and Helen separated. When they divorced and Helen remarried in 1972, James was living in Washington, DC.[25] Thomas married Mary Alice Richardson in 1952 and had two children—Brenda born in 1952 and Gregory in 1955. The couple separated in 1958 and divorced in 1972.[26]

The insecure employment of both sons may help to explain why Mable continued to work well into her eighties. Although her son James gave up alcohol for a while, he was drinking with his son Reginald one night in December 1978 when a fire broke out; Reginald survived, but James died from smoke inhalation. Thomas continued to drink heavily. It is clear from the interview that even at the end of Mable's life, when she was sick with lung cancer, Thomas was incapable of caring for himself or his mother; he still lived in her house because he had nowhere else to go. The pastor told us that Mable had asked him to be the executor of her estate because she did not trust Thomas and wanted someone else to manage the money she left him. Before Mable's death, Violet Price had kept her checkbook and written the checks. Price explained that Mable feared Thomas would "interfere."

The stories Mable's grandchildren recounted of their early lives demonstrated both the ongoing impact of structural racism and a deep reliance on extended kin, most of whom had few resources to share. During our visit to Charlottesville, the grandchildren told us not only about the poverty they had endured but also about their pride in their survival and their gratitude toward family members who offered critical support. Their great-uncle Henry, Mable's youngest brother, had been the most important. (He also, they repeatedly noted, had had impressive skills as a car mechanic). Their mother's parents, Lonnie and Bessie Vest, had provided much of their daily care; Charles, one of the oldest of James's children, suggested he had relied more on them than on his own parents. Mable and Dora had often intervened as well. Theresa remembered spending summers in the house on Ridge Street while the rest of her family remained in Staunton; she also recalled how terrified she had been when she had had to ride home alone on the train at the age of seven after one of her visits.

LOSSES

We assume Mable was Dora's primary caregiver during the years Dora was bedridden and that Mable experienced her death in September 1978 (a few months before Mable's son James died) as a terrible blow. Since Mable's birth nearly seventy years earlier, the women's lives had been closely entwined. During the relatively few years in which they did not share a house, Dora cared for Mable's children while Mable provided much of the financial support.

One by one, Mable's siblings died—Lawrence and Thomas in 1984, Henry in 1987, and Beatrice in 1992.[27] The oldest of five children, she remarked that now there was "Nobody left but Mable." Beatrice had been living in the back cottage with her daughter Mary Anna, who was disabled. When Beatrice died, Mary Anna moved into the main house where Mable could care for her.

In her interview, Mable told the story of yet another loss—the destruction of her house on Ridge Street, the "beautiful home" with all the appurtenances that had given her such great pleasure and of which she was so proud. Months later the shock of that tragedy was still clear; so too was Mable's deep religious faith:

> [w]hen the tree fell, I heard this noise. My niece and I met in the hall, "what is that?" I looked out the front door and all I could see was limbs, but I didn't know what it was. And I couldn't get to—and I went to the side door. There were branches, and we were trapped in there. . . . It came over the kitchen, smashed the kitchen in (Chuckle), and some of the ceiling from the dining room fell. But, I couldn't see the tree from the

Fallen tree on 409 Ridge Street. (Courtesy of Jean Hiatt)

> back, you know, from in the house. 'Cause, it fell—it came down in the kitchen. And I was not in the kitchen. *The Lord had told me to get out of that kitchen and go in my room, and that's where I was when the tree fell.* [Emphasis added.][28]

Although no one was hurt, almost all of Mable's possessions were gone, including her furniture, clothes, and a lifetime's accumulation of photographs.

The trauma of the accident remained vivid for most people we interviewed. Mable's granddaughter Theresa lived on a street behind Mable's and could see the house from her backyard. Hearing the noise, she was terrified that something had happened to her Grandma Mable. The pastor recounted the story about the tree as well, remembering that Mable had had fire and wind insurance, but nothing that would cover a tree destroying her house. Charles told the story both on the phone and again when we were all together. Claudia Jessup remembered that she had been in Charlottesville at the time because she was getting her parents' house ready to go on the market. She wrote that "at Mable's bidding" her husband "crawled through a window of the condemned house (yellow police tape all around it) & retrieved the mink coat that [her] mother had given to [Mable]." Cast-off clothes were one of the gifts White employers frequently gave Black domestic workers, sometimes in lieu of decent wages.[29]

But Mable's coat may have meant much more to her than as a token of Mamie Jessup's generosity. "There is a sense among black women that cultural disavowal of fur has coincided with our increased ability to purchase it," wrote Jasmine Sanders in 2019. A famous model and fashion writer born to a German mother and African American father, Sanders added that the two furs owned by her mother "are her insistence on public elegance in a world frequently inhospitable to her. It is a point of pride that she wears and will pass down to me." Sanders noted that Black performers have often clad themselves in fur. The mink coat worn by the opera singer Marian Anderson when she sang on the steps of the Lincoln Memorial after having been refused space at Constitution Hall in 1939 "seemed to steel her, offering protection from many bitter elements."[30] Robin Givhan, fashion editor of the *Washington Post*, remarked that Aretha Franklin typically appeared on stage in a fur coat which she slid off before she began to sing: "Watching Franklin toss her furs to the ground was a glorious sight . . . It was more resonant than a diva move. It meant watching a black woman declare her talent, her presence as valuable and special."[31] A woman who took great pains with her clothes, Mable may have wanted the mink coat to continue to declare her worth after losing the beautiful house that had signaled her place in the world.

After the accident, Mable stayed two weeks with her next-door neighbor Elizabeth Dawson and then for another two weeks with her daughter-in-law Helen. It was not easy to find a new place to live. According to a 1991 study, housing policies in Charlottesville had "limited the quality of affordable housing available to the poor and especially to low-income blacks."[32] In the end, Mable moved to a rental apartment on Brown Street, which she clearly did not like. Jean Hiatt, who interviewed her there, described it as "gloomy."[33] Mable missed being able to visit regularly with Mrs. Dawson. And she had to walk upstairs to her bedroom, a considerable burden as she became sicker and sicker. Thomas moved with Mable to the apartment and was present during the interview, interrupting when Mable was telling the story of the tree. "Shhh!" she said to him; he responded, "Yes ma'am." She still went to church every Sunday—when she could. The Mt. Zion bus came by her house to pick her up; but getting out was harder and harder, and Mable acknowledged that after a life of continuous work and care for others she now often just stayed home: "I just take it easy, do what I have to do. Take it easy, take it easy." She died a few months later, on June 26, 1995.

AFTERWORD

MABLE JONES WAS EMBLEMATIC of her race, gender, time, and place in significant ways. Like many African Americans born in the late nineteenth and early twentieth centuries, she lived first in a rural community before moving to a city. She had to leave school after eighth grade. She began her career as a domestic worker in an era when few other jobs were open to African American women, and she remained in that occupation throughout much of her life. She experienced racism in both the North and the South. And although she played critical roles in her extended family, the care she provided for others often came at the expense of her kin.

A quarter century after Mable Jones's death, it is still all too easy to find evidence of systemic injustice in the lives of subsequent generations of African American women as well as in the places she lived and the kind of employment she held.

AFRICAN AMERICAN WOMEN

African American women remain clustered in low-wage employment. Although no longer confined to domestic labor, as many as 28 percent have service sector jobs.[1] "Ironically," Premilla Nadasen writes, "working-class black women who left private household labor often ended up in occupations that resembled the social reproductive labor they had previously engaged in, albeit in different settlings. . . . The proliferation of hospitals, schools, nursing homes, and restaurants changed the nature of social reproductive care and relocates some of the work that had previously taken place in the home into institutional settings."[2] Institutional jobs have clear benefits over those in private households. They tend to be less lonely, offer basic labor protections, and enable workers to cover for each other and join together to protest employment conditions.[3] But Black women often occupy the lowest rung of service jobs, doing the most menial work, receiving the smallest wages and fewest benefits, and having the least flexible hours.[4]

Today, as in in the past, Black women remain in the labor force when they have children. More than 80 percent of Black mothers work for pay, and their earnings are vital to sustaining their households. They either are sole earners or contribute at least 40 percent of the household income. But combining work and family remains extremely difficult. More than a third of Black working mothers lack access to paid sick leaves, and the cost of childcare is prohibitive for many.[5]

As was true for Mable's mother Dora Walls and eventually for Mable as well, elderly African Americans provide the safety net for their families. African American grandparents are three times as likely as White ones to raise their grandchildren.[6] In 2000, more than 8 percent of African Americans aged sixty to sixty-four provided such care.[7] The bulk of the work falls on women. African American men who serve as caregivers are far more likely than African American women to be married and thus far less likely to have sole responsibility for children.[8] Grandparental caregiving has deep roots in African American history and culture, but studies suggest it can have serious consequences for finances and both physical and mental health.[9]

THE PLACES MABLE JONES LIVED

Louisa County

Since the end of the Civil War, Louisa County's population has more than doubled, from 16,701 to 35,380. As African Americans left rural areas, the county's racial composition changed dramatically. Once more than half (62 percent) of the population, African Americans now represent just 15 percent. Farming no longer dominates the economy; less than one percent of the employed civilian population works in farming, fishing, and forestry occupations. As elsewhere in Virginia and the nation, African Americans earn less than Whites. In 2018 the median household income was $51,209 for African Americans and $62,421 for Whites.[10]

Shortly after World War II, Mable's aunts and uncles who were still living in Louisa County moved from Quarlestown to a place on Route 15 about a mile outside of Gordonsville—a distance of about two miles as the crow flies. Seven years old at the time, Chuck Lewis helped his grandparents (Dora's sister Lucy and her husband Charles Winston) move their possessions—and their house itself—to this new "little area, which consisted of a few houses grouped together and which didn't even have a name."[11] Thomas Edler, the grandson of another one of Dora's sisters, Mattie Ellis, still owns two acres of undeveloped land in Quarlestown, adjacent to land owned by other relatives. In March 2021 Gloria Gilmore and Robin Patton (co-founders of One Shared Story) tried to locate this land with the help of a lifelong Louisa County resident. They traveled as far as they could on a dirt road through "silent wooded areas—no houses, just trees, mostly tall pines." When they could drive no further, they began to walk, finding "areas with cement blocks and bricks" that they believed were once foundations for homes. "Yucca plants and small areas of sprouting daffodils dotted these locations along with broken glass containers—canning jars, petroleum jelly & small medicine bottles, tin tubs, pieces of old license plates, tin kerosene lanterns."[12] They also found a small knoll with sunken graves and a few headstones. Only one stone was clear; it marked the grave site of Mable's father, Oscar Walls.

Thomas Edler also owns two acres on Route 15 where his grandparents' home still stands. The house itself has fallen into disrepair and will probably be torn down. Behind it is a small, private cemetery in which Thomas's grandmother and other Hughes family members are buried. As far as we know, these bits of land, graves, and homes in disrepair are the only traces of Mable's family left in Louisa County.

The Edler home. (Courtesy of Gloria Gilmore)

Charlottesville

The shock of the Unite the Right rally in August 2017 propelled many Charlottesville residents to investigate not only the city's racist history but also the continuing legacy of that past today. A headline in the *Washington Post* in August 2020 read, "White supremacists made Charlottesville a symbol of racism. Black residents say it still is."[13] Recent studies have focused on racial disparities in two areas: education and the juvenile justice system. A 2018 *New York Times* article written in conjunction with ProPublica noted that White students were "four times as likely to be in Charlottesville's gifted program, while black students are more than four times as likely to be held back a grade and almost five times as likely to be suspended from school." Moreover, the evidence suggested that the achievement gap between White and Black students, rather than diminishing over time, had widened in the previous decade in nearly all subjects. And residential segregation still resulted in segregated elementary schools. White students predominate at three elementary schools, Black students at the other three. Nikuyah Walker, the first Black woman mayor after

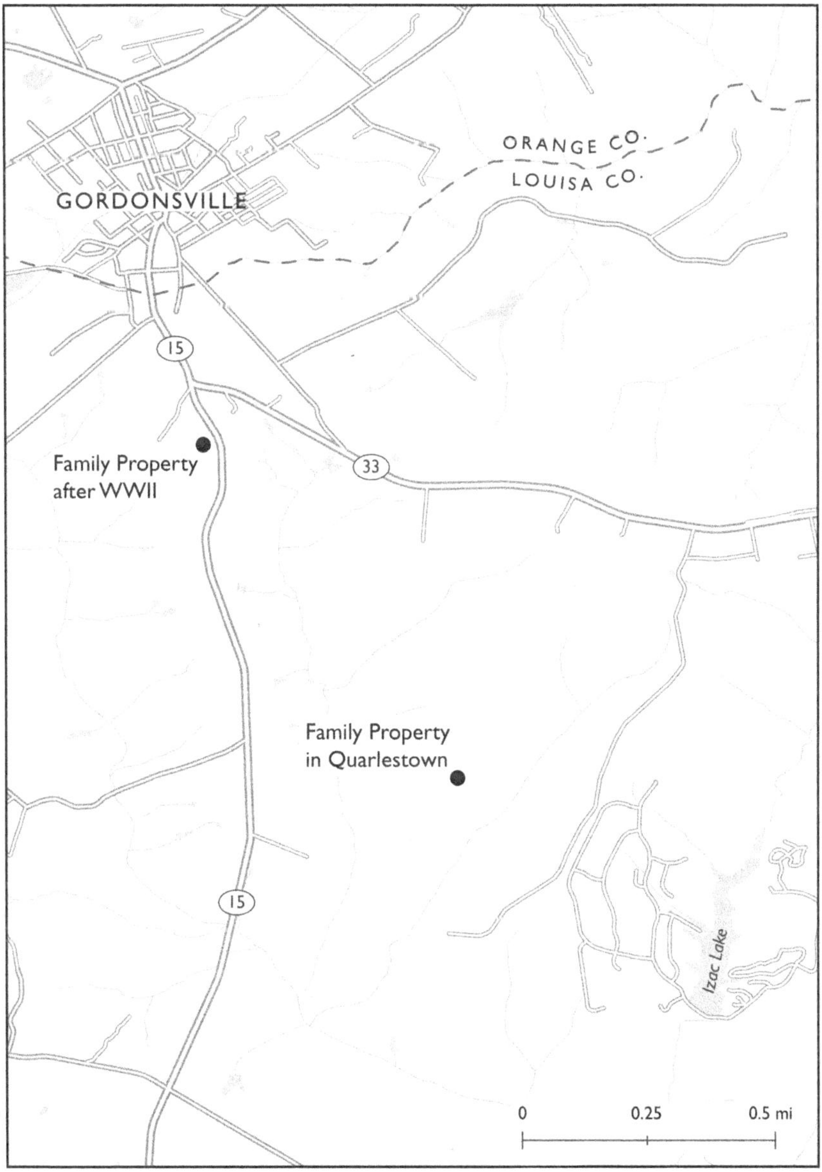

Location of property belonging to members of Mable Jones's extended family in Quarlestown and near Gordonsville, Louisa County, Virginia

the events of 2017, explained that Charlottesville was "beautiful physically and aesthetically pleasing, but a very ugly in the soul place. No one has ever attempted to undo that, and that affects whether our children can learn here."[14] The Charlottesville Task Force on Racial Disparities and Disproportionality reported that African American children were arrested, stopped and frisked, sent to court, and placed on probation far more often than White children were.[15]

Years of segregation and discrimination have left their mark on the adult Black population of the city as well. In 2018, 80 percent of African Americans had completed a high school education and only 10 percent had a Bachelor's degree; by contrast, 95 percent of Whites had graduated from high school and two-thirds (64 percent) from college. White average household incomes continue to be considerably higher than those of African Americans ($87,224 versus $54,896). More African Americans live in poverty (31 percent) than do Whites (21 percent), and the unemployment rate for African Americans (4.3 percent) is one and a half that of Whites (2.9 percent).[16] As we write this, COVID-19 is devastating marginalized communities in Charlottesville, as in Virginia and the nation as a whole. By May 20, 2020, 290 people in the Thomas Jefferson Health District (which serves the counties of Albemarle, Fluvanna, Greene, Louisa, and Nelson and the City of Charlottesville) had tested positive for COVID-19. Although African Americans represented 13 percent of the population in that district, they accounted for 27 percent of the cases and approximately half of the sixty-seven hospitalizations.[17]

Larchmont

Larchmont's least popular resident today may be Gavin McInnes, a far-right political commentator and the founder of Proud Boys, the extremist group Donald Trump urged to "stand back and stand by" in his first debate with Joe Biden and that helped to organize the January 6, 2021, attempted coup. McInnes mocked his neighbors who posted "Hate Has No Home Here" on their front lawns, calling them "retards." In response, many more anti-hate signs appeared.[18] But African Americans, too, seem to have no home in Larchmont. Sixty years after we lived there, they represent just 1.73 percent of the population.[19] And Larchmont continues to be bastion of privilege. In 2017, households in Larchmont had a median annual income of $198,661 (three times that of the United States as a whole). The median property value stood at $118 million.[20]

THE EMPLOYMENT MABLE JONES HELD

Most of the 2.5 million private household workers in the United States today are immigrant women from Asia, Africa, the Caribbean, and Latin America.[21] As the population ages, these workers increasingly care for elderly people as well as children. In significant ways, however, domestic service remains remarkably similar to the occupation Mable entered a century ago. Household workers are now entitled to receive Social Security, but fewer than 9 percent of employers pay into the system.[22] In addition, domestic workers still lack basic job protections. Three major pieces of legislation—the Civil Rights Act of 1964, the Americans with Disabilities Act of 1967, and the Age Discrimination in Employment Act of 1971—do not cover those in jobs with single employees. The Occupational Safety and Health Act of 1970 explicitly excludes domestic workers.[23] More than half of immigrant household workers are undocumented and thus unlikely to be covered by any labor laws.

With few legal safeguards, private household workers remain vulnerable to exploitation and abuse. Nearly a fourth are paid beneath the state minimum wage; more than two-thirds receive less than fourteen dollars an hour. As many as 60 percent spend more than half of their wages on housing. A third report working long hours without a break in the past year; another third report having been injured or exposed to toxic chemicals on the job.[24] Fearful of deportation, undocumented workers are especially wary of complaining about employment conditions.

And household service work continues to tear families apart. Like Mable, large numbers of workers leave children behind, in the care of grandparents and other kin. Although some take advantage of modern communication methods like Skype, the periods and distances of separation are far greater than they were for Mable and her sons. Undocumented workers face overwhelming obstacles when they try to travel home or bring their children to the United States.[25]

For many White, upper-middle-class women in our mother's generation, domestic workers ensured leisure. Today, a similar socioeconomic status depends on having two adults in the labor force and thus on shifting much household labor—including caregiving—to private domestic workers. As a result, the care domestic workers provide to the children of their employers continues to diminish both the quality and quantity of care they can render their own children. The sociologist Mary Romero argues that the workers' offspring not only have fewer years of childhood dependency but also are deprived of the "intensive mothering" that is a hallmark of social reproduction today.[26] In short, the exploitation of domestic workers continues to both thrive on and intensify vast social inequalities.

As an isolated and largely invisible labor force, domestic workers are notoriously difficult to organize. New groups of activists, however, have taken up the challenge. Founded in 2007, the National Domestic Workers Alliance (NDWA) is a network of advocacy organizations including four local chapters and sixty-three affiliate groups. The director is Ai-jen Poo, the child of Taiwanese immigrant parents and a recipient of a MacArthur "genius grant." Poo views herself as building on the successes of her predecessors, most notably Dorothy Lee Bolden, who helped workers in Atlanta win inclusion in labor laws in the 1960s and 1970s.[27] In addition to launching a broad-based political campaign, the NDWA sponsored the first national survey of household workers, drafted a Domestic Workers Bill of Rights (including overtime pay, one day off each week, and protection under state human rights laws), and then lobbied to secure its passage in Congress and various state legislatures. During the COVID-19 pandemic, the group raised money to provide emergency assistance to domestic workers to enable them to stay home. Poo acknowledges that bringing household workers together to fight for better employment conditions might be "a never-ending project." The emergence of a powerful new movement for workers' rights, however, offers considerable hope.[28]

This social movement has arrived too late for Mable and most of her heirs. Even so, we learned that some of Mable's grandchildren had been able to take advantage of the new opportunities available to African Americans in the South, constructing lives that were far more stable than those of their fathers. Charles served in the military reserves following a tour of duty in Vietnam and worked for a power company for four decades. Gregory, Thomas' only son, has been a patient care specialist at the University of Virginia Medical Center for almost three decades. Both men, like Charles's sister Theresa, enjoyed long marriages. They also reported the educational attainments of members of subsequent generations. One of Gregory's daughters had graduated from college and one of Charles's granddaughters was about to do so. We can well imagine Mable's pride in their achievements.

INTERVIEW OF MABLE WALLS JONES

BY JEAN HIATT AND DIANE BERKELEY OF THE RIDGE STREET ORAL HISTORY PROJECT, FEBRUARY 10, 1995

Biographical Information

MABLE JONES MOVED WITH her mother to Ridge Street in 1957. She lived in the house there until 1994 when a rotten tree collapsed onto it and caused enough damage that the house had to be demolished. In this interview, she and her son Thomas Jones share their memories of Ridge Street and their lives growing up in Charlottesville. They talk about schooling, working in the area, and their involvement in their church, Mt. Zion Baptist Church.

Project Description

Race and Place is a project of the Virginia Center for Digital History and the Carter G. Woodson Institute for Afro-American and African Studies. The goal of the project is to chronicle the life of African Americans in the Charlottesville, Virginia area during the period of segregation. As part of this project we have conducted a series of interviews with current residents of the Charlottesville area who were alive during that period. The project has also incorporated oral interviews conducted by other Charlottesville institutions which cover the appropriate subject area.

Notes about Our Transcription

The transcripts represent what was said in the interview to the best of our ability. It is possible that some words, particularly names, have been misspelled. Where we did not feel sure of spellings we have indicated this by the use of the term "phonetically" in parentheses following the word in question. Places where words were unclear are noted by "inaudible." We have made no attempt to correct mistakes in grammar.

Q: Today is Friday, February 10, and this is Jean Hiatt and D. Berkley interviewing Mrs. Mable S. Jones, a longtime resident of 409 Ridge Street.

A: (Inaudible)

Q: Do you have any pictures, of when you were a child? (Inaudible)

A: No. Yes! Plenty of them.

Q: Plenty of them?

A: Yes, but they in the trashcan. My house went down.

Q: Oh!

A: Everything. Everything in my house went down.

Q: That's a, a major tragedy. Well, Mrs. Jones, were you born in Charlottesville?

A: No. I was born in Gordonsville, in Louisa County. Louisa County.

Q: When were you born?

A: July the 29th, 1909.

Q: 1909? Oh. And then did you grow up (Inaudible)?

A: No. I came to Charlottesville when I was sixteen, and I went to Jefferson School.

Q: You went to Jefferson School?

A: (Indicates yes).

Q: And did you continue going there?

A: No. No. I quit in the eighth grade.

Q: Was that because it didn't continue—I know that—

A: No, I just quit!

Q: You just chose not to continue? I know that the school didn't—at one point didn't (Inaudible).

A: It's still going on.

(General chuckling)

Q: When you first—where did you live when you moved (Inaudible)

A: I lived—when I first come to Charlottesville, I lived on Dice Street. Dice Street.

Q: Das? D.A.S.?

A: D.I.C.E. Dice.

Q: Dice Street. I know that street. I said I'm familiar with that street. And then, at that point you started working?

A: No. I was sixteen. And I got married at age twenty. And I had lived in and out—I hadn't always lived in Charlottesville. I've lived in New York.

Q: (Inaudible).

A: Yes.

Q: So—

A: Let's see. Then I left Dice Street. (Pause several seconds) I don't know.

Q: When you moved from Dice Street, (Inaudible)?

A: No, No, No. I'm trying to think—Dice Street. I guess I moved in—well I used to—we used to go back and forth to Gordonsville in the summer, and then we'd come back to Dice Street. But when we left Dice Street, I guess I moved to Gordon Avenue and stayed there a few years.

Q: On Gordon Avenue? That's close to where I live. Um, your parents—were they—did they--

A: My mother—my father is dead. My mother is dead too. But my father died when I was ten years old, and my mother raised the five children. Three boys and two girls. Nobody left but Mable.

(General chuckling)

Q: What was your father's name?

A: Oscar.

Q: Oscar Jones?

A: No.

Q: Oh, no?

A: W.A.L.L.S.

Q: Wells?

A: Walls. And my mother's name was Dora Hughes Walls.

Q: And Hughes is a—

A: It's her maiden name. H.U.G.H.E.S.

Q: And were they—did they grow up in the Gordonsville area?

A: Mm-hm, mm-hm.

Q: So they—were they—was your home as a child—was it a place in the country?

A: Mm-hm.

Q: And did you have a farm-type situation, or was it a garden in the backyard, or something like that?

A: When I was a child?

Q: Uh-huh.

A: I reckon so. I can't even remember that far back. (Chuckle)

Q: I imagine most people had gardens.

A: Yeah I know my mother did. She—Yeah, we had a garden. In the country.

Q: Well—and so you were one of five children? And did your brothers and sisters stay in the area or did they wind up in other places?

A: They moved to other places.

Q: Outside of—

A: After they grew up they married. Yes. And they moved. One brother lived in Staunton, and one lived in Waynesboro, and one lived with Momma and me, on Ridge Street. We moved up, mm—I guess in 1957 was when we moved to (Inaudible) on Ridge Street. So then everybody's grown and married and away, and it's just my mother and me.

Q: So when—you, you moved to Ridge Street, you came with your mother. You and your mother—

A: My mother and I had always lived together.

Q: Uh-huh. And so you were—uh—

A: I'm the oldest of five children.

Q: You were grown up when you moved to Ridge Street?

A: Yeah, grown and married and had children. (Laughter)

Q: You had—

A: Two boys.

Q: Two boys.

A: James and Thomas. And my husband died in the '60s I think.

Q: Your husband died when?

A: In the '60s I believe, yeah.

Q: What was your husband's name?

A: James Jones.

Q: And what kind of—did he come from another area, or was he from Charlottesville?

A: He was from Simeons I think, wherever that is. Somewhere other than Charlottesville.

Q: Simeons?

A: Simeons.

Q: I don't know. Something like S.I.M.E.O.N.S. There's a, a orchard called Simeons. So he—(Inaudible)

A: But I met him in Charlottesville. I think Simeons's where he was born. (Inaudible)

Q: You met him in Charlottesville.

A: I met him in Charlottesville.

Q: Where, where—how did you meet him? Through, uh—

A: I don't know.

Q: Through the neighborhood or something? (Chuckle)

A: I don't know.

Q: How old were you when you got married?

A: Twenty. (Loudly) Twenty.

Q: Twenty? A young one.

Q: I was twenty.

Q: You were twenty too? (Laughter) I was a lot older. And, what kind of uh, work did he do?

A: He was a waitress. (Inaudible)

Q: At the Monticello Hotel?

A: Mm-hm.

Q: Which was, was that, the one—where's that?

Q: That's across from the courthouse.

A: Yeah, mm-hm.

Q: Which just closed, very recently.

Q: It's now I think apartments.

A: I think so, yeah. It's been so many years ago.

Q: It was a very fine restaurant. Did he work there—I mean, did he work there as a young man too, and continue to work there?

A: Mm-hm, until he left Charlottesville. He moved to New York.

Q: Uh-huh. And when did you start working? (Inaudible)

A: I started working when I was thirteen years old.

Q: Oh, no!

(General Laughter)

A: Just working all around.

Q: Did you—

A: But no, um, when I went to New York, I was a children's nurse in a private home. So, that's what I did. I had five kids, and then when I came back to Charlottesville, I worked as a domestic for Mrs. Claude Jessup for thirty-five years.

Q: Could you spell the name Claude Jessup?

A: Claude Jessup for thirty-five years.

Q: J.E.S.S.U.P. That's a famous name in Charlottesville.

Q: Did you say Claude or Clyde?

A: Claude.

Q: C.L.A.U.

A: D.E. Everybody ought to know him, he owns everything in Charlottesville. (Chuckle)

Q: I know the name. Actually D. is new to Charlottesville.

A: Aww!

Q: I've lived here a year now. I moved here last April. (Inaudible)

A: Oh, yes. Aw!

Q: The Jessups own the land where Seminole Square is now, right?

A: I don't know.

Q: I think that was (Inaudible).

A: But I know the Pepsi Cola plant, the City Laundry, the cemeteries. Just so much in Charlottesville that they own.

Q: That they own. No I think you're right. Where was their house where you worked?

A: Farmington. I started with them on Lewis Mountain Road, and then they lived in Farmington.

Q: How did you—how did you get out there everyday?
A: I had a ride.
Q: Oh. And you were there, like full-time.
A: Yeah, I was there five days a week.
Q: Uh huh. Well I know that's a well-known family.
A: Yeah and she died last year. Her birthday was yesterday and I put flowers on the cemetery.
Q: Oh. So you were pretty good friends then?
A: Very close. Very close, yeah. (Inaudible).
Q: Um, so when you went to New York, how did you manage to do that? Did you know people there? Did you—how did you find that out?
A: Yes. There was a family that I met in Washington and I went to New York, and I worked up there about fourteen years.
Q: Oh fourteen years? (Inaudible)
A: I cared for the children. And then I came back to Charlottesville.
Q: And when you were doing—
A: When my—
Q: You were married at the time?
A: Yeah but I was divorced, at uh, my husband died in '60s, that means divorce was—(Inaudible).
Q: So you were married, and then divorced, and then went to New York?
A: No I divorced while I was in New York.
Q: Uh-huh. Your uh,—what kind of work did your father do?
A: My father died in 19 and 20, I was ten years old. So I can't tell you what he did.
Q: That's a sad thing when parents die early.
A: Uh-huh. Yeah and I was young. But I think my mother said he was a railroad man. I think. And my mother was a seamstress. She used to make clothes for everybody (Chuckle) in Charlottesville almost.
Q: Oh that's great.
A: She got her diploma. I guess that went down with the house too. Um, but he worked on the railroad, and my mother was a dressmaker.
Q: Well, there's quite a few people that worked on the railroad. Virginia Ross had family, or her, her husband worked—
A: Yeah, yeah my father did. My momma said.

Q: So when you moved to Ridge Street, that was, you said, was in the '50s.

A: Mm-hm.

Q: And was it—did you move directly to 409 Ridge Street? So you've been there forever then?

A: Until the tree went down. Fifty some years.

Q: It was a wonderful house.

A: It was. A beautiful home.

Q: Can you tell us a little bit about the house? I saw it from the outside, but what was it like on the inside?

A: Very nice.

Q: How many rooms did you have?

A: I had, I guess, fourteen rooms in all.

Q: That's a big—

A: Yes. Big house. Lots of closets, hardwood floors and everything. It was beautiful!

Q: There was a—

A: (Coughing) Inside we had a fireplace in the hall, a fireplace upstairs, and we had, I think we had about three fireplaces, but I never used them. (Inaudible) Mantelpieces, beautiful mantelpieces in the hall and the living room, and in a upstairs bedroom. The mantles.

Q: It was—I've been told it was the oldest house on Ridge Street.

A: That's what they say.

Q: (Inaudible)

A: (Inaudible) (Coughing)

Q: Can you tell me about the little—the little, the building behind, in the backyard?

A: That—that's a cottage back there. That has three rooms and a shower.

Q: Do you think it was a kitchen at one time, or did anyone say anything about that? Used to have in the older houses, used to have a—have a kitchen separate from the main house.

A: No. It wasn't separate.

Q: That was saved though. You were next door to the (Hartman's?), the Gibsons, Beverly Gibson (Inaudible)

A: Mm-hm. Yeah but they weren't there when I, when we bought that.

Q: They arrived shortly after the war I guess.

A: I remember when my mother speak of the Hartmans (phonetically) and there was somebody else over there, I don't know, that made potato chips. I can't think who they were, though. On Ridge Street.

Q: (Inaudible) potato chip factory, or—?

A: No, it wasn't a factory. No. Just a home. I was very young. I was living on Dice Street then, but I remember.

Q: So there was a lot of businessmen—there were a lot of businesspeople that lived on Ridge Street at one time?

A: Yes.

Q: Well, when you went to—when you were on Dice Street and Ridge Street, did you—you—which church did you—

A: Mt. Zion has always been my church. I joined Mr. Zion when I came to Charlottesville.

Q: Uh-huh. And this is still a very active church?

A: Yes.

Q: How about shopping, where did you—what stores were available, like, for groceries and so forth? Where did you go? Early, in the early times.

A: I don't know in the early times. I guess my mother did the shopping. (Chuckling)

Q: When—how about in the—when you moved to Ridge Street in the '50s, did you—

A: Yeah, I used to deal with the style shop and the young men's shop, and whatever grocery store there was down on the mall, now, I used to shop there. M.C. Thomas.

Q: St. Thomas?

A: (Loudly) M.C. Thomas. Grand Piano now, isn't it? Yeah, that's what they call.

Q: But it says M.C. Thomas, I think, on the building.

A: Yes, uh-huh. I used to shop with them in the '50s.

Q: That was what kind of store?

A: Furniture.

Q: Furniture?

A: Yeah. Grand Piano furniture store. And the style shop was a ladies clothing store.

Q: The Style shop?

A: The Style shop. Uh-huh.

Q: And that was right down, like, where the mall is now?

A: It used to be. Uh-huh.

Q: How about, where did you—did you ever use the—weren't there some little tiny grocery stores on Ridge Street?

A: Not that I know of.

Q: I guess toward where Hartmans Mills Road is.

A: No.

Q: That might have been before you moved here, that they had those stores.

A: Well it could have been, but I don't go down, you know—but uh, Mrs. Dawson lived down on that end of Ridge Street, but I don't know—.

Q: Then she was—

A: —much. Then she moved to 413 before I did.

Q: She was there before you?

A: Mm-hm.

Q: (Inaudible) Tell us some things about the—that neighborhood or at least the several blocks that—where you lived. Did you get to know most of the people?

A: I knew most of the people on that block. Mrs. Ophelia Smith, and Mrs. Safronia Jackson, Mrs. Elizabeth Dawson.

Q: Mrs. Ophelia Smith—

A: Mrs. Safronia Jackson.

Q: How do you spell that? (Chuckling)

A: S.A.F.R.O.N.I.A.

Q: S.A.F.—

A: R.O.N.I.A., Jackson. She's there now.

Q: Oh. And is she a long-time resident also?

A: Yes.

Q: And Mrs. Elizabeth—

A: Dawson.

Q: And that's who we, she's been interviewed hasn't she? But, when you first moved to Ridge Street, that was before some of the buildings were taken down, before they expanded Cherry Avenue, so what—can you sort of tell us about what it looked like?

A: I don't know, because I wasn't here long enough to pay attention. I was going back and forth. Where I worked in New York, she was a writer, and if she would write and call and say, would you come up for six months or a year or what, take care of the children while I write, and I'm gone, so, things happened on Ridge Street that I didn't know about until I come home, and my mother or somebody would tell me, but I just don't know.

Q: You were moving around quite a bit?

A: Yes. Yes. My brother told me once that I had bought the Pennsylvania Railroad (Interviewer laughs), because I used to ride the train all the time. But all of those people that I knew there were very nice. And all of us went to the same church and everything.

Q: How about—how has Ridge Street changed in the last twenty years or so?

A: Don't ask me honey. (Chuckling) I don't know.

Q: Well, some other time. It's gotten—seems like it's gotten, did lose, you know, some of the nice buildings. Down Ridge Street.

A: Yeah. Where were the buildings? In my block?

Q: One block down where Cherry Avenue—

A: Yeah well see I don't know down like that.

Q: (Inaudible) So Nolan's was built on Ridge Street, did that happen when you were—

A: Nolan's? Was it, Tom?

Mr. Jones: (Inaudible)

A: I don't know. Nolan's was built (Inaudible).

Mr. Jones: (Inaudible)

Q: But they took down some nice houses, I think, (Inaudible)—Were you going to say something?

Mr. Jones: No I'm just trying to think back now. I think uh, I'm trying to think what was on the corner, see Nolan's was where the (new museum?) is now. Since we were there. '57. (Inaudible) I'm trying to think what was on the corner there. (Inaudible) It wasn't a funeral home I'm pretty sure. And John (Inaudible)he lived cross the street there.

A: When what?

Mr. Jones: (Inaudible) the store right there. You know I worked with John (Inaudible) his house. When we were first there. When I go back in the service. (Inaudible)

A: I don't know. Tell me about it, I don't know (Chuckle). Tell me about it, I don't know.

Mr. Jones: (Inaudible)

Q: Well, what uh, I was going to ask about your son. What kind of work have you been, did you do, and (Inaudible)?

Mr. Jones: Well uh, I worked at the University for a while when I first came out of the service, then I worked at—I was a cook at Cedars Nursing Home, the one that's out on Barracks road. Then I worked for Greencroft Nursery. I don't know where that's located now, and I also worked for E.C. Ferron, which is a—

A: Construction firm.

Q: Oh construction. E.C. Ferron? F.—?

Mr. Jones: Ferron. Yeah, Allied bought them out. It's HFE.R.R.O.N.

A: Who's H.E.?

Mr. Jones: Ferron. F.E.R.R.O.N.

A: Oh yeah, F.

Mr. Jones: Allied bought them out.

Q: So you were in the service?

Mr. Jones: Yes, ma'am.

Q: So what—what years were you in the service?

Mr. Jones: Uh, '50—'51. I was wounded, that's the reason I didn't stay that long.

Q: You said you worked at uh, Sears?

Mr. Jones: Cedars.

Q: Cedars?

A: Nursing Home.

Mr. Jones: It was right off of Barracks road. (Inaudible) I was the morning cook over there. That's, I worked in Charlottesville, for about, I spent quite a time away from here, quite a bit of time here. But most of my work was in Coopersville, except once I drove a—

Q: You were a cook.

A: (Chuckling) Yeah, a cook.

Mr. Jones: I drove a (Inaudible) trucks for a while, in Washington, but most of my other time I was cooking.

Q: So this is why—this is lucky for you that he could cook, huh?

(General Laughter)

(Inaudible)

Q: And you have, your other son?

A: He died. My mother died in 1978, in August, and my son died in 1978 in December.

Q: That was an unhappy year then. And you had—

A: And my mother was ninety-six years old.

Q: Ninety-six? Well that's pretty wonderful.

A: Isn't it though?

Q: Long lived.

A: Yes.

Q: Pretty remarkable. Did, you and she spent the whole, your whole lives together?

A: We lived together, yes.

Q: That's really (Inaudible)

A: When I left New York, I came home to take care of my mother.

Q: Did—you said you were, you always attended Mt. Zion. What kind of entertainment activities did you enjoy? Was it—

A: I was a Sunday school teacher, and I sang in the choir. And I belonged to the Industrial Club.

Q: Industrial?

A: Club.

Q: Was that connected with the church?

A: Oh yes, that's a club in the church. The Daughters of Ruth, that's in the church, and the Missionary Society. (Inaudible) So I was busy.

(Laughter)

Q: What did the Daughters of Ruth do?

A: Well, (Inaudible), men and young women, and we talked and, you know, and we would go around and visit the sick, put on programs, we used to put on a lot of programs, and we got a lot of things for the church that the Daughters of Ruth did. Don't ask me what 'cause I've forgotten. But we did a lot, the Daughters of Ruth. The Industrial Club—

Q: It's kind of like a service club (Inaudible).

A: The Industrial Club, I'm an honorary member there now. But they just take care of the sick. And the missionary (Inaudible)

Q: (Inaudible) plus I'm sure there's (Inaudible) social as well.

A: Yeah.

Q: So are—do you still participate in some of those organizations?

A: Mm-hm. I'm an honorary member of the Industrial Club, but I'm still in the Daughters of Ruth. I don't attend all the meetings—I'm eighty-five years old and with lung cancer, I just take it easy, do what I have to do. Take it easy. Take it easy. I go to Sunday School and church when I can.

Q: Well when, when the weather's bad.

A: 'Cause the bus comes right past here.

Q: Oh, it does?

A: Uh-huh. Mt. Zion bus. And the, if the weather's nice I go, every Sunday. Go to Sunday School, and stay to church.

Q: And it's, that's a nice program. I attended a program there recently at the Martin Luther King memorial service. It was very nice.

A: Yeah, I was there in all that rain, and gloom.

Q: Uh-huh, good for you! (Chuckle)

A: But it was nice.

Q: Did—tell us about when the trees came down (Inaudible).

A: (Inaudible) when the trees came down, it was on the Monday, no I guess, or a Tuesday, I don't know but anyhow, around 10:30, and I had breakfast heating in the stove, and had come back out of the kitchen and was sitting in my room reading the bible, and I heard this boom noise. And I got up, and my niece was in another room across from me, and she—we met in hall—and she said, what was that? And I said, I don't know. And I looked out the front door and I looked out the back door, and we were trapped. We were trapped in by branches. The lady at the day-care called to see if I was all right. And I said, fine! Call somebody. (Laughter)

Q: (Laughter) The phone was working and everything?

A: Yes it was. And I said, call somebody. And she said, okay. And a few minutes, everybody in Charlottesville was there from the fire department and all. And there were men working on up—(Tape stopped briefly)

Q: Was there an attic in the house?

A: No. No.

Q: Second floor. And, and there you saw it, next to you? Or,—

A: No. No.

Q: Did you see it? The tree?

A: I—when the tree fell, I heard this noise. My niece and I met in the hall, "what is that?" I looked out the front door and all I could see was limbs, but I didn't know what it was. And I couldn't get to—and I went to the side door. There were branches, and we were trapped in there.

Q: So the tree didn't—

A: It came over the kitchen, smashed the kitchen in (Chuckle), and some of the ceiling from the dining room fell. But, I couldn't see the tree from the back, you know, from in the house. 'Cause, it fell—it came down in the kitchen. And I was not in the kitchen. The Lord had told me to get out of that kitchen and go in my room, and that's where I was when the tree fell. And these men—

(Inaudible from other person present)

Q: It didn't?

A: It didn't. Now that I think of it, but at first, I was just as happy. It was shock. That's all, that's right, it was shock. But these men—

Mr. Jones: (Inaudible) Salvation Army (Inaudible)

A: —three—two men working for the city came and—Shhh! (to Mr. Marshall who is talking while she is talking)—

Mr. Jones: Yes ma'am.

Q: You've got more information for us.

A: —these men working for the city came up and broke a window, and lifted me and my niece out through that window.

Q: Oh my god.

Q: Was this in a terrible—

A: No wind. No wind. No nothing. Beautiful. A beautiful day.

Q: What caused—it became—(Inaudible).

A: They said that when the tree fell—they said that it was rotten on the inside. But from the outside, you couldn't say that.

Q: It looked good?

A: Yes. Yes.

Q: So it was just the tree was, was rotting away? (Inaudible) It was a very big tree. I took have pictures of it, actually.

A: You did?

Q: Would you like some?

A: Yes.

Q: I'm sure you would.

A: Oh, that's the biggest tree.

Q: It was enormous. It was a beautiful tree.

Mr. Jones: (Inaudible)

A: Yes, it was. It was. Beautiful. Yes. But it—and Mrs. Dawson wasn't home when this happened. She was out shopping. So when she came home, here I am in her yard, and all these people in her yard. And she, somebody met her outside before she came to the house, to tell her what had happened, so she wouldn't have a heart-attack.

Q: Oh, good. Were you able to save much furniture or?

A: No, no. Not too much. The upstairs, I had two rooms, actually three rooms of things that I could not get, and clothing and furniture.

Q: Oh that's awful. You couldn't get it because it was too dangerous?

A: Yes. They didn't want us to, because they didn't know—

Q: Yes sir?

Mr. Jones: I just had a thought, just came to me. (Inaudible) Okay, there was a white house on that corner, it had a very big tall yard to it, and it had a cottage in the back, just like the (Inaudible). A weather built house (Inaudible).

A: I don't know nothing about that.

Mr. Jones: (Inaudible)—call Mrs. Dawson and ask her. I remember (Inaudible) before the war. And they had a cottage in the back like we did. But the yard was way up in the air. They cut that yard down when (Inaudible). (Inaudible) down to the Street. (Inaudible).

Q: (Inaudible) just very sad. Thank you for finding that out.

Q: Just flattened down?

Q: Took the land right out. Well I know you're glad—

A: And some of my dishes in the dining room, because the ceiling, you know, continued to fall and we were afraid to go in there because you didn't know what was going to fall on your head. So some of my dishes I didn't get.

Q: Did they send anybody in there to get as much as they could though?

A: Yes. My grandchildren went in there and got what they could, but—

Q: It sounds like (Inaudible) earthquakes. The same situation, they wouldn't let you go—

A: No, they wouldn't. They had the yellow ribbons all around, right.

Q: Well, when they demolished the house, did you watch that, or—

A: No. No, no, no.

Q: It was too depressing. Well when they did it—

A: I saw some of it, I was over there. But they didn't demolish the house until after I had gone, left Mrs. Dawson's.

Q: Right. They waited to see if it would stand.

A: Yeah. But I would go over some days, and I (Inaudible). But I didn't see it when they got the tree off. I didn't see that.

Q: That took a long time to take the tree off.

A: Long time, mm-hm. There was a lot of wood there too. (Chuckle)

Q: Tragedy, for that to happen.

A: Yeah.

Q: There was a man in my building who was cutting down, I guess a couple of years ago, cutting down a tree, with a chainsaw, and I guess he was—didn't really know how to do this, because it (Sound of phone)—the tree he cut down knocked down another tree, as I understand it, and it fell on him, and he is—both his arms and legs were paralyzed, you know, and he was crushed under this (Inaudible).

A: He was crushed?

Q: Yes. He survived, but he's paralyzed.

A: Yes, uh-huh. Aww. That's tragic. Yeah that is dangerous. I am—I could have been in, walking in my backyard when that tree went down. Did you see how that—

Q: I saw it—I went over to Oak Street and looked.

A: Uh-huh, and I usually—and he was downtown when that happened.

Q: Your son was?

A: Uh-huh. And I usually sit on the front porch all the time in the summer, and when he came home and saw this tree, somebody had to grab him because he almost came screaming. Because he just knew that I was on that porch, under the tree. Thank the Lord—

Q: It was a relief.

A: It was. Yeah. It was something.

Q: Is that one of the most frightening things that ever happened to you, closest you've come—

A: That ever happened to me. Mm-hm. But, like we were saying, I didn't get excited, I was just laughing and acting crazy and all. But after it all over—after it was all over, I started thinking how blessed I was that I didn't get hurt and I started thinking about things that could have happened to me, you know. But right at that minute, think nothing (Inaudible).

Q: Do you miss living over there?

A: I certainly do.

Q: Terribly.

A: Yes. I had been over there so long. And with Mrs. Dawson, my neighbor, we would run—we had a path that we would run from one house to the other.

Q: You beat a path?

A: Yes. And I certainly do miss that.

Q: She says she miss—she feels lonely with that empty space, and not having you there.

A: I know. She's—she's, yes.

Q: It was a wonderful, mutual relationship—

A: —relationship we had.

Q: Well now at least you can talk on the phone and still go over there.

A: And go over. I do. Yes.

Q: And she took care—you stayed with her for a few weeks?

A: About three weeks. Then when I left there, I went and stayed with my daughter-in-law for about three weeks.

Q: She's in—

A: Charlottesville. Mm-hm, on 9th Street. Carmilla. And I stayed with her three weeks, and then we started looking for a place to live, and this was all I could find right then.

Q: I think it's good to find someplace close. Nearby . . . so you can see her. Well, getting back to some other questions about life on Ridge Street, where did you go when you were sick? Did you have a doctor nearby?

A: What do you mean, when I was sick?

Q: Well a doctor, did you have a doctor nearby?

A: Oh, Dr. Jennings was my doctor.

Q: Dr. Jones?

A: Jennings. And I'd go to him, to his office, yes.

Q: Was he a long-term doctor?

A: As far as I know, yes. I've had him for a long time. Dr. Jennings. And he's still my doctor.

Q: Did you go to—you were talking about going to Martha Jefferson, is that where you would go instead of the University?

Q: (Inaudible)—my grandson was born, ten years ago.

A: Martha Jefferson? Yes. Ohh. My children were born in University Hospital.

Q: Were you born at home, yourself?

A: Uh-huh, I guess, I'm not sure. (Chuckle) Yes I was born at home.

Q: Now it's changed, well now they push people out of the hospital in a very quick fashion. Used to be you could stay there a few days when you had children, but now, it's very short-term.

A: Yeah, that's what I hear. I heard that. Yes. I think I stayed there about two weeks.

Q: Oh that's nice, that's what my mother did. Two weeks.

Q: Three weeks?

Q: Two weeks.

Q: Oh mine was three weeks. She was perfectly healthy, no problems. Three weeks (Inaudible).

A: Yeah yeah. And then come home and stayed.

(Laughter)

Q: Relax.

A: Yeah. For another two weeks. Yeah.

Q: Well, that sounds like fun to me. Well, when the Civil Rights Movement came along, did you get involved in that?

A: Mm-hm, I used to go to some of their meetings and marches.

Q: Oh, you did? Good. How about you? Did you get involved in the Civil Rights Movement or were you too young?

Mr. Jones: Well, I was—no, I wasn't here. I didn't get around too much. I had my hip replaced twice and I was just able to get around myself. (Inaudible). I couldn't do any walking.

Q: Uh-huh, so your mom had to do it?

(Laughter)

Mr. Jones: Well yes. I had my hip replaced twice in two years. Same hip.

Q: Same hip? When was that?

A: Well that was just here lately.

Mr. Jones: (Inaudible)

Q: Was the activity—was the church active? Did you get active in—

A: In the Civil Rights Movement? Yes, yes. (Inaudible).

Q: The Mount Zion—

Q: So you say you went on marches. Where?

A: Well we marched from downtown, downtown. Some church down—downtown, up until Mt. Zion church. Just short. Real short. Just one Sunday. Just one Sunday. You know, I didn't go to Washington Park. We just walked down. The church was real nice from one church to another.

Mr. Jones: (Inaudible)—down to Tonsler Park.

A: Not me. No.

Q: Some other people huh?

A: Yeah a lot of people.

Q: Did you—were there—I don't know about this but were there any sort of famous people that came to Ridge Street that you know about that stayed at people's homes or maybe were involved in the Civil Rights Movement?

A: Mm-mm. No. Not that I know of. Not that I know of.

Mr. Jones: Yeah. What was his name, he came here one time. (Inaudible).

Q: I know Jesse Jackson has been here, but that's fairly recent.

A: Yeah but I can't think of anybody.

Mr. Jones: (Inaudible) he was a kind of older fellow (Inaudible)

Q: Oh I know who you're talking about. That's recent. Dick Gregory (Phonetically). That was like three or four years ago. I went on that march. That was good. And it ended out at Tonsler Park. I know him. I have a picture of myself standing next to him in fact.

A: Oh, you do? Hmm.

Q: Did you have some questions to ask?

Q: No, I can't think of any.

Q: How about when your family bought the Ridge Street house? Was that the first time that you purchased a house, or was that back in Gordonsville and then Dice Street?

A: No. No.

Q: It was harder for African Americans to (Inaudible)—

A: The first house that we owned was on—the first house—the first house we owned was Parrot Street. Now it's another name. Yeah but it was Parrot Street.

Q: How do you spell that?

A: P.A.R.R.O.T. Yeah.

Mr. Jones: (Inaudible)

A: No. No. That's way back Thomas. Parrot Street is down there off of the cemetery. Down in there.

Q: Okay. Uh-huh.

Q: What's your name?

A: Thomas Marshall Jones.

Q: Mable, what does S. stand for, Mable?

A: Serena.

Q: Serena. Oh that's (Inaudible).

A: That's what my momma said.

Q: That's her middle name. How do you spell that?

A: S.E.R.E.N.A. My mother did all spelling. M.A.B.E.L. . . . M.A.B.L.E. She spelled it. M.A.B.L.E. was the way my momma spelled it. Some people spell it differently.

Mr. Jones: Didn't your brothers use that middle name. (Laughter) I don't remember, they never used it.

Q: So you bought the house on Parrot Street, and then came to Dice, and then Ridge?

A: I didn't own anything on Dice Street.

Q: Oh, that was your parents that had that. Was it hard to borrow money from the bank?

A: I didn't buy that house on Parrot Street. My brother gave it to my mother, and my mother sold it, and we bought on Ridge Street. And we had no trouble with the mortgage or anything because momma put the money from the house that she sold on Ridge Street.

Q: That was a nice gift.

A: It was—my brother gave it to my mother.

Q: Wonderful.

Q: You said that you started working when you were thirteen. As a baby-sitter or?

A: No, I think I used to wash dishes for somebody (Chuckle) in a home, and go to school. It's been so long ago.

Q: So when you left school, you were glad to leave school, or—

A: Yeah because I wanted to get a better job and help my mother. She had raised five children and I'm being the oldest and only ten or twelve when my father died. So she had, my mother had a lot of responsibility.

Q: You were the youngest?

A: I'm the oldest.

Q: The oldest of five.

A: Of five.

Q: And you're the only one still living? What kind of work did you do during those years, from the time you left school until you got married?

A: I just said, taking care of children.

Q: Oh that was when you were (Inaudible). This is all on tape so I'm writing it so if I don't understand something you can check it.

A: That's all right.

Q: Then your—did your brother stay in Charlottesville that gave your mother the house?

A: No.

Q: He went on.

A: He went to service. And when he came home from service, he lived in Staunton, Virginia, and he gave my mother the house then. He gave my mother that house when he came out of service. He bought it. And that was her baby. And that was her baby.

Q: No kidding. Shows a lot of love. So the children loved their mother quite a bit.

A: Yes. Yes. All of them, all of them. All the children.

Q: What church did you go to when you lived out in Gordonsville?

A: Oak Grove. Oak Grove Baptist Church.

Q: Do you know if it's still there?

A: No it isn't. I think they merged with some other church.

Q: But the church was a big part of your life all along?

A: While I was, you know, growing up, and lived down in Gordonsville. But I came to Charlottesville when I was sixteen. My mother moved to

Charlottesville. But we would go back and forth. Summer in the country, and winter in Charlottesville.

Q: Huh, pleasant (Chuckle). And did you still have relatives in Gordonsville area? So it'd be a pleasant place to go back.

A: Yes, we had my home down there.

Q: And, your family, you kept it? (Inaudible) Did you come to Charlottesville because it was more work? Is that why your mom—

A: Yes, because, mm-hm. And the schools were better for the children. She moved.

Q: Better schools. Did you go to the—You were still going to the ele—at ten years old, oh no, sixteen, there was another elementary school that was next to Jefferson.

Mr. Jones: Both of them were named Jefferson.

Q: Oh, they both liked the same name. Where did you go to school?

Mr. Jones: I went to Mechanicsville. That's down in Louisa County. I went to Jefferson. I went to Christianburg Industrial Institute. That's over in Christianburg.

Q: Uh-huh. Industrial Institute. Is that—did you get sort of, did you learn about cooking there, or did you just learn that on your own?

Mr. Jones: No I didn't. I didn't. (Inaudible)—my brothers (Inaudible). Oh the name of Parrot Street is Oakmont, used to be Parrot Street. That's down off of (Inaudible), between Oak and Dice (Inaudible).

Q: Okay. Good, thank you.

Q: What was your other son's name?

A: James.

Q: And his—he did some cooking too? He was a chef or a cook?

A: James? I guess. (Inaudible) He did a lot of—

Mr. Jones: (Inaudible)—on Rugby Road. And I was a baker's second. And he was a cook's second. And we kind of got (Inaudible) during the school time, school years.

Q: Oh at one of the fraternities or—

Mr. Jones: Well there was a townhouse—on Rugby Road the old brick apartments, I think it was an apartment there. The basement used to be Rugby cafeteria.

Q: Oh no kidding? I didn't know that. There are beautiful old apartments out there. Is, there's one on, is that Gordon Avenue?

Mr. Jones: No this is Rugby Road. If you cross the bridge, coming from, going from the north or south, yeah south, going that way, you cross the bridge and it's right on the left hand side (Inaudible) down at the bottom.

Q: Oh okay. When you moved to Ridge Street, did you, that was the time when there was, African American families were moving in, and some white families were leaving? Did you find—

A: No problem. No problem.

Q: white families, reacting negatively or was it sort of—

A: No, not to me. No problem.

Q: Oh. That's good. People were pretty courteous and—

A: In my—up in my—in the 400 block—I had no trouble. (Inaudible) Mm-hm.

Q: Well I think some people moved out, from what I understand was just because the houses were big, and their children were grown, and more businesses coming in, that affected the change. Is there some things that you would like to add to this? Other thoughts on Ridge Street?

A: No. I just miss my home on Ridge Street. (Inaudible) (Laughter)

Mr. Jones: Wouldn't mind having three bedrooms on one floor, wouldn't have to go upstairs. (Inaudible).

A: He wouldn't mind having a home with three bedrooms so that I wouldn't have to go up and down the steps.

Q: Are you renting this house—

A: Yes. No I'm too old to buy anything now.

Q: That was, the timing on that tree falling down, that was pretty terrible.

A: Yeah, but I don't intend to stay here. Ma'am?

Q: What was the date, of the, what date?

A: I think it was about the 22nd of August. That's when the tree fell.

(Inaudible)

Q: I brought the clipping in.

A: Yeah I think it was the 22nd of August. I think it was the 22nd of August.

Q: So you hoped that—you planned that, this is a temporary situation.

A: Yes.

Mr. Jones: 22nd of August. (Inaudible).

A: All right! (Chuckle)

Q: Well, I appreciate very much you talking with us. And thank you—

A: Sorry I can't give you enough.

(Thereupon this interview was concluded.)

NOTES

ABBREVIATIONS

Esmont — *Esmont Oral History Project: Building Digital Communities, Race and Place: African American Community History, Albemarle County, Virginia*. Prepared by the Virginia Center for Digital History, Charlottesville, VA, 2001–2002, http://www2.vcdh.virginia.edu/afam/raceandplace/oralhistory_esmont1.html.

GMI — *The Great Migration: Stories from the South to the North,* Oral History Project, Hudson River Museum, Yonkers, New York, 2002.

McG — Florence Coleman Bryant, *Rebecca Fuller McGinness: A Lifetime, 1892–2000,* Charlottesville: Van Doren Co., 2001 (based on interviews Bryant conducted in 1991).

MJ — Mable Wall[s] Jones, interview by Jean Hiatt and Diane Berkeley, February 10, 1995, "Ridge Street Oral Histories," *Ridge Street Oral History Project: A Supplement to the Survey of the Ridge Street Historic District and Proposal for Local Designation*. Prepared by the Preservation Piedmont for the Department of Community Planning, Charlottesville, VA, December 1995, http://www2.vcdh.virginia.edu/afam/raceandplace/orals/mjones.html.

PSP — *From Porch Swings to Patios: An Oral History of Charlottesville's Neighborhoods*. Prepared by the Department of Community Planning Advisory Board and students of the University of Virginia, Charlottesville,

	VA, 1982–84, http://www2.vcdh.virginia.edu/afam/raceandplace/oralhistory_porchswings.html.
Ridge	"Ridge Street Oral Histories." *Ridge Street Oral History Project.* Prepared by Preservation Piedmont for the Department of Community Planning, Charlottesville, VA, December 1995, http://www2.vcdh.virginia.edu/afam/raceandplace/oralhistory_ridge.html.
Ridge Street Project	*Ridge Street Oral History Project: A Supplement to the Survey of the Ridge Street Historic District and Proposal for Local Designation.* Prepared by Preservation Piedmont for the Department of Community Planning, Charlottesville, VA, December 1995.
VH	James Robert Saunders and Renae Nadine Shackelford, *Urban Renewal and the End of Black Culture in Charlottesville, Virginia: An Oral History of Vinegar Hill* (Jefferson, North Carolina: McFarland, 1998).

INTRODUCTION

1. The interview was part of a project designed to support an application to create a protected historic district: *Ridge Street Oral History Project.* Prepared by Preservation Piedmont for the Department of Community Planning (Charlottesville, VA, December 1995). The tapes and their transcripts are now included in "Race and Place," which is a project of the Virginia Center for Digital History and the Carter G. Woodson Institute for Afro-American and African Studies (http://www2.vcdh.virginia.edu/afam/raceandplace/transcripts/mjones.html) (hereafter MJ).
2. MJ.
3. MJ.
4. Mable also lived briefly in Washington, DC. We discuss this period of her life in chapter 3.
5. Frederick Buechner, *Sacred Journey: A Memoir of Early Days* (San Francisco: Harper, 1982), 13–14.
6. Leith Mullings, "Uneven Development: Class, Race, and Gender in the United States before 1900," in *Women's Work,* eds. E. Leacock and H. I. Safa (South Hadley, MA: Bergin & Garvey, 1986), 50.
7. See Maxine Baca Zinn, "The Family as a Race Institution," in *The SAGE Handbook of Race and Ethnic Studies,* eds. John Solomos and Patricia Hill Collins (London: Sage, 2010), 357–82.

8. Kwame Anthony Appiah, "The Case for Capitalizing the 'B' in Black," *Atlantic,* June 18, 2020, https://www.theatlantic.com/ideas/archive/2020/06/time-to-capitalize-blackand-white/613159/. For another argument on capitalizing both *Black* and *White* see Nell Irvin Painter, "Opinion: Why 'White' Should Be Capitalized, Too," *Washington Post,* July 22, 2020, https://washingtonpost.com/opinions/2020/07/22/why-white-should-be-capitalized.
9. We located her living relatives with the help of several people-finding search engines. We also uncovered information about two families for whom Mable had worked in Charlottesville.
10. Paul Laurence Dunbar, "We Wear the Mask," from *The Complete Poems of Paul Laurence Dunbar* (New York: Dodd, Mead and Company), Poetry Foundation, accessed October 9, 2019, https://www.poetryfoundation.org/poems/44203/we-wear-the-mask.
11. For exceptions, see Bonnie Thornton Dill, *Across the Boundaries of Race and Class: An Exploration of Work and Family among Black Female Domestic Servants* (New York: Garland Publishing, Inc., 1994); Andrew Wiese, *Places of Their Own: African American Suburbanization in the Twentieth Century* (Chicago: University of Chicago Press, 2004).
12. John Darnton, *Almost a Family* (New York: Anchor, 2011), 80.
13. Sau-ling C. Wong, "Diverted Mothering: Representations of Caregivers of Color in the Age of 'Multiculturalism,'" in *Mothering: Ideology, Experience, and Agency,* eds. Evelyn Nakano Glenn, Grace Chang, and Linda Rennie Forcey (New York: Routledge, 1994), 67–91.
14. We told it for the first time, together, after our father died. We wrote an article published in the *American Prospect* that focused on the caregiver we had hired for our father. In that essay, we gave Mable the pseudonym Martha. Emily K. Abel and Margaret K. Nelson, "Intimate Care for Hire," *American Prospect* 12 (May 21, 2001): 26–31.
15. In a recent, best-selling book, Robin DiAngelo defines White fragility as "a state in which even a minimum amount of racial stress becomes intolerable, triggering a range of defensive moves. These moves include the outward display of emotions such as anger, fear, and guilt, and behaviors such as argumentation, silence, and leaving the stress-inducing situation." Robin DiAngelo, *White Fragility: Why It's So Hard for White People to Talk about Racism* (Boston: Beacon Press, 2018), 2.
16. Zinn, "The Family," 372.
17. Darlene Clark Hine, "Rape and the Inner Lives of Black Women in the Middle West: Preliminary Thoughts on the Culture of Dissemblance," *Signs* 14, no. 41 (1981): 916.

18. For some of those criticisms, see Valerie Smith, "Black Women's Memories and *The Help*," *Southern Cultures* 20, no. 1 (2014): 26–37, https://doi.org/10.1353/scu.2014.0000; "History and *The Help*," Harvard University Press Blog, https://harvardpress.typepad.com/hup_puublicity/2012/02/history; "Historians on 'The Help': Vanessa May and Rebecca Sharpless Respond," https://uncpressblog.com/2011/08/24/; "Open Statement from the Association of Black Women's Historians (ABWH) to Fans of *The Help*," August 12, 2011, abwh.org/2011/08/12/; C. Garcia, V. Young, and Charise Pimentel, *From "Uncle Tom's Cabin" to "The Help": Critical Perspectives on White-Authored Narratives of Black Life* (New York: Palgrave Macmillan, 2014).

1. "WE HAD MY HOME DOWN THERE"

1. This information is available through the Louisa County Historical Society's project, The Land Between the Rivers: Piedmont Virginia Digital History: Converting Slavery Documents to Geospatial Information: A Storymap: http://lch.maps.arcgis.com/apps/MapSeries/index.html?appid=a95d3ff3e0ec4458a3d56f8bc935a380.
2. Amy Morsman, Professor of History at Middlebury College, email to authors, November 15, 2019.
3. Crandall A. Shifflett, *Patronage and Poverty in the Tobacco South: Louisa County, Virginia, 1860–1900* (Knoxville: University of Tennessee Press, 1982).
4. Eric Foner, *Reconstruction: America's Unfinished Revolution, 1863–1877*, rev. ed. (New York: HarperPerennial, 2014); Virginia Writers' Project, *The Negro in Virginia* (Winston-Salem: John F. Blair, 1994).
5. Virginia Department of Health; Richmond, Virginia; Virginia Deaths, 1912–2014, Ancestry.com.
6. The structure of African American families and, in particular, the women-centeredness of those families, has been an issue of great debate among anthropologists and sociologists. For some of these debates, see Natalia Sarkisian and Naomi Gerstel, "Kin Support among Blacks and Whites: Race and Family Organization," *American Sociological Review* 69 (December 2004): 812–37; Carol Stack, *All Our Kin: Strategies for Survival in a Black Community* (New York: Harper and Row, 1974); Marietta Morrissey, "Gender, Race, and Kinship: Searching for the Matrifocal Family," *Critical Sociology*, 18, no. 2 (Summer 1991): 103–15.
7. The exception is the 1890 census, which was destroyed.

8. *Esmont Oral History Project: Building Digital Communities, Race and Place: African American Community History, Albemarle County, Virginia*, Prepared by the Virginia Center for Digital History (Charlottesville, VA, 2001–2002), http://www2.vcdh.virginia.edu/afam/raceandplace/esmont_info.html#project (hereafter Esmont).
9. Esmont.
10. Foner, *Reconstruction*, 84.
11. We know less about this Serena because she died in 1871 at approximately age forty-six and thus appeared with her full name in only one census after the Civil War. (Her maiden name might have been Kinney, Kenney, or Kemmly.) Shortly before her death, Serena lived with her husband and five of their children; two other children were living elsewhere (US Bureau of the Census, 1870, Northern District, Louisa, VA, roll M593_1660, page 364B, Family History Library Film 553159, accessed through Ancestry.com). Soon after Serena died, Stephen Johnson remarried a considerably younger woman—Peachy Scott—with whom he continued to have children until he had fathered seventeen altogether (US Bureau of the Census, 1900, Green Spring, Louisa, VA, page 7, enumeration district 0061; FHL microfilm 1241716, accessed through Ancenstry.com). These relatives remained present in the lives of Dora, Mable, and Mable's sons well into the 1940s.
12. Louisa County Courthouse, Deed Book 1, 253. According to Robin Patton, co-founder of One Shared Story, the size and price were typical for African Americans at the time.
13. Two African American families named Hughes lived in Louisa County. One was descended from the Hemings of Monticello, but we were unable to ascertain whether that was the family into which Mable was born. (Personal communication between Gloria Gilmore, co-founder of One Shared Story and authors, at Louisa County Historical Society, December 19, 2019.)
14. Louisa County Courthouse, Deed Book 23, 16–17.
15. At some other point in time, Thomas Hughes acquired an additional 4⅜ acres. We suspect he gave at least one plot of land to one of his children because at the time of his death in 1940 (some twenty years after his wife had died) he owned only two of the three plots of land he had purchased (Louisa County Courthouse, Deed Book 163, 384–85).
16. This is precisely what happened to the land originally owned by Harriet Walls, the mother of Dora's husband, Oscar Walls. She died in 1927, leaving six children and no will. All of her children had died by 1980. That year, five of her descendants (Mable and her four siblings) and their spouses jointly sold their grandmother's 8⅞ acres of land for ten dollars. (Louisa County Courthouse, Deed Book 233, 565–66).

17. US Bureau of the Census, 1880 Green Spring, Louisa, VA, roll 1376, page: 200A, enumeration district 144, accessed through Ancestry.com.
18. US Bureau of the Census, 1880, Green Spring, Louisa, VA, roll 1376, page 195C, enumeration district 144, accessed through Ancestry.com.
19. In the census, Serena's name is given as "Sererua." (US Bureau of the Census, 1910, Green Spring, Louisa, VA, roll T624_1634, page 4A, enumeration district 0077, FHL microfilm 1375647, accessed through Ancestry.com.)
20. US Bureau of the Census, 1940, Green Spring, Louisa, VA, roll: m-t0627-04274, page 5B, enumeration district 55-5, accessed through Ancestry.com.
21. Chuck Lewis and Amy Lemley, *All the Riches of Job: A True Story of Success and What Came After* (Charlottesville: Serendipity Press, 1993), 14.
22. Louis M. Kyriakoudes, "'Lookin' for Better All the Time': Rural Migration and Urbanization in the South, 1900–1950," in *African American Life in the Rural South: 1900–1950*, ed. R. Douglas Hurt (Columbia: University of Missouri Press, 2003), 10–26.
23. Under the category "Mother of How Many Children," the census in that year has separate columns for "number born" and "number now living."
24. US Bureau of the Census, 1880, Green Spring, Louisa, VA, roll 1376, page 195C, enumeration district 144; US Bureau of the Census, 1880, Green Spring, Louisa, VA, roll 1376, pages 200A, enumeration district 144; US Bureau of the Census, 1910, Green Spring, Louisa, VA, roll T624_1634, page 4A, enumeration district 0077, FHL microfilm 1375647 (all accessed through Ancestry.com). Marshall Walls and Thomas Hughes may have met during this time and introduced their children, Oscar and Dora, respectively, who were both living in Scottsville, Virginia. Walls and Hughes may have accumulated enough resources to purchase relatively large plots of land. In any case, we suspect that Stephen Johnson (with his two wives and seventeen children) had enough land to share with his children; Walls's landownership seems a bit more tenuous.
25. Tera W. Hunter, *To 'Joy My Freedom: Southern Black Women's Lives and Labors after the Civil War* (Cambridge: Harvard University Press, 1997), 25.
26. Mary Stark, interview by Sarah Lawrence, Esmont, May 24, 2002.
27. Virginia Department of Historic Resources, 2801 Kensington Avenue, Richmond, VA 23221, "054–0111 Green Springs Historic District," accessed October 15, 2019, https://www.dhr.virginia.gov/historic-registers/054-0111/.
28. According to the census, only 13 percent of African American farmers in Louisa County in 1900 were sharecroppers. US Bureau of the Census, 1900, digitally transcribed by Inter-university Consortium for Political and

Social Research, edited, verified by Michael Haines, compiled, edited, and verified by Social Explorer, *Social Explorer Dataset (SE)*, T54, Farm Ownership Status (Colored Farmers) [7] (https://www.socialexplorer.com/data/Census1900/metadata/?ds=SE&table=T054).

29. Even though some land was distributed to people who were formerly enslaved, White landowners in Louisa County maintained—and even increased—their control of the land after emancipation (Shifflett, *Patronage and Poverty*).
30. Jettie F. Gardner-Hardy, interview by Bernie Jones and Deva Woodley, Esmont, August 14, 2001.
31. William N. Rush, interview by Mieka Brand, Esmont, April 25, 2002.
32. This was Peachy's son, Charles L. Johnson (US Bureau of the Census, 1910, Green Spring, Louisa, VA, roll T624_1634, page 4A, enumeration district 0077, FHL microfilm 1375647; US Bureau of the Census, 1920, Green Spring, Louisa, VA, roll T625_1894, page 3B, enumeration district 81; US Bureau of the Census, 1930, Green Spring, Louisa, VA, page 11B, enumeration district 0003, FHL microfilm 2342183, all accessed through Ancestry.com).
33. US Bureau of the Census, 1940, Green Spring, Louisa, VA, roll m-t0627-04274, page 5B, enumeration district 55–5, accessed through Ancestry.com. Relying on the adjacent pages in the census, we learned that other people in the neighborhood reported wages of $200 as a farm laborer, $440 as the minister of the Baptist church, $720 and $450 as laborers on the railroad, and $160 and $240 as laborers at the sawmill. Another man is listed as having worked fifty-two weeks and making $0 on his own farm; one man worked as a "house ward," maybe in a private home, and worked thirty-two weeks for $150; a night watchman at a mill worked for twenty-two weeks and earned $300, and a farm laborer earned $360. By these standards, Mable's aunt and uncle seem to be doing quite well. They might also have been supporting much of their community at that time since the only additional influx of cash would have come from Mable herself, who earned $416 that year as a live-in maid in a town near Charlottesville (US Bureau of the Census, 1940, Ivy, Albemarle, VA, roll m-t0627-04242, page 12A. enumeration district 2-5, accessed through Ancestry.com).
34. Esmont.
35. US Bureau of the Census, 1870, Northern District, Louisa, VA, roll M593_1660, page 364B, FHL microfilm 553159, accessed through Ancestry.com.
36. US Bureau of the Census, 1900, Scottsville, Albemarle, VA, enumeration district 0012, FHL microfilm 1241698, accessed through Ancestry.com.
37. US Bureau of the Census, 1910, Green Spring, Louisa, VA, roll T624_1634,

page 3B, enumeration district 0077, FHL microfilm 1375647, accessed through Ancestry.com.

38. US Bureau of the Census, 1920, Green Spring, Louisa, VA, roll T625_1894, page 3B, enumeration district 81, accessed through Ancestry.com.
39. "Louisa County School Board Ledger, 19125–26," Box 1560, Louisa County Historical Society.
40. Psyche A. Williams-Forson, *Building Houses out of Chicken Legs: Black Women, Food, and Power* (Chapel Hill: University of North Carolina Press, 2006). The names of the chicken ladies include Winston, a name in Mable's extended family.
41. Dylan C. Penningroth, *The Claims of Kinfolk: African American Property and Community in the Nineteenth Century* (Chapel Hill: University of North Carolina Press, 2003), 164.
42. Williams-Forson, *Building Houses out of Chicken Legs*, 34.
43. Foner, *Reconstruction*, 85–87.
44. James Jordan, interview by Sarah Lawrence, Esmont, October 10, 2001, and October 16, 2001.
45. Steve Jakobovic, "A Handbook for Citizens of Louisa County, 1953," April 5, 2018, https://louisahistory.org/blog/f/a-handbook-for-citizens-of-louisa-county-1953.
46. Jakobovic, "A Handbook for Citizens of Louisa County, 1953."
47. Lewis and Lemley, *All the Riches of Job*, 14.
48. Sharla M. Fett, *Working Cures: Healing, Health, and Power on Southern Slave Plantations* (Chapel Hill: University of North Carolina Press, 2002), 2, 196.
49. Florence C. Bryant, *Memoirs of a Country Girl* (New York: Vantage Press, 1988), 12, 4.
50. Ruth Brooks, interview by Sarah Lawrence, Esmont, February 21, 2002; Agnes Louise Rush, interview by Mieka Brand, Esmont, May 5, 2002; Lorraine Paige, interview by Sarah Lawrence, Esmont, February 7, 2002, and February 14, 2002.
51. AFL-CIO, "Atlanta's Washerwomen Strike," https://aflcit.org/history/labor, accessed September 11, 2019. Constance Carter, "Transcript of The History of Household Technology," www.loc.gov/rr/program/journey/household-transcript.html, accessed September 11, 2019.
52. Luella Swift-Gohaner and Luella Gohaner-Lyles, interview by Lois McKenzie and Mary Gilliam, February 17, 1995, "Ridge Street Oral History," *Ridge Street Oral History Project*. Prepared by Preservation Piedmont for the Department of Community Planning, Charlottesville, VA, December 1995, http://www2.vcdh.virginia.edu/afam/raceandplace/oralhistoryridge.html (hereafter Ridge).
53. Hunter, *To 'Joy My Freedom*, 91.

54. Bryant, *Memoirs of a Country Girl*, 46.
55. William N. Rush interview; Reverend Carlton Luck, interview by Mieka Brand, Esmont, October 25, 2001, and October 16, 2001; Jordan interview.
56. Quoted in "Mt. Garland: A History of Negro Education in Louisa County," The African-American Schools of Louisa County, Virginia, Louisa County Historical Society, http://louisaheritage.org/schools/mtgarland.htm (the school was located at the conjunction of Route 33 and 15, near Gordonsville); "Koontztown Elementary School," The African-American Schools of Louisa County, Virginia, Louisa County Historical Society, http://louisaheritage.org/schools/koontztowna.html.
57. "Mt. Garland: A History of Negro Education in Louisa County."
58. Scot A. French, "1865–1926: African American Civic Activism and the Making of Jefferson High School," in *Pride Overcomes Prejudice: A History of Charlottesville's African American School*, ed. Andrea Douglas (Charlottesville: Jefferson School African American Heritage Center, 2013), 47. Darlene Clark Hine and Kathleen Thompson, *A Shining Thread of Hope: The History of Black Women in America* (New York: Broadway Books, 1999), 206.
59. "Mechanicsville," The African-American Schools of Louisa County, Virginia, Louisa County Historical Society, http://louisaheritage.org/schools/mechanicsville.htm.
60. Quoted in "Mechanicsville."
61. William N. Rush interview.
62. In Toni Morrison's *Beloved*, Sethe heads to the woods to find the Clearing, described as "a wide-open place cut deep in the woods nobody knew for what at the end of a path known only to deer and whoever cleared the land." This is taken to be "a literary depiction of a brush harbor." (Alphonso F. Saville IV, "Where Are Our Brush Harbors Today??," *Patheos*, August 1, 2017, https://www.patheos.com/blogs/rhetoricraceandreligion/2017/08/brush-harbors-today.html.)
63. Louisa County Historical Society, "Bright Hope Baptist Church" and "Oak Grove Baptist Church." In her interview, Mable mentioned the merging of the churches, which occurred long after she had left her home in Louisa County, suggesting that she had maintained ties to the community and was aware of what happened to the places important in her childhood (MJ).
64. Lewis and Lemley, *All the Riches of Job*, 14.

2. "WHILE JIM CROW RULED THE SOUTH"

1. "Charlottesville Dedicates Historical Marker Remembering Lynching," Equal Justice Initiative, July 12, 2019, https://eji.org/news/charlottesville

-dedicates-historical-marker-on-lynching. In July 2019, a historical marker was placed at the site.

2. Maurie D. McInnis, "Introduction: Dialogues on Race and Inequity at the University of Virginia," in *Charlottesville 2017: The Legacy of Race and Inequity*, ed. Louis P. Nelson and Claudrena N. Harold (Charlottesville: University of Virginia Press, 2018), 3–4.
3. See Tera W. Hunter, *To 'Joy My Freedom: Southern Black Women's Lives and Labor after the Civil War* (Cambridge: Harvard University Press, 1997), 219–22; William Sturkey, *Hattiesburg: An American City in Black and White* (Cambridge: Harvard University Press, 2019), 132–33.
4. McInnis, "Introduction," 3–6.
5. Quoted in McInnis, 7.
6. Quoted in McInnis, 5–6.
7. McInnis, 5.
8. McInnis, 5–10.
9. McInnis, 11.
10. Louis P. Nelson and Maurie D. McInnis, "Landscape of Slavery," in *Educated in Tyranny: Slavery at Thomas Jefferson's University*, ed. Maurie D. McInnis and Louis P. Nelson (Charlottesville: University of Virginia Press, 2019), 47.
11. Lisa Woolfork, "'This Class of Persons': When UVA's White Supremacist Past Meets Its Future," in *Charlottesville 2017*, 101.
12. Maurie D. McInnis, "Violence," in *Educated in Tyranny*, 97–112.
13. McInnis, "Introduction," 13.
14. McInnis, "Introduction," 13.
15. Quoted in Woolfork, "UVA's White Supremacist Past," 103.
16. Kirt von Daacke, "UVA and the History of Race: When the KKK Flourished in Charlottesville," *University News*, September 25, 2019, https://news.virginia.edu/content/uva-and-history-race-when-kkk-flourished-Charlottesville.
17. Charles E. Wynes, "The Evolution of Jim Crow Laws in Twentieth-Century Virginia," *Phylon* 28, no. 4 (1967): 416–25.
18. *From Porch Swings to Patios: An Oral History of Charlottesville's Neighborhoods*, prepared by the Department of Community Planning Advisory Board and students of the University of Virginia (Charlottesville, VA, 1982–84), 55 (hereafter *PSP*).
19. Lucille Woodfolk Jones, interview by Ashlin Smith and Kara Cox, Ridge, May 19, 1995.
20. MJ. University of Virginia, Office of the Dean of Students, Fraternity & Sorority Life, https://fsl.virginia.edu/sites/fsl.virginia.edu/files/FSL%20Facility%20Map_1.pdf.

21. McInnis, "Introduction," 18.
22. Personal communication with Gregory Jones and Theresa Jones, grandchildren of Mable Jones.
23. Richard B. Sherman, "'The Last Stand': The Fight for Racial Integrity in Virginia in the 1920s," *Journal of Southern History* 54, no. 1 (February 1988): 69–72.
24. Florence Coleman Bryant, *Rebecca Fuller McGinness: A Lifetime, 1892–2000* (Charlottesville: Van Doren Co., 2001), 22 (hereafter McG).
25. Ruth Ward and Nancy Luck, interview by Bernie Jones and Deva Woodley, Esmont, August 14, 2001; William N. Rush, interview by Mieka Brand, Esmont, April 25, 2002.
26. Jettie F. Gardner-Hardy, interview by Bernie Jones and Deva Woodley, Esmont, August 14, 2001; Ruth Brooks, interview by Sarah Lawrence, Esmont, February 21, 2002.
27. Marjorie Felice Irwin, "The Negro in Charlottesville and Albemarle County" (master's thesis, University of Virginia, 1929), 18.
28. Helen Camp de Corse, "Charlottesville: A Study of Negro Life and Personality" (master's thesis, University of Virginia, 1933), 18.
29. Irwin, "Negro in Charlottesville," 19.
30. Sanborn Company, *Insurance Maps of Charlottesville, Virginia* (New York: Sanborn Company, 1929).
31. de Corse, "Charlottesville," 10.
32. de Corse, 9–10.
33. US Bureau of the Census, 1930, Charlottesville (Independent City), VA, page 12B, enumeration district 0007, FHL microfilm 2342200, accessed through Ancestry.com.
34. de Corse, "Charlottesville," 10.
35. John Hammond Moore, *Albemarle: Jefferson's County, 1727–1976* (Charlottesville: University Press of Virginia, 1976), 427.
36. MJ.
37. Brian J. Daugherity, *Keep On Keeping On: The NAACP and the Implementation of* Brown v. Board of Education *in Virginia* (Charlottesville: University of Virginia Press, 2016), 7.
38. McG, 49–51.
39. McG, 36.
40. "History," Hampton University, http://www.hamptonu.edu/about/history.cfm.
41. Quoted in Scot A. French, "1865–1926: African American Civic Activism and the Making of Jefferson High School," in *Pride Overcomes Prejudice: A History of Charlottesville's African American School*, ed. Andrea Douglas (Charlottesville: Jefferson School African American Heritage Center, 2013), 63.

42. Virginia Writers' Project, *The Negro in Virginia* (Winston-Salem: John F. Blair, 1994), 301.
43. Florence C. Bryant, *Memoirs of a Country Girl* (New York: Vantage Press, 1988), 154.
44. For example, see *Reflector*, November 11, 1933, 4, and December 23, 1933, 3.
45. MJ; Lawrence Marshall Walls, Draft Registration Card for Virginia, 10/16/1940–03/31/1947, roll 44044_04_00150, Records of the Selective Service System, 1940–, Record Group 147, National Archives in St. Louis, MO, accessed through Ancestry.com, https://www.fold3.com/image/598127514?xid=1022&xid=1945.
46. Lawrence Marshall Walls draft registration card.
47. A school for White "Deaf, Dumb and Blind" students had opened in Staunton seventy-one years earlier.
48. US Bureau of the Census, Newport News, Newport News (Independent City), VA, page 9B, enumeration district 0014, FHL microfilm, 2342203.
49. Thomas Walls, Draft Registration Card for Virginia, 10/16/1940–03/31/1947, Records of the Selective Service System, 1940–, Record Group 147, National Archives in St. Louis, MO, accessed through Ancestry.com, https://www.ancestry.com/imageviewer/collections/2238/images/44044_04_00150-00858.
50. Henry Philip Walls, Draft Registration Card for Virginia, 10/16/1940–03/31/1947, Records of the Selective Service System, 1940–, Record Group 147, National Archives in St. Louis, MO, accessed through Ancestry.com, https://www.ancestry.com/imageviewer/collections/2238/images/44044_04_00150-00752.
51. MJ.
52. Mable refers to her mother having a "diploma" (MJ).
53. Jacqueline Jones, *Labor of Love, Labor of Sorrow: Black Women, Work, and the Family from Slavery to the Present* (New York: Basic Books, 2009), 123, 149, 153.
54. *Reflector*, in 1934, reported that "in Cville, 85% of the Negro wage-earners are engaged in domestic labor" ("Facts to Remember about Charlottesville," *Reflector*, April 7, 1934, 2).
55. MJ.
56. Sarah Patton Boyle, *The Desegregated Heart: A Virginian's Stand in Time of Transition* (New York: William Morrow, 1962), 14.
57. Boyle, 12.
58. Boyle, 44–45.
59. *PSP*, 85.
60. *PSP*, 90.

61. *PSP*, 90.
62. *PSP*, 64.
63. *PSP*, 24.
64. *PSP*, 17.
65. *PSP*, 24.
66. James Jordan, interview by Sarah Lawrence, Esmont, October 10, 2001, and October 16, 2001.
67. Tera W. Hunter, "Domination and Resistance: The Politics of Wage Household Labor in New South Atlanta," *Labor History* 34, no. 2–3 (Spring-Summer 1993): 205–20.
68. Quoted in Rebecca Sharpless, *Cooking in Other Women's Kitchens: Domestic Workers in the South, 1865–1960* (Chapel Hill: University of North Carolina Press, 2010), 82.
69. McG, 36–37.
70. McInnis, "Introduction," 2.
71. James Worsham Barksdale, "A Comparative Study of Contemporary White and Negro Standards in Health, Education, and Welfare, Charlottesville, Virginia" (master's thesis, University of Virginia, 1950), 9.
72. Nicholas Lemann, *The Promised Land: The Great Black Migration and How It Changed America* (New York: Vintage, 1992); Carole C. Marks, *"Farewell—We're Good and Gone": The Great Black Migration* (Bloomington: Indiana University Press, 1989); Isabel Wilkerson, *The Warmth of Other Suns: The Epic Story of America's Great Migration* (New York: Vintage, 2011).
73. McG, 6.
74. "Society Notes of Charlottesvillians," *Reflector*, January 27, 1934, 3; "Church Notes," *Reflector*, February 17, 1934.
75. Evelyn Brooks Higginbotham, *Righteous Discontent: The Women's Movement in the Black Baptist Church, 1880–1920* (Cambridge: Harvard University Press, 1993), 5.
76. de Corse, "Charlottesville, " 22.
77. McG, 69–70.
78. "Mount Zion First African Baptist Church," Charlottesville, Albemarle, Virginia, https://www.visitcharlottesville.org/listing/mount-zion-first-african-baptist-church/3188/. On its website, the church explains that the location, at the entrance to Ridge Street "became symbolic of the integrated nature of that most prestigious residential street." "Our History," Mt. Zion First African Baptist Church, https://www.mtzionfabc.org/our-history. In 2003, the church moved to its present location on 105 Lankford Avenue. The original church building is now the Music Resource Center Music Resource

Center. "History," Music Resource Center, https://musicresourcecenter.org/about/history/.

79. Virginia Foundation for the Humanities, "Mount Zion First African Baptist Church," http://www.aahistoricsitesva.org/items/show/286.
80. "Mt. Zion Baptist Church One of Largest in City," *Norfolk Journal and Guide*, June 24, 1933.
81. Virginia, Select Marriages, 1785–1940, accessed through Ancestry.com.
82. US Bureau of the Census, 1920, Charlottesville Ward 2, Charlottesville (Independent City), VA, roll T625_1882, page 12B, enumeration district 24, accessed through Ancestry.com. The area was razed in the 1960s to make way for the public housing project, Westhaven (https://www.cvillepedia.org/Cox%27s_Row).
83. McG, 11–12.
84. US Bureau of the Census, 1930, Charlottesville, Charlottesville (Independent City), VA, page 12B, enumeration district 0007, FHL microfilm 2342200, accessed through Ancestry.com.
85. U.S. City Directories, 1822–1993, accessed through Ancestry.com.
86. MJ. From a letter she wrote to our older sister, we know that Mable also spent several months in the hospital in the mid-1950s.
87. Esmont.
88. James Robert Saunders and Renae Nadine Shackelford, *Urban Renewal and the End of Black Culture in Charlottesville, Virginia: An Oral History of Vinegar Hill* (Jefferson, North Carolina: McFarland, 1998) (hereafter VH).
89. Barksdale, "Comparative Study," 42. Distrust of White medical care also must have impelled African American patients to leave prematurely. See Emily K. Abel, *Hearts of Wisdom: American Women Caring for Kin, 1890–1940* (Cambridge: Harvard University Press, 2000), 63; Vanessa Northington Gamble, "Under the Shadow of Tuskegee: African American Health Care," in *Tuskegee's Truths: Rethinking the Tuskegee Syphilis Study*, ed. Susan M. Reverby (Chapel Hill: University of North Carolina Press, 2000), 431.
90. Herbert G. Gutman, *The Black Family in Slavery and Freedom, 1750–1925* (New York: Random House, 1976).
91. Virginia, Select Marriages, 1785–1940, accessed through Ancestry.com.
92. Death certificates, 1906–1967, certificate number range 009601–012450, Pennsylvania Historic and Museum Commission, Harrisburg, PA, accessed through Ancestry.com.
93. US Bureau of the Census, 1850, Fluvanna, VA, roll M432_944, page 26B, image 58; Virginia Deaths, 1912–2014, Virginia Department of Health, Richmond, VA.

94. Virginia Deaths, 1912–2014, Virginia Department of Health, Richmond, VA. Thomas Walls Jr.'s obituary can be found online at *Daily Progress*, February 23, 2015, http://www.dailyprogress.com/obituaries/walls-thomas/article_99cda8a0 5b8d-5c3a-bb57-16e21bc93001.html. Information about the nickname is from a Thomas Edler (a relative), private communication, August 2020.
95. US Bureau of the Census, 1880, Green Spring, Louisa, VA, roll 1376, page 200A, enumeration district 144, accessed through Ancestry.com.

3. SURVIVING IN THE GREAT DEPRESSION AND WORLD WAR II

1. Ronald L. Heinemann, *Depression and New Deal in Virginia: The Enduring Dominion* (Charlottesville: University Press of Virginia, 1983), 82–83.
2. Patricia P. Martin and David A. Weaver, "Social Security: A Program and Policy History," *Social Security Bulletin* 66, no. 1 (2005), https://www.ssa.gov/policy/docs/ssb/v66n1/v66n1p1.html.
3. Martin and Weaver, "Social Security."
4. Rebecca Sharpless, *Cooking in Other Women's Kitchens: Domestic Workers in the South, 1865–1960* (Chapel Hill: University of North Carolina Press, 2010), 86.
5. Heinemann, *Depression and New Deal in Virginia*, 82–83.
6. Agnes Louise Rush, interview by Mieka Brand, Esmont, May 5, 2002.
7. Jacqueline Jones, *Labor of Love, Labor of Sorrow: Black Women, Work, and the Family from Slavery to the Present* (New York: Basic Books, 2009), 182–83. See also Vanessa H. May, *Unprotected Labor: Household Workers, Politics, and Middle-Class Reform in New York, 1870–1940* (Chapel Hill: University of North Carolina Press, 2011), 133–37; Phyllis Palmer, *Domesticity and Dirt: Housewives and Domestic Servants in the United States, 1920–1945* (Philadelphia: Temple University Press, 1989), 89–110.
8. "Anonymous to Mr. Theodore Roosevelt, April 25, 1941," in *Black Women in White America: A Documentary History*, ed. Gerda Lerner (New York: Random House, 1972), 404.
9. Rose Agee, interview by Mieka Brand, Esmont, September 27, 2001, and October 4, 2001.
10. Her husband might still have been alive and working in Simeon as a laborer until at least 1959 (Provo, UT, U.S., City Directories, 1822–1995, accessed through Ancestry.com). We have no way of knowing whether he contributed at all to his wife and children's well-being.

11. W. H. Brown, *The Education and Economic Development of the Negro in Virginia* (Charlottesville: University Press of Virginia, 1924), 113.
12. US Bureau of the Census, 1930, Charlottesville, Charlottesville (Independent City), VA, page 18B, enumeration district 0008, FHL microfilm 2342200, accessed through Ancestry.com.
13. US Bureau of the Census, 1940, Green Spring, Louisa, VA, roll m-t0627-04274, page 5B, enumeration district 55-5, accessed through Ancestry.com. US Bureau of the Census, 1940, Ivy, Albemarle, VA, roll m-t0627-04242, page 12A, enumeration district 2-5, accessed through Ancestry.com.
14. This was especially the case in Charlottesville, which had a large Black community. Marjorie Felice Irwin, "The Negro in Charlottesville and Albemarle County" (master's thesis, University of Virginia, 1929).
15. Elizabeth Clark-Lewis, *Living In, Living Out: African American Domestics in Washington, D.C., 1910–1940* (Washington, DC: Smithsonian Books, 1994); David M. Katzman, *Seven Days a Week: Women and Domestic Service in Industrializing America* (Urbana: University of Illinois Press, 1978); May, *Unprotected Labor.*
16. U.S., City Directories, 1822–1995, accessed through Ancestry.com.
17. U.S., City Directories, 1822–1995; James Walls, Selective Service System Registration Cards, Records of the Selective Service System, 1938–1946, Record Group 147, Box 403, National Archives, St. Louis, MO; US Bureau of the Census, 1930, Charlottesville, Charlottesville (Independent City), VA, page 12B, enumeration district 0007, FHL microfilm 2342200, accessed through Ancestry.com.
18. Heinemann, *Depression and New Deal in Virginia.*
19. Mary Anderson, "The Plight of Negro Domestic Labor," *Journal of Negro Education* 6, no. 1 (January 1936): 67.
20. Heinemann, *Depression and New Deal in Virginia*, 37.
21. Nannie H. Burroughs, "Domestic Workers Excluded," *Atlanta Daily World*, June 21, 1937.
22. This figure is calculated from the 1940 census, which lists earnings of individual workers. US Bureau of the Census, 1940, Ivy, Albemarle, VA, roll m-t0627-04242, page 12A, enumeration district 2-5, accessed through Ancestry.com.
23. The other members of this household included C. Armonde Paxson's wife, Elizabeth; her son by her first marriage (Lindsey B. Mount, born in 1925, later mayor of Charlottesville); and their daughter, Eliza (born in 1937). "Paxson Eighth Generation," accessed April 29, 2019, https://sites.rootsweb.com/~paxson/Paxson8Gen.html.

24. Susan Tucker, *Telling Memories among Southern Women: Domestic Workers and Their Employers in the Segregated South* (Baton Rouge: Louisiana State University Press, 1988), 27.
25. *Reflector*, December 16, 1933, and January 6, 1934, "Race & Place: Newspapers," Virginia Center for Digital History, The Carter G. Woodson Institute, University of Virginia.
26. US Bureau of the Census, 1930, Charlottesville, Charlottesville (Independent City), VA, pages 15B, enumeration district 0008, FHL microfilm 2342200; US Bureau of the Census, 1940, Green Spring, Louisa, VA, roll m-t0627-04274, page 6A, enumeration district 55-5, accessed through Ancestry.com.
27. Jillian Jimenez, "The History of Grandmothers in the African-American Community," *Social Service Review* 76, no. 4 (December 2002): 523–51.
28. Chuck Lewis and Amy Lemley, *All the Riches of Job: A True Story of Success and What Came After* (Charlottesville: Serendipity Press, 1993), 9.
29. Katherine van Wormer, David W. Jackson III, and Charletta Sudduth, eds., *The Maid Narratives: Black Domestics and White Families in the Jim Crow South* (Baton Rouge: Louisiana State University Press, 2012), 109–10.
30. Lewis and Lemley, *All the Riches of Job*, 14.
31. Lewis and Lemley, 9–10.
32. Lewis and Lemley, 19.
33. We have no information about what happened to James after he and Mable separated in 1944. His grandchildren remember meeting him only once. Whatever his life had been before he was drafted in World War II, it might have been even more difficult after the war when Black soldiers faced both violence and continued segregation at home. Alexis Clark, "Returning from War, Returning to Racism," *New York Times*, July 30, 2020, https://www.nytimes.com/2020/07/30/magazine/black-soldiers-wwii-racism.html.
34. Jones, *Labor of Love*, 185.
35. US Bureau of the Census, 1940, Green Spring, Louisa, VA, roll m-t0627-04274, page 6A; enumeration district 55-5, accessed through Ancestry.com.
36. Heinemann, *Depression and New Deal in Virginia*, 38.
37. Elliot Carter, "Washington during Wartime," Architect of the Capital, August 11, 2016, https://architectofthecapital.org/posts/2016/7/30/washington-at-war.
38. Robert D. Manning, "Multicultural Washington, DC: The Changing Social and Economic Landscape of a Post-Industrial Metropolis," *Ethnic and Racial Studies* 21, no. 2 (January 1998): 334, https://doi.org/10.1080/014198798330043.

39. Clark-Lewis, *Living In, Living Out*, 70–71.
40. John Darnton, *Almost a Family* (New York: Anchor, 2011), 60.
41. *PSP*, 56.
42. Manning, "Multicultural Washington, DC," 335.
43. James Borchert, *Alley Life in Washington: Family, Community, Religion, and Folklife in the City, 1850–1970* (Urbana: University of Illinois Press, 1980), quotations on xi–xii.
44. William H. Chafe, "History Resources: 1945 to the Present," Gilder Lehrman Institute of American History, https://www.gilderlehrman.org/history-resources/essays/1945-present.
45. Elaine Tyler May, *Homeward Bound: American Families in the Cold War Era* (New York: Perseus Group, 2008), 59.
46. "It's an Employe's [*sic*] Market Today with Quality Down and Wages Up You Have Maid Trouble," *Washington Post*, August 1943.
47. Darnton, *Almost a Family*, 60.
48. Premilla Nadasen, *Household Workers Unite: The Untold Story of African American Women Who Built a Movement* (Boston: Beacon, 2015), 109.
49. George Q. Flynn, "Selective Service and American Blacks during World War II," *The Journal of Negro History* 69, no. 1 (January 1984): 14–25, https://doi.org/10.2307/2717656.
50. "Pay of the WW2 Enlisted Man," Hardscrabble Farm, http://www.hardscrabblefarm.com/ww2/payscale.htm.
51. U.S., World War II Army Enlistment Records, 1938–1946, accessed through Ancestry.com.

4. "THE SOCIAL PARADOX IN THE NORTH"

1. Becky Nicolaides and Andrew Wiese, "Suburbanization in the United States after 1945," *Oxford Research Encyclopedia of American History*, April 2017, https://oxfordre.com/americanhistory.
2. Sandra L. Colby and Jennifer M. Ortman, *The Baby Boom Cohort in the United States, 2012 to 2060: Population Estimates and Projections* (Washington, DC: United States Census Bureau, May 2014), 2.
3. Elaine Tyler May, *Homeward Bound: American Families in the Cold War Era* (New York: Perseus Group, 2008).
4. "Larchmont Temple History," Larchmont Temple, https://www.larchmonttemple.org/larchmont-temple-history.
5. Virginia Divorce Records, 1918–2014, Virginia Department of Health, Richmond, VA, roll 101296631, accessed through Ancestry.com.

6. Charles Jones (grandson of Mable Jones), in conversation with authors, along with Theresa Williams, and Walter Jones, Charlottesville, VA, July 3, 2019.
7. Jordy Yager, "Searching for Solutions: Why Are Black Kids Arrested More Often than White Kids?" www.c-ville.com/searching-solutions-black-kids-arrested-often-white-kids/.
8. Richard Rothstein, *The Color of Law: A Forgotten History of How Our Government Segregated America* (New York: W. W. Norton, 2017).
9. Tract 46, page 64, Sanborn Map Company, *Insurance Maps of Charlottesville, Virginia, 1929* (New York: Sanborn Map Company, 1929), Special Collections, University of Virginia Library, Charlottesville, VA. This extension is an unnamed alley on contemporary maps. See Google Maps https://www.google.com/maps/place/Oakmont+St,+Charlottesville,+VA+22902/@38.0276491,-78.4851774,20.25z/data=!4m5!3m4!1s0x89b386233f7dc61f:0x16943e08f253535c!8m2!3d38.0272509!4d-78.48539820.
10. Nicholas Lemann, *The Promised Land: The Great Black Migration and How It Changed America* (New York: Vintage Books, 1992); Isabel Wilkerson, *The Warmth of Other Suns: The Epic Story of America's Great Migration* (New York: Vintage, 2011); Carole Marks, *"Farewell—We're Good and Gone": The Great Black Migration* (Bloomington: Indiana University Press, 1989).
11. GMI.
12. Alberta Wren, interview by Ebony Williams, GMI, December 9, 2001; Eva Lillian Goode Jones, interview by L. McGahran, GMI, December 4, 2001; Calvin O'Neal, interview by Jamie Mariconda, GMI, September 30, 2001.
13. Eva Lillian Goode Jones interview.
14. *Charlottesville-Albemarle Tribune*, September 22, 1950. On that trip, Dora also visited with a sister, Anna Hughes Watson, who was living in Lakewood, NJ.
15. Frank E. Sanchis III, "The Suburban Home," in *Westchester: The American Suburb*, ed. Roger Panetta (New York: Fordham University Press, 2006), 234.
16. Virginia Writers' Project, *The Negro in Virginia* (Winston-Salem: John F. Blair, 1994), 266.
17. William H. Chafe, Raymond Gavins, and Robert Korstad, eds., *Remembering Jim Crow: African Americans Tell about Life in the Segregated South* (New York: New Press, 2001), xxx, xxxii, 1.
18. Wilkerson, *Warmth of Other Suns*, 391.
19. Essie Mae Washington-Williams, *Dear Senator* (New York: HarperCollins), 25–26, Kindle.
20. *PSP*, 56.

21. Theodore Kornweibel, Professor of African American History at San Diego State University, personal correspondence with authors, December 3, 2018.
22. MJ.
23. "Penn. R.R. Says JC Is 'Convenient,'" *New York Amsterdam News*, August 3, 1947.
24. Quoted in Theodore Kornweibel Jr., *Railroads in the African American Experience: A Photographic Journey* (Baltimore: Johns Hopkins University Press, 2010), 256; see "Jim Crow Riding from NY to Southland Is Outlawed," *New York Amsterdam News*, October 22, 1949.
25. GMI.
26. National Museum of African American History and Culture, "This Segregated Railway Car Offers a Visceral Reminder of the Jim Crow Era," https://www.smithsonianmag.com/smithsonian-institution/, accessed February 20, 2019.
27. Quoted in Thomas J. Sugrue, *Sweet Land of Liberty: The Forgotten Struggle for Civil Rights in the North* (New York: Random House, 2008), xiv.
28. Sherrill D. Wilson, "African Burial Ground," in *Slavery in New York*, ed. Ira Berlin and Leslie M. Harris (New York: New Press, 2005), 7.
29. Ira Berlin and Leslie M. Harris, "Introduction: Uncovering, Discovering, and Recovering," in *Slavery in New York*, 4.
30. Berlin and Harris, "Introduction."
31. See Eric Foner, "Eric Foner's Report: Columbia University and Slavery." https://columbiaandslavery.columbia.edu/content/eric-foners-report.
32. Foner, "Columbia University and Slavery."
33. Marcy S. Sacks, "Re-Creating Black New York at Century's End," in *Slavery in New York*, 329–30.
34. Jacqueline Jones, *Labor of Love, Labor of Sorrow: Black Women, Work, and the Family from Slavery to the Present* (New York: Basic Books, 2009), 171–72.
35. Ella Baker and Marvel Cooke, "The Slave Market," *The Crisis*, 42 (November 1935), https://caringlabor.wordpress.com/2010/11/24/.
36. Bonnie Thornton Dill, *Across the Boundaries of Race and Class: An Exploration of Work and Family among Black Female Domestic Servants* (New York: Garland Publishing, Inc., 1994), 101.
37. Dill, 101–2.
38. "Slavery Laid to Jerseyites," *New York Amsterdam News*, June 15, 1935.
39. Eileen Boris, Hull Professor in the Department of Feminist Studies, University of California, Santa Barbara, letter to Nadine Zimmerli, April 2, 2020.
40. Roger Panetta, "Westchester, The American Suburb: A New Narrative," in *Westchester*, 3–76.

41. Quoted in Kenneth T. Jackson, *Crabgrass Frontier: The Suburbanization of the United States* (New York: Oxford University Press, 1985), 94–95.
42. Kate Stone Lombardi, "County's Rails Tell of Past and Future," *New York Times*, December 22, 1996.
43. Jackson, *Crabgrass Frontier*, 95.
44. As they increasingly locate, analyze, and digitize new kinds of records, local historians report that, like the city with which it has always been closely linked, Westchester once included a sizeable enslaved population. Moreover, many of the financiers and businessmen who settled in Westchester became wealthy from the New York City slave trade (Berlin and Harris, *Slavery in New York*, 3–27).
45. Earl Lewis and Heidi Ardizzone, *Love on Trial: As American Scandal in Black and White* (New York: W. W. Norton, 2001).
46. Eva Lillian Goode Jones interview.
47. Addie Fields, interview by Michael Murray, GMI, November 15, 2001.
48. Rothstein, *Color of Law*, 80. Exceptions typically were made for live-in servants; Martha Biondi, *To Stand and Fight: The Struggle for Civil Rights in Postwar New York City* (Cambridge: Harvard University Press, 2003), 114.
49. Jeanne Theoharis, "What King Said about Northern Liberalism," *New York Times*, January 20, 2019.
50. GMI.
51. Quoted in Wilkerson, *Warmth of Other Suns*, 341.
52. Henrietta Mills, interview by Marion Forstall, 1980, "Voices and Profiles of New Rochelle's Rich, Color-Full History," Marion Forstall Oral History Project, New Rochelle Library, New Rochelle, NY.
53. Quoted in Andrew Wiese, *Places of Their Own: African American Suburbanization in the Twentieth Century* (Chicago: University of Chicago Press, 2004), 57.
54. Wiese, 57.
55. Sugrue, *Sweet Land of Liberty*, 190–91.
56. Pauline Billups Flippin, interview by Doris Rollins and Catherine Moore, October 23, 1987, "New Rochelle Tricentennial Oral History Collection," New Rochelle Public Library, New Rochelle, NY.
57. Elaine Pagels, *Why Religion? A Personal Story* (New York: HarperCollins, 2018), 148.
58. "Adelaide Hall's Neighbors Irate," *New York Amsterdam News*, August 24, 1932.
59. "Court Battle Won by Adelaide Hall," *New York Amsterdam News*, February 8, 1933.
60. "Adelaide Louise Hall's Rich Harlem History, 1901–1993 (Audio

Video)," Harlem World Magazine, February 4, 2018, https://www.harlemworldmagazine.com/adelaide-louise-halls-rich-harlem-history-1901-1993-audio-video/; "Why Can't the Stars Live Where They Please?," *Afro-American*, 3 August 1935.

61. See Biondi, *To Stand and Fight*, 82–83, 86; Susan Tucker, *Telling Memories among Southern Women: Domestic Workers and Their Employers in the Segregated South* (Baton Rouge: Louisiana State University Press, 1988), 235–36.

5. "WOULD YOU COME UP FOR SIX MONTHS OR A YEAR?"

1. MJ.
2. Judith Rollins, *Between Women: Domestics and Their Employers* (Philadelphia: Temple University Press, 1985), 94.
3. Sherry B. Ortner, *New Jersey Dreaming: Capital, Culture, and the Class of '58* (Durham: Duke University Press, 2003), 60–62.
4. Vanessa H. May, *Unprotected Labor: Household Workers, Politics, and Middle-Class Reform in New York, 1870–1940* (Chapel Hill: University of North Carolina Press, 2011), 107.
5. Charlottesville, VA, U.S., City Directories, 1822–1995, accessed through Ancestry.com.
6. The *Charlottesville-Albemarle Tribune* recorded one visit Mable's mother Dora took to New York to visit Mable on September 22, 1950, and a trip home Mable took (along with her son, James, who was a private in the army) on May 5, 1951. The *Norfolk Journal and Guide* noted that Mable visited her mother on October 24, 1953. We do not know if there were other visits during the years Mable worked for us.
7. Premilla Nadasen, *Household Workers Unite: The Untold Story of African American Women Who Built a Movement* (Boston: Beacon, 2015), 66; David M. Katzman, *Seven Days a Week: Women and Domestic Service in Industrializing America* (Urbana: University of Illinois Press, 1978), 132–33.
8. May, *Unprotected Labor*, 44–45.
9. Rollins, *Between Women*; Bonnie Thornton Dill, *Across the Boundaries of Race and Class: An Exploration of Work and Family among Black Female Domestic Servants* (New York: Garland Publishing, Inc., 1994).
10. "400,000 White Maids Quit, Colored Increased 50,000," *Afro-American*, March 3, 1945.

11. Jacqueline Jones, *Labor of Love, Labor of Sorrow: Black Women, Work, and the Family from Slavery to the Present* (New York: Basic Books, 2009), 210.
12. Dill, *Across the Boundaries*, 15.
13. Heywood Broun, "Domestics Must Form Own Organization, Says Broun," *Afro-American*, June 15, 1935.
14. "Low Pay, Neurotic Employers Merely Two of Many Problems," *Afro-American*, February 8, 1941.
15. US Bureau of the Census, 1940, Larchmont Village, enumeration district ED 60–107 to 60–111, accessed through Ancestry.com, https://www.ancestry.com/interactive/2442/m-t0627-02805-00381?backurl=&ssrc=&backlabel=Return#?imageId=m-t0627-02805-00382.
16. We also recorded information about every household (rather than one in ten) for the most fashionable section of town, known as "the Manor." Here both the number of households with paid domestic workers (61 percent as opposed to 25 percent in Larchmont as a whole) and the number of servants per household (1.5 percent compared to 1.3 percent in the town as a whole) were higher (US Bureau of the Census, 1940, Larchmont Village, enumeration district ED 60–107 to 60–111, accessed through Ancestry.com, https://www.ancestry.com/interactive/2442/m-t0627-02805-00381?backurl=&ssrc=&backlabel=Return#?imageId=m-t0627-02805-00382).
17. Jamie Bernstein, *Famous Father: A Memoir of Growing Up Bernstein* (New York: Harper, 2018); John Darnton, *Almost a Family* (New York: Anchor, 2011); Laura Furman, *Ordinary Paradise* (Houston: Winedale, 1998); Dorien Grunbaum, "Clara," unpublished paper, in possession of the authors; Adam Hochschild, *Half the Way Home: A Memoir of Father and Son* (New York: Viking, 1986); Marie Killilea, *With Love from Karen* (New York: Dell Publishing, 1963); Arthur Kleinman, *The Soul of Care: The Moral Education of a Husband and a Doctor* (New York: Viking, 2019); Richard Lempert, "A Personal Odyssey Toward a Theme: Race and Equality in the United States, 1948–2009," *Law and Society Review* 44, no. 3–4 (2010): 431–62; Reeve Lindbergh, *Under a Wing: A Memoir* (New York: Simon and Schuster, 1998); Christopher Lukas, *Blue Genes* (New York: Doubleday, 2008); Jay Neugeboren, *Imagining Robert: My Brother, Madness, and Survival; A Memoir* (New York: William Morrow, 1997); Allen Shawn, *Wish I Could Be There: Notes from a Phobic Life* (New York: Penguin Books, 2007), Carly Simon, *Boys in the Trees* (Los Angeles: Warner Bros. Publications, 1978); Sarah Payne Stuart, *My First Cousin Once Removed: Money, Madness, and the Family of Robert Lowell* (New York: Harper Collins, 1998); Elaine M. Strauss, *In My Heart I'm Still Dancing* (New Rochelle, NY: Elaine M. Strauss, 1979); Alexandra Styron, *Reading My Father* (New York: Scribner, 2011); Cathy

Wilkerson, *Flying Close to the Sun: My Life as a Weatherman* (New York: Seven Stories Press, 2010).

18. *Martha and Ethel* (1994), directed by Jyll Johnstone, written by Alysha Cohen, Barbara Ettinger, Christine Houlihan, Jyll Johnstone, Frank Ortega, Sharon Wood.
19. Lempert, "Personal Odyssey," 433.
20. Wilkerson, *Flying Close to the Sun*, 14–15.
21. Kleinman, *Soul of Care*, 18.
22. Lempert, "Personal Odyssey," 453.
23. Hochschild, *Half the Way Home*, 79.
24. Grunbaum, "Clara," 1.
25. Michael Adelson, interview by Margaret K. Nelson, July 10, 2019.
26. Adelson interview.
27. Wilkerson, *Flying Close to the Sun*, 14.
28. Kleinman, *Soul of Care*, 18.
29. Furman, *Ordinary Paradise*, 74.
30. Lukas, *Blue Genes*, 61.
31. Lindbergh, *Under a Wing*, 4.
32. Susan Tucker, *Telling Memories among Southern Women: Domestic Workers and Their Employers in the Segregated South* (Baton Rouge: Louisiana State University, 1988), 107.
33. Mario L. Barnes, "Racial Paradox in a Law and Society Odyssey," *Law and Society Review* 44, no. 3–4 (2010): 476–77.
34. Lukas, *Blue Genes*, 60–61.
35. Killilea, *With Love*, 70.
36. Killilea, 84.
37. Killilea, 266.
38. *Martha and Ethel.*
39. Rose Lambert, interview with Emily K. Abel, September 2, 2019.
40. Styron, *Reading My Father*, 21.
41. Darnton, *Almost a Family*, 80–81.
42. John Rosenthal, interview by authors, June 10, 2019.
43. Lambert interview.
44. Furman, *Ordinary Paradise*, 74.
45. *Martha and Ethel.*
46. Lambert interview.
47. Stuart, *My First Cousin*, 134–36.
48. Hochschild, *Half the Way Home*, 201.
49. Hochschild, 79.
50. Hochschild, 61, 140.

51. Dill, *Across the Boundaries*, 90.
52. Naomi Rogers, *Dirt and Disease: Polio before FDR* (New Brunswick: Rutgers University Press, 1992), 49–50.
53. Charles V. Craster, "Medical Examination of Domestic Servants," *American Journal of Public Health* 23, no. 1 (May 1, 1933): 436.
54. *New York Amsterdam News*, June 26, 1937.
55. Quoted in Vanessa May, *Unprotected Labor*, 167–68.
56. *New York Amsterdam News*, June 26, 1937.
57. Vivian Morris and Dora Jones, *Domestic Workers' Union*, New York City, NY, February 7, 1939, Library of Congress, https://www.loc.gov/item/wpalh001484/.
58. Marvel Cooke, "Help Wanted for the Help: Sorry Plight of Domestics Sore Problem," *New York Amsterdam News*, October 7, 1939.
59. "Worthy of Their Hire," *New York Amsterdam News*, November 14, 1939.
60. M. S. Stuart, "Southern Say-So: Field of Domestic Service Deserves a Greater Measure of Respect," *Pittsburgh Courier*, April 10, 1943.
61. The following citations refer to the edition of the collected stories: Alice Childress, *Like One of the Family: Conversations from a Domestic's Life* (Boston: Beacon, 1986).
62. Childress, 2.
63. Childress, 129–32.
64. Childress, 3.
65. Childress, 43.
66. Nadasen, *Household Workers Unite*.
67. Dill, *Across the Boundaries*.
68. Dill, 87.
69. Dill, 83–84.
70. Dill, 91.
71. Dill, 91–92.
72. Dill, 97.
73. Dill, 91.
74. Michael Botwinick, "Introduction," in *Westchester: The American Suburb*, ed. Roger Panetta (New York: Fordham University Press, 2006), 1.
75. Tucker, *Telling Memories*, 145–51; Mary Romero, *Maid in the U.S.A.* (New York: Routledge, 1992).
76. U.S., World War II Army Enlistment Records, 1938–1946, accessed through Ancestry.com.
77. Virginia Divorce Records, 1918–2014, Richmond, VA, Virginia Department of Health, roll 101296631, accessed through Ancestry.com.
78. Our parents probably also helped her sign up for Social Security. Her Social

Security card was issued in New York in 1951. (US, Social Security Death Index, 1935–2014, NY, issue date 1951, accessed through Ancestry.com.)

79. Kellie Carter Jackson, "'She Was a Member of the Family': Ethel Phillips, Domestic Labor, and Employer Perceptions," *Women's Studies Quarterly* 45, no. 3–4 (2017): 165, https://doi.org/10.1353/wsq.2017.0053.
80. Tucker, *Telling Memories*, 121.

6. "WE MARCHED FROM DOWNTOWN . . . UP UNTIL MT. ZION CHURCH"

1. "Discrimination at the University Hospital," *Charlottesville-Albemarle Tribune*, May 21, 1951.
2. "Bryan McKenzie, Civil Rights Leaders Reflect on Charlottesville Segregation 50 years after King speech," *Daily Progress*, August 24, 2013.
3. *Charlottesville-Albemarle Tribune*, September 22, 1951.
4. "Gregory Swanson, First African American Admitted to the University of Virginia, *Encyclopedia Virginia*, https://www.encyclopediavirginia.org/media_player?mets_filename=evm00001276mets.xml.
5. Eudora D. Lias, "Gregory Swanson Heard in Charlottesville," *Norfolk Journal and Guide*, November 4, 1950.
6. James Worsham Barksdale, "A Comparative Study of Contemporary White and Negro Standards in Health, Education, and Welfare, Charlottesville, Virginia" (master's thesis, University of Virginia, 1950), 56–57.
7. Florence C. Bryant, *Memoirs of a Country Girl* (New York: Vantage Press, 1988), 142.
8. Brian J. Daugherity, *Keep On Keeping On: The NAACP and the Implementation of* Brown v. Board of Education *in Virginia* (Charlottesville: University of Virginia Press, 2016).
9. Quoted in VH, 49.
10. Dallas Randall Crowe, "Desegregation of Charlottesville, Virginia Public Schools, 1964–1969: A Case Study" (PhD diss., University of Virginia, 1971), 60–62.
11. Sarah Patton Boyle, *The Desegregated Heart: A Virginian's Stand in Time of Transition* (New York: William Morrow, 1962), 253.
12. Quoted in VH, 59.
13. Quoted in VH, 59.
14. Andrew B. Lewis, "Emergency Mothers: Basement Schools and the Preservation of Public Education in Charlottesville," in *The Moderates' Dilemma: Massive Resistance to School Desegregation in Virginia*, ed. Matthew D.

Lassiter and Andrew B. Lewis (Charlottesville: University Press of Virginia, 1998), 110.

15. Daugherity, *Keeping On Keeping On*, 87, 113; Lewis, "Emergency Mothers."
16. Lewis, "Emergency Mothers," 95.
17. Boyle, *Desegregated Heart*, 287.
18. Paul M. Gaston, "Public School Desegregation: Charlottesville, Virginia," in *Pride Overcomes Prejudice: A History of Charlottesville's African American School*, ed. Andrea Douglas (Charlottesville: Jefferson School African American Heritage Center, 2013), 100.
19. Daugherity, *Keep On Keeping On*, 101.
20. "Charlottesville Twelve," https://www.cvillepedia.org/Charlottesville_Twelve, accessed September 28, 2019.
21. Bryant, *Memoirs of a Country Girl*, 144.
22. Paul M. Gaston and Thomas T. Hammond, *Public School Desegregation: Charlottesville, Virginia, 1955–62* (Charlottesville: University Press of Virginia, 1962), 7 (A report presented to the Nashville Conference on "The South: The Ethical Demands of Integration," a consultation sponsored by the Southern Regional Council and the Fellowship of Southern Churchmen. December 28, 1962).
23. "*Rising Up* Biographies," Virginia Center for Digital Humanities, www2.vcdh.virginia.edu/risingup/bios.html.
24. Ridge.
25. Ridge.
26. Ridge.
27. Quoted in Louis Nelson, "An Oral History of Starr Hill," Center for Christian Study, https://www.studycenter.net/lectures/oral-history-starr-hill.
28. Gaston, "Public School Desegregation," 100.
29. Ridge.
30. Anna Holden, *The Bus Stops Here: A Study of School Desegregation in Three Cities* (New York: Agathon Press, 1974), 55–61.
31. Gaston and Hammond, *Public School Desegregation*, 10. In 1980, enrollment in the city's private schools stood at 5.7 percent. In the subsequent decades, an increasing proportion of Charlottesville K–12 students enrolled in private schools: 8.5 percent in 2000 and 12 percent in 2017. Private school enrollment in 2017 was especially high among K–8 students at 16 percent (for 1980 and 2000, see US Bureau of the Census, 2000, Table P36, "Sex by School Enrollment by Level of School by School Type for the Population over 3 Years"; for 2017, see "Charlottesville Virginia Education Data," TownCharts, https://www.towncharts.com/Virginia/Education/Charlottesville-city-VA-Education-data.html).
32. Daugherity, *Keep On Keeping On*, 101.

33. Bryant, *Memoirs of a Country Girl*, 147.
34. Bryant, 90.
35. Bryant, 91.
36. J. Douglas Smith, *Managing White Supremacy: Race, Politics, and Citizenship in Jim Crow Virginia* (Chapel Hill: University of North Carolina Press, 2002).
37. Kristen Green, *Something Must Be Done about Prince Edward County: A Family, a Virginia Town, a Civil Rights Battle* (New York: HarperCollins, 2015), 137.
38. Darlene Clark Hine, "Rape and the Inner Lives of Black Women in the Middle West: Preliminary Thoughts on the Culture of Dissemblance," *Signs* 14, no. 41 (1981): 916.
39. Quoted in VH, 44.
40. Paul M. Gaston, *Coming of Age in Utopia: The Odyssey of an Idea* (Montgomery: NewSouth Books, 2010), 208–44.
41. Gaston, 215–16.
42. Gaston, 223.
43. Reverend Alvin Edwards, interview by Emily K. Abel and Margaret K. Nelson, July 2, 2019, Mt. Zion African Baptist Church.
44. "It Is Now the Law," *Daily Progress*, July 3, 1964, 4, https://search.lib.virginia.edu/catalog/uva-lib:2676979/view#openLayer/uva-lib:2676983/3611/2553.5/0/1/0.
45. "Restaurant Closed in Protest," *Daily Progress*, July 3, 1964, 1, https://search.lib.virginia.edu/catalog/uva-lib:2676979/view#openLayer/uva-lib:2676983/3611/2553.5/0/1/0.
46. Quoted in VH, 47.
47. Andrew Small, "The Wastelands of Urban Renewal," CityLab, February 17, 2017, https://www.bloomberg.com/news/articles/2017-02-13/how-the-bulldozer-became-an-urban-block-buster.
48. Richard Rothstein, *The Color of Law: A Forgotten History of How Our Government Segregated America* (New York: W. W. Norton, 2017), 127.
49. Quoted in VH, 21.
50. Agnes Louise Rush, interview by Mieka Brand, Esmont, May 5, 2002.
51. Quoted in VH, 23–24.
52. Quoted in VH, 25.
53. Quoted in VH, 29.
54. Quoted in VH, 29.
55. Quoted in VH, 31.
56. Robin D. G. Kelley, "'We Are Not What We Seem': Rethinking Black

Working-Class Opposition in the Jim Crow South," *Journal of American History* 80, no. 1 (June 1993): 79.

57. Carlton Andrew Luck Sr., interview by Mieke Brand, Esmont, October 25, 2001, and November 1, 2001.
58. Luella Swift-Gohaner and Luella Gohaner-Lyles, interview by Lois McKenzie and Mary Gilliam, Ridge, February 17, 1995.
59. Quoted in VH, 31.
60. Quoted in VH, 40.
61. US Bureau of the Census, 1940, Ivy, Albemarle, VA, roll m-t0627-04242, page 12A; enumeration district 2-5, accessed through Ancestry.com.
62. Quoted in VH, 67.
63. Rothstein, *Color of Law*.
64. Wyatt Massey, "Photographer Documents Historic Neighborhood Destroyed by Racism," *Frederick News Post*, February 26, 2019.
65. VH, 81.
66. Quoted in VH, 78–79.
67. Quoted in VH, 78.
68. McG, 23.
69. Quoted in VH, 19.
70. Joan Woodfolk and Theresa Woodfolk, interview by Lois McKenzie and Kay Peaslee, Ridge, February 24, 1995.
71. "That World Is Gone: Race and Displacement in a Southern Town," Field Studio, www.fieldstudiofilms.com/that-world-is-gone.
72. Mindy Thompson Fullilove, *Root Shock: How Tearing Up City Neighborhoods Hurts America, and What Can We Do About It* (New York: New Village Press, 2016), 11–12.
73. Carolyn Ferlic, Conner Gentil, Adam Matthews, Alison Tramba, and Brooke Yamakoshi, "Westhaven and the Charlottesville Redevelopment and Housing Authority: Community Design and Engineering in Public Housing," paper prepared for the Charlottesville Redevelopment and Housing Authority and the University of Virginia Double Hoo Community-Based Research grant program, 2007, https://citeseerx.ist.psu.edu/viewdoc/download?doi=10.1.1.623.5963&rep=rep1&type=pdf.
74. MJ.
75. Elizabeth F. Dawson, interview recorded in *Ridge Street Oral History Project: A Supplement to the Survey of the Ridge Street Historic District and Proposal for Local Designation*. Prepared by Preservation Piedmont for the Department of Community Planning, Charlottesville, VA, December 1995 (hereafter Ridge Street Project), 55.

76. MJ.
77. "Ridge Street Historic District," Living Places, https://www.livingplaces.com/VA/Independent_Cities/Charlottesville_City/Ridge_Street_Historic_District.html.
78. John Frederick Harlan Jr., Ridge Street Project, 10.
79. Eugene Williams and Lorraine Williams, Ridge Street Project, 77.
80. Swift-Gohaner and Gohaner-Lyles interview.
81. "City Seeks to Re-Zone Ridge Street," *Charlottesville-Albemarle Tribune,* November 1, 1957.
82. Woodfolk and Woodfolk interview.
83. Ridge Street Project, 2–3.
84. Woodfolk and Woodfolk interview.

7. "NOBODY LEFT BUT MABLE"

1. Eudora D. Lias, "Charlottesville Baptists Attend General Meeting," *Norfolk Journal and Guide*, July 8, 1950.
2. "Mount Zion First African Baptist Church," AfroVirginia: Virginia Humanities, http://places.afrovirginia.org/items/show/286.
3. Blanche L. Garland, "Charlottesville," *Norfolk Journal and Guide*, December 22, 1956.
4. Blanche L. Garland, "Charlottesville," *Norfolk Journal and Guide*, July 13, 1957; Blanche L. Garland, "Charlottesville, *Norfolk Journal and Guide*, January 18, 1958.
5. P. Uhlenberg and J. B. Kirby, "Grandparenthood Over Time: Historical and Demographic Trend," in *Handbook on Grandparenthood*, ed. Maximiliane E. Szinovacz (Westport, CT: Greenwood Press, 1998), 45.
6. Enobong Hannah Branch and Caroline Hanley, "Interrogating Claims of Progress for Black Women Since 1970," *Journal of Black Studies* 44, no. 2 (2013): 203–26.
7. Bob Gibson, "Sam Jessup: Beyond the Success of His Pepsi Bottling Business, He Served on City Council for Eight Years," *Daily Progress*, May 3, 2017, https://dailyprogress.com/business/sam-jessup-beyond-the-success-of-his-pepsi-bottling-business-he-served-on-city-council/article_22898d54-3004-11e7-9a5c-cb888f533a57.html.
8. "Farmington Neighborhood Guide," Nest Realty, https://www.nestrealty.com/charlottesville/neighborhood-guides/farmington.
9. "Farmington Neighborhood Guide."
10. "Chronology," *Charlottesville 2017: The Legacy of Race and Inequity*, ed.

Louis P. Nelson and Claudrena N. Harold (Charlottesville: University of Virginia Press, 2018), xiii.

11. "Jeffersonian Dilemma," *Time*, February 9, 1976, 50.
12. MJ.
13. Claudia Jessup, letter to authors, July 2, 2020.
14. Jessup letter.
15. Jessup letter.
16. Ridge Street Project, 49.
17. *News Leader*, June 23, 1951, 2.
18. Morris J. MacGregor Jr., *Integration of the Armed Forces, 1940–1965* (Washington, DC: Center of Military History, United States Army, 1981).
19. Quoted in Jordy Yager, "Searching for Solutions: Why Are Black Kids Arrested More Often than White Kids?," *C-Ville Weekly*, June 15, 2016, https://www.c-ville.com/searching-solutions-black-kids-arrested-often-white-kids/.
20. James Worsham Barksdale, "A Comparative Study of Contemporary White and Negro Standards in Health, Education, and Welfare, Charlottesville, Virginia" (master's thesis, University of Virginia, 1950), 111–119.
21. On the low upward mobility of Black men throughout the twentieth century, see William J. Collins and Marianne H. Wanamaker, "Up from Slavery? African American Intergenerational Economic Mobility since 1880," National Bureau of Economic Research Working Paper (2017), www.nber.org/papers/w23395.
22. MJ; Charlottesville, VA, 1950, 1956, 1958, U.S., City Directories, 1822–1995, accessed through Ancestry.com.
23. "Obituary: Thomas Walls," *Daily Progress*, February 23, 2015 (https://www.dailyprogress.com/obituaries/walls-thomas/article_99cda8a0-5b8d-5c3a-bb57-16e21bc93001.html).
24. Virginia Department of Health; Richmond, Virginia; Virginia Marriages, 1936–2014; Roll: 101168227; Virginia Department of Health; Richmond, Virginia; Virginia Divorce Records, 1918–2014; Roll: 101176401. Ancestry.com.
25. Virginia Department of Health; Richmond, Virginia; Virginia Deaths, 1912–2014; Virginia Department of Health; Richmond, Virginia; Virginia Divorce Records, 1918–2014; Roll: 101176401; Virginia Department of Health; Richmond, Virginia; Virginia Marriages, 1936–2014; Roll: 101142196. Ancestry.com.
26. Virginia Department of Health; Richmond, Virginia; Virginia Marriages, 1936–2014; Roll: 101169167; Virginia Department of Health; Richmond, Virginia; Virginia Divorce Records, 1918–2014; Roll: 101176446. Ancestry.com.
27. Virginia Department of Health; Richmond, Virginia; Virginia Deaths, 1912–2014. Ancestry.com.

28. MJ.
29. Susan Tucker, *Telling Memories among Southern Women: Domestic Workers and Their Employers in the Segregated South* (Baton Rouge: Louisiana State University Press, 1988).
30. Jasmine Sanders, "A Black Legacy, Wrapped Up in Fur," *New York Times*, January 31, 2019.
31. Robin Givhan, "Aretha Franklin, Secret Style Icon: With the Drop of a Fur Coat, She Proclaimed Her Worth," *Washington Post*, August 17, 2018.
32. William M. Harris Sr. and Nancy Olmsted, "Public Housing in Charlottesville: The Black Experience in a Small Southern City," *Review of Black Political Economy* (Winter-Spring 1991): 161.
33. Jean Hiatt, President, Preservation Piedmont, interview, Charlottesville, July 2019.

AFTERWORD

1. Asha DuMonthier, Chandra Childers, and Jessica Milli, *The Status of Black Women in the United States*, (Washington, DC: Institute for Women's Policy Research, n.d.), 18.
2. Premilla Nadasen, *Household Workers Unite: The Untold Story of African American Women Who Built a Movement* (Boston: Beacon, 2015), 152.
3. See Emily K. Abel and Margaret K. Nelson, "Circles of Care: An Introductory Essay," in *Circles of Care: Work and Identity in Women's Lives*, eds. Abel and Nelson (Albany: State University of New York Press, 1990); Dan Clawson and Naomi Gerstel, *Unequal Time: Gender, Class, and Family in Employment Schedules* (New York: Russell Sage Foundation, 2014).
4. Nadasen, *Household Workers Unite*, 152; Clawson and Gerstel, *Unequal Time*.
5. DuMonthier, Childers, and Milli, *Status of Black Women*, 19, xii, 18.
6. Fengyan Tang and Heejung Jang, "Challenges and Resilience in African American Grandparents Raising Grandchildren: A Review of the Literature with Practice Implications," *GrandFamilies: Contemporary Journal of Research, Practice, and Policy* 2, no. 2 (2015).
7. Meredith Minkler and Esme Fuller-Thomson, "African American Grandparents Raising Grandchildren: A National Study Using the Census 2000 American Community Survey," *Journals of Gerontology: Series B* 60, no. 2 (March 2005): S82–S92.
8. Minkler and Fuller-Thomson, "African American Grandparents Raising Grandchildren."

9. Minkler and Fuller-Thomson, "African American Grandparents Raising Grandchildren"; Dorothy Smith-Ruiz, "African American Grandmothers Providing Extensive Care to Their Grandchildren: Sociodemographic and Health Determinants of Life Satisfaction," *Journal of Sociology and Social Welfare* 35, no. 4 (December 2008): 29–52.
10. U.S. Census Bureau; Social Explorer Tables: ACS 2018 (5-Year Estimates) (SE). Tables A14007. Median Household Income by Race (In 2018 Inflation Adjusted Dollars) [10]; B17008. Occupation for Employed Civilian Population 16 Years and Over [14]; A03001. Race [8]. Accessed June 11, 2021.
11. Chuck Lewis and Amy Lemley, *All the Riches of Job: A True Story of Success and What Came After* (Charlottesville: Serendipity Press, 1993), 14.
12. Gloria Gilmore, email message to authors, March 13, 2021.
13. Ian Shapira, "White Supremacists Made Charlottesville a Symbol of Racism. Black Residents Say It Still Is." *Washington Post,* August 11, 2020, https://www.washingtonpost.com/local/white-supremacists-made-charlottesville-a-symbol-of-racism-black-residents-say-it-still-is/2020/08/11/7455df10-da61-11ea-809e-b8be57ba616e_story.html.
14. Erica L. Green and Annie Waldman, "'You Are Still Black': Charlottesville's Racial Divide Hinders Students," *New York Times,* October 16, 2018.
15. "Letter to City Council from Members of the Disproportionate Minority Contact in Juvenile Justice System Task Force," *Daily Progress,* June 6, 2015; Jordy Yager, "Searching for Solutions."
16. "Charlottesville, Virginia Population," World Population Review, http://worldpopulationreview.com/us-cities/charlottesville-population/; Social Explorer Tables: ACS 2017 (5-Year Estimates) (SE), ACS 2017 (5-Year Estimates), Social Explorer; U.S. Census Bureau, https://www.socialexplorer.com/tables/ACS2017_5yr/R12277090.
17. *Thomas Jefferson Health District: Mobilizing for Action through Planning and Partnerships,* December 2012, https://www.naccho.org/uploads/downloadable-resources/TJHD-MAPP-2-Health-2-7-13.pdf.
18. Andy Campbell, "Gavin McInnes Is Losing the Battle to Win Over his Neighbors," *Huffington Post,* January 15, 2019.
19. "Larchmont, New York Population," World Population Review, http://worldpopulationreview.com/us-cities/larchmont-ny-population/.
20. "Larchmont, NY," Data USA, https://datausa.io/profile/geo/larchmont-ny.
21. In fact, African American women are no longer confined to this work: less than 1 percent of all Black women over the age of sixteen who were employed in 2017 were private household workers. ("Labor force characteristics by race and ethnicity, 2017," *BLS Reports,* August 2018, U.S. Bureau of

Labor Statistics, United State Department of Labor [https://www.bls.gov/opub/reports/race-and-ethnicity/2017/home.htm]).

22. Linda Burnham and Nik Theodore, *Home Economics: The Invisible and Unregulated World of Domestic Labor* (New York: National Domestic Workers Alliance, 2012), xi.
23. Michelle Chen, "Home-Care Workers Are Now Protected by Minimum-Wage Laws," *The Nation,* July 1, 2016, https://www.thenation.com/article/homecare-workers-are-now-protected-by-minimum-wage-laws/.
24. Burnham and Theodore, *Home Economics*, xi–xii.
25. Joanna Dreby, *Divided by Borders* (Berkeley: University of California Press Press, 2010); Pierrette Hondagneu-Sotelo and Ernestine Avila, "I'm Here, But I'm There," *Gender and Society* 11 (October 1997): 562; Cecilia Menjivar and Leisy Abrego, "Parents and Their Children across Borders," in *Across Generations: Immigrant Families in America*, ed. Nancy Foner (New York: New York University Press, 2009), 160–189.
26. Mary Romero, "Unraveling Privilege: Workers' Children and the Hidden Cost of Paid Childcare," *Chicago-Kent Law Review* 76, no. 2 (2001): 1651–72. On intensive mothering, see Sharon Hays, *The Cultural Contradictions of Motherhood* (New Haven: Yale University Press, 1996).
27. Herb Boyd, "Dorothy Bolden, Civil Rights Activist and Visionary Labor Leader," *New York Amsterdam News,* March 7, 2019; Daniel E. Slotnik, "Overlooked No More: Dorothy Bolden, Who Started a Movement for Domestic Workers," *New York Times,* February 20, 2019.
28. Quoted in Lauren Hilgers, "Out of the Shadows," *New York Times Magazine,* February 21, 2019.

INDEX

Italicized page numbers refer to illustrations.